D1069980

Phil Nuxhall's

Stories IN THE Grove

Phil Nuxhall's
Stories IN THE Grove

Phillip J. Nuxhall

Orange *frazer* Press
Wilmington, Ohio

ISBN 978-1939710-086
Copyright©2014 Phillip J. Nuxhall

No part of this publication may be reproduced in any material form (including photocopying or storing in any medium by electronic means and whether or not transiently or incidentally to some other use of this publication) without the written permission of the copyright holder except in accordance with the provisions of the Copyright, Designs and Patents Act 1988.

Published for Phil Nuxhall by:
Orange Frazer Press
P.O. Box 214
Wilmington, OH 45177
Telephone: 800.852.9332 for price and shipping information.
Website: www.orangefrazer.com
www.orangefrazercustombooks.com

Book and cover design: Brittany Lament, Orange Frazer Press
Photographs on back cover: David Paul Ohmer
Author photo on flap: Kessler Photography

Library of Congress Control Number 2013957955

Printed in China

Photos courtesy of the Boyer Guild of Women in Architecture on page 126; photo courtesy of Christ Church Cathedral on page 37; photo courtesy of the Kenton County Public Library, Covington, Kentucky, on page 124; photos courtesy of the Public Library of Cincinnati and Hamilton County on pages 26, 95, 102, 212, and 223; photos courtesy of the Rookwood Pottery Company on pages 87 and 88; photos courtesy of Michael O'Bryant on pages 24, 42, 61, 92, 109, 176, 231, 241, and 251; photos courtesy of the Library of Congress on pages 106, 107, 115, 203, 204, and 240; photos courtesy of the Heinz History Center on pages 144, 146, and 147; photo courtesy of Renfro Funeral Services on page 139; photo courtesy of David Paul Ohmer on page 108; photos courtesy of Richard Titus on pages 209 and 211; photos courtesy of Kevin Grace and the Archives and Rare Books Library, University of Cincinnati on pages 43, 60, 89, 58, 59, 101, 102, 118, 119, 134, 162, 187, 191, 200, 201, 224, 230, 234, 235, 237, 243, 247, and 252; photo from the Collection of Henry Ford on page 166; photos from Kenny's *Illustrated Cincinnati* on pages 11, 16, 109, 156, and 158; photos from William's *Cincinnati Directory* on pages 121 and 172; photo courtesy of Brad Smith on page 196; photo courtesy of Nancy Kohnen Black on page 238; photo courtesy of Christ Church Cincinnati on page 37; photos courtesy of Charles Gast on pages 9, 15, 19, 29, 35, 51, 53, 64, 67, 111, 151, 160, 169, 218, and 251; photo courtesy of Sandy Hamilton on page 193; photos courtesy of Clay Huff on pages 256 and 257; photos courtesy of Betsy Jo Outten on pages 4 and 5; photo courtesy of Jennifer Palanci on page 93; photos courtesy of Herb and Suzie Reisenfeld on pages 214 and 215; photo courtesy of Judy Stewart on page 226; photos courtesy of the Fed Suhre collection on page 39; photo courtesy of Ann Drackett Thomas on page 206; photos courtesy of the Nantuckett Historical Association on pages 99 (P217525) and 100 (PC Humor); All other photos courtesy of Phil Nuxhall and Spring Grove Cemetery.

Every effort has been made to trace the copyright holders of photographs and illustrations reproduced in this book. Mr. Nuxhall will be pleased to rectify any omissions or inaccuracies in the next printing.

This book is dedicated to my supportive friend and Spring Grove Heritage Foundation President Thomas Huenefeld, and the Volunteer Docents for The Spring Grove Heritage Foundation. Without your support, dedication, and passion to share the history, art, architecture, and landscape of Spring Grove, my work on behalf of historic preservation would have been impossible. You are the true stewards of this national treasure.

ACKNOWLEDGMENTS

Heather Amos

John Baskin

Joe Besecker

Nancy Kohnen Black

Dave Bossart

Carolyn M. Bowers

Venita Brown

Debbie Budke

Jim & Carol Buquo

Mary Ann Burkhardt

Frank Chambers

Cecie & Jay Chewning

Brent Coleman

David C. Conzett

Sandi Cook

Louise Cottrell

Cincinnati Enquirer

Cincinnati Historical
   Society

Cincinnati Magazine

Cincinnati Mercantile
   Library

Cincinnati Preservation
   Association

Cincinnati Public Library

Scott Darrah

Barbara and David Day

Pam Deschler

Michelle Devine

Jackie DeWitt

Christina DiBari

Kathleen Doane

Margaret Dodds

Cassie Eckhardt

Janice Ellis

John E. Esley

Robert Eveslage

Tim Fauley

James K. Fitton

Robert Flischel

Janice Forte

Charles Frank

Gary Freytag

Mark Funke

Paul Gallaher

Charles Gast

Mary Gilbert

Barb Gloeckner

Stephen C. Gordon

Kevin Grace

Sandy Hamilton
Cornelius, Janet, and
    John Hauck
Marcy Hawley
Sarah Hawley
Brian Heinz
Leigh Hensley
Miguel Hernandez
Janet Heywood
Sharon Hill
Greg Hoard
Joanna Hobler
Skip Holmes
Linda Holthaus
William H. Hopple
Jennifer Howe
Jody Howison
Betty Hoyt
Thomas E. Huenefeld
Jeannette Humphries
Marcha Hunley
Denise A. Hunyadi
Eric Johnson
Monika Jorg
Aaron Kash
Michael Kelley
Greg Kent

Winifred Beam Kessler
Richard Kesterman
John Kiesewetter
Tina Klemann
Joy Kraft
Karen Kramer
Marie & Mark Lager
Brittany Lament
Walter Langsam
Marsha Lindner
Jack MacAffee
Jewell & Judy McClure
Suzanne Maggard
Diane Mallstrom
Elizabeth and Thom
    Mariner
Sondra Merusi
Fred & Hope Miller
Susan Moerlein
Julie Molleran
Mike Morgan
Nancy Hannaford &
    William Nadeau
Shawn Nicholson
Craig Niemi
Michael O'Bryant
Brian O'Donnell

Beth Ferguson Oeters
David Oeters
Cate O'Hara
Susan Olsen
Betsy Jo Neff Outten
Jennifer Palanci
Kevin Pape
Mary Peterson
Tom Pfeifer
Lynn H. Pierce
Brian Powers
Gary Profitt
Albert Pyle
Meredith Raffel
David Reidel
Herb & Suzie Reisenfeld
Greg Rhodes
Helen Rindsberg
Bart Rosenberg
James "Aldo" Ross
John A. Ruthven
Richard Ryan
Elaine Rysiewicz
Brian Sahd
Elizabeth Scheurer
Tim Shaffer
David A. Simmons

Chris Smith
Thomas Smith
Betty Smiddy
Spring Grove Heritage
    Foundation
Judy Stewart
Eira Tansey
Jim Tarbell
Anne Drackett Thomas
Richard Titus
John Toale
Don Heinrich Tolzmann
Patricia VanSkaik
John & Valerie Ventre
Karen Wais
Heather Weilnau
Jack Wood
Owen I. Wrassman
Richard Zinicola

TABLE OF CONTENTS

FOREWORD

John A. Ruthven

◦ ◇ ◦

MUCH HAS BEEN SPOKEN AND WRITTEN
about the beauty of Spring Grove Cemetery &
Arboretum. It goes without question that
the vivid descriptions of the many beautiful monuments and lakes, along with the
varied species of trees and plants, make
this place special.

Over many years, notable and interesting people have been laid to rest,
and are now intertwined amongst a visual feast of beautifully landscaped roads.
Here, you don't get a forlorn feeling that
many cemeteries give you. Indeed, the people
who rest here are very much in touch with the living.

The author and John Ruthven at the dedication of the Joseph R. Mason marker.

Start your walk on one of the painted lines on the main roads and wind your way
past history. At the Civil War statue of an armed soldier, you can't help feeling that
you might have known him in another life. His fellow combatants lie in a great circle
around him. All of them reflect a sense of patriotism that makes your spine tingle.

You will pass many names that are familiar but it's difficult to place them in
your mind. Then you come close to names that you know, like the great leaders of
industry in Cincinnati, such as the Procters, the Gambles, the Fleischmanns, and
the Huenefelds. If one is interested in finding dozens of notables who are interned
here, the main office can furnish an extensive list.

My association with Spring Grove Cemetery & Arboretum began as a young
boy growing up in Cincinnati. I have always been aware of the cemetery's beauty,

Stories in the Grove

but after I was discharged from the Navy in 1946, I became involved in the study of bird life in the Grove. Being a member of the Cincinnati Bird Club, it was common practice to "band" and identify the many species that are found in the botanical landscape. Often, we would actually discover new species to the southern Ohio area. Too, we would often spot one of its many resident animals, a fox, a rabbit, a squirrel (Fox, Gray, and Flying), and even a mink!

The flora, the fauna, the people, the stories—together, they make Spring Grove Cemetery & Arboretum a Cincinnati gem.

INTRODUCTION

◦ ◇ ◦

WE USUALLY THINK OF A STORYTELLER as a person who tells a story through written or spoken words. As children and adults, we go to bookstores and libraries for stories. We may attend a lecture, poetry reading, or story hour to listen to others share stories. Sometimes the words can be silent, as in pantomime; or the words can appear in a song. Dance and movement can visually tell a story, and art can use a variety of mediums to convey one.

In *Stories in the Grove* you'll discover that Spring Grove Cemetery & Arboretum is an archive (a national treasure!) with a stellar collection of biographies, recollections, tales, mysteries, and remembrances—all given new life for those willing to listen. In this book, you'll find stories of the cemetery's founding, and stories forgotten, mysterious, artistic, historical, competitive, inventive, and musical.

My journey as a Spring Grove storyteller began when I started walking in the cemetery as part of a weight loss program. It seems astounding to me now, but I had never stepped foot in Spring Grove until I was in my 40s. Before then, I thought of Spring Grove as a big, creepy, old cemetery. How wrong I was! From the beginning, it seemed as though I was walking through a beautiful history book.

Every time I noticed a familiar name, it was like turning another page in the book. I wanted to learn the stories behind names such as Longworth, Taft, Procter, Gamble, and Moerlein. There were stories waiting behind each statue, no matter how large or small. What about the stories of the cemetery's founding? Think about it. More than two hundred thousand deceased, each with their own story. Some stories are modest. Others are simply unbelievable. Some are sad. Others are inspirational. A cemetery is more than a place to bury our dead, but a place to celebrate lives and remember deeds. It's the variety that makes Spring Grove Cemetery & Arboretum the place it is today.

When I wrote my first book, *Beauty in the Grove,* I didn't understand the term *less is more.* I wanted the book to be all-inclusive. There was so much to share, but it didn't take long to realize the impossibility of such a lofty goal. The book would have been too heavy for one person to carry! So I slowly started narrowing the list to a reasonable number, and quickly discovered less really *was* more, but I was left with so many stories still waiting to be told. Actually, even before *Beauty in the Grove,* I knew that I needed to write its sequel. There was too much to keep to myself. The stories needed to be shared.

Deciding on what to include was an overwhelming task. I realized that no matter what I chose for a book, it would never be enough. Someone would certainly point out a story I missed, or I'd discover another tale previously hidden. I was constantly frustrated in choosing stories to include, but the reality was, when dealing with more than two hundred thousand lives, someone is not going to be included. I did the best I could!

From the beginning, I knew I wanted an easy book to read. This is not an academic book. You can find plenty of those! My goal is for the reader to say, "Wow! I had no idea!" or, "That's amazing!" and then plan another trip to Spring Grove. I want it to seem as if you're on a tour right now, and you're hearing tales about the people, the buildings, and the monuments that make Spring Grove Cemetery & Arboretum unique.

These stories come from a variety of sources—many of them unexpected—their discovery is as much a part of the tale as the story itself. You'd be amazed at how many I hear through living descendants. Phone calls, handwritten letters, email messages, spontaneous conversations, and lectures are all potential sources. Over the years, I've accumulated books on Cincinnati's history that help fill in the gaps.

I found out about the Drackett family when I serendipitously met Anne Drackett Thomas at a private dinner party. She had heard I was writing a book and politely mentioned she had family in Spring Grove. I asked her the family name and before I knew it, I had a fantastic story about the founders of the Drackett Company. Some stories are told by tour participants. Once in a while, a living descendant will send

◇ Sketch of the original front entrance buildings of Spring Grove.

me a letter, filled with previously unknown information about their ancestor. I knew nothing of John A. Audubon's assistant, Joseph R. Mason, until I spoke with famed wildlife artist John Ruthven. Within a week of learning about Mason, I had interviewed John, written Mason's story, and attended the ceremony and reception to unveil a beautiful new bronze memorial for Mason. The more I wrote, the more information I received—which is the way of so many untold stories. Many stories I thought I knew, only to learn there was more waiting to be told.

A few words about my writing style, which is (I admit) non-traditional. There's a frequent joke among my family, friends, and co-workers about how dramatic and excitable I can be at times. I respond with one phrase: joie de vivre, or "joy of life." I have it and I'm proud of it, which is why I use so many exclamation points! As I tell everyone, particularly my editor, "I am a walking exclamation point!" He often reminded me to stop using them when I write, and I attempted to heed his advice; but the more I wrote, the more excited I became. There was just *so* much to tell! It's difficult for me to hold back my excitement when I'm sharing Spring Grove's story. So sit back, relax, and allow me to do just that—with and without exclamation points!

—*Phil Nuxhall*

Phil Nuxhall's
Stories IN
THE Grove

HISTORY AND MYSTERY

Isabella Freeman Neff (1796-1844)
Peter Neff (1798-1879)

◦ ◇ ◦

THERE ARE MORE THAN TWO HUNDRED THOUSAND SOULS who lie at rest in Spring Grove Cemetery & Arboretum, and all those souls found a beautiful home because of the love Peter Neff felt for his wife, Isabella. Sandy Cohan, an expert Spring Grove Volunteer docent, has always referred to the story of Peter, Isabella, and Spring Grove as "a love story."

This "love story" pre-dates the cemetery by a year. Isabella succumbed to cancer in the spring of 1844. Her husband, Peter, was grief-stricken. In Cincinnati, there were twenty-three overcrowded, unkempt burial grounds, three of which were located across from Music Hall where Washington Park now sits. At the time, Victorians filled their graveyards, as well as their homes, with clutter and decorations. Urban cemeteries were filled with victims from epidemics that only added to the cramped cemeteries. Grounds maintenance was minimal at best, so the statuary and monuments quickly became hidden by overgrown foliage. Poor Peter was left with no good options for his wife's burial grounds, but Peter was not going to give up (after all, this is a love story).

Isabella Freeman Neff

Peter had his wife's body temporarily held in a friend's burial vault in the Presbyterian burial grounds. It is rumored the friend was a fellow Spring Grove resident, Judge Jacob Burnet, who helped shape Ohio's first constitution. In the same year as Isabella's death, Peter went to the Cincinnati Horticultural Society and urged the group to consider the establishment of a new venue to bury loved ones.

He sought a place of beauty and tranquility, devoid of gloomy, crowded conditions. The Society listened to his wishes and began traveling across America and Europe for inspiration for a rural cemetery. They visited famous Père Lachaise in Paris, known for its serene, park-like setting, and found their inspiration. The group returned to Cincinnati, and scouted the countryside. It might be hard to believe, but Spring Grove Cemetery & Arboretum was indeed created from more than fifty-two private parcels of farm land.

Peter Neff

Spring Grove was a labor of love for Peter Neff, but Peter isn't the only Neff with a connection to the cemetery. In 2006, I met the great-great granddaughter of Isabella and Peter's son, Colonel Peter Rudolph Neff, when she was visiting from Florida in search of family burial sites. Last year, I received a letter and phone call from the great granddaughter of another Neff ancestor, George Washington Neff, who (at a spry 93 years old) inquired about donating original oil paintings of G.W. and his wife, Maria White Neff. She described the subjects as "Both rather attractive and don't have faces that would stop a clock!" Obviously, the love story didn't end with Isabella and Peter Neff—it continues today, with their descendants' love for preserving family history.

George W. Neff was an insurance man who volunteered for a Cincinnati militia company. He was eventually commissioned as a lieutenant colonel in the 2nd Kentucky Volunteer Infantry. Captured in West Virginia he spent a year in various Southern prisons barely escaping being hung. Returning to Cincinnati after a prisoner exchange he defended Camp Dennison during Morgan's Raid. By the end of the war he achieved the rank of Brevet brigadier-general. In addition to the portrait paintings, the *Richmond Times-Dispatch* wrote that the great granddaughter has G.W. Neff's sword "mounted in a shadow box with his belt and his insignia as an original companion of the Military Order of the Loyal Legion of the United States."

◇

According to the Ohio Historic Inventory, compiled by the Ohio Historical Society in 1992, Isabella's Italian marble sarcophagus in Spring Grove was laid out by the cemetery's first landscape designer, the prominent Philadelphia architect, John Notman. He modeled the monument after Rome's tomb of Scipio. The sarcophagus was one of the first funerary monuments in the cemetery. Near the sarcophagus is the Portland stone octagonal monument of the George Neff family relatives, created by James G. Batterson.

The First Burials
in the Cemetery

I'M FREQUENTLY ASKED BY TOUR PARTICIPANTS AND VISITORS, "Who was the first person to be buried in Spring Grove?" For years it was assumed the first burials were two sisters, but in doing extensive research in the Spring Grove records, I finally solved the mystery and sorted out the stories of the first cemetery inhabitants.

Answering questions regarding the first burial is a bit tricky because the first person buried in Spring Grove is no longer in Spring Grove. Her name was Mary Julia Brisbane and she lived in the Cheviot area of Cincinnati's West side. Her father, Dr. William Brisbane, was a nationally known anti-slavery physician. He once owned slaves, freed them, and became a staunch abolitionist. In fact, Dr. Brisbane delivered an address at the Anti-Slavery Convention in 1840, in Hamilton, Ohio, my family's hometown.

Mary Julia was only two years old when she died from whooping cough and her body was first placed in the Baptist Burying Grounds near downtown's Music Hall. Little Mary was reinterred to Spring Grove on September 1, 1845, and then disinterred to Arena, Wisconsin, in 1879, as was her brother, Bentley H. Brisbane (1829-1846). Their father moved the family to Wisconsin, where he became chief clerk of the state senate in 1857.

The second burial has now become the official "first to be buried (and is still) in Spring Grove" burial. Martha Louisa Ernst was buried on September 18, 1845,

(the original interment incorrectly lists her burial date as 1846). She was entered in the original Spring Grove records as being the second burial because Mary Brisbane had not been disinterred to Wisconsin until 34 years later. Confused yet? Martha Louisa died at the age of 33 from "perpetual fever" and her body was removed from the Baptist Burying Grounds on September 18, 1845, and buried in Spring Grove the same day.

The family plot of Spring Grove's "official" first burial has another notable attribute. An unusual monument, a tree without branches, stands at the top of the hill on the Ernst family plot. The tree was carved out of sandstone by Leopold Fettweiss in 1866 and erected by Andrew Ernst's friends. The purposeful cutting off of branches on this type of funerary art symbolizes the cutting off of life, or the end of a life cut short.

At the top of a knoll in Section 23, the Ernst tree stone monument appears eerie, but if you view it closely, you will see intricate carvings of plant life, including a lily and ivy creeping around the tree stone.

◇ Ernst marker, one of the first in Spring Grove.

Stories in the Grove

This was no coincidence because Andrew H. Ernst, Sr. was a horticulturist, landscape architect, and land speculator who owned an estate called *Spring Garden* with many greenhouses. He was known primarily for his collection of beautiful orchids and helped form the Cincinnati Horticultural Society in 1843. Fittingly enough, the monument was brought from the same downtown cemetery that Mary Julia and Martha Louisa were originally buried.

The first burial issue often reminds me of the old Abbott & Costello skit, "Who's on first?" because of the confusing "truth" about the facts. In Spring Grove's case, we finally know who's on first, in this case, the first to be buried in the cemetery.

Gano Family Monument

◇ ◇ ◇

NOTABLE SCULPTOR, TED GANZ, once remarked to me that the Gano monument might be the oldest piece of outdoor art in the entire area. Its history is remarkable and I most likely would know less about it had I not contacted a family descendant in Swampscott, Massachusetts, over ten years ago. I had become concerned that the shrubbery in front of the monument was covering some of the most significant iconography on the base: Carved cherubs, drums, father time, etc. It is

Leopold Fettweiss was the son of the founder of Fettweiss Marble Works, a prominent monument maker at the close of the Civil War.

Another notable member of the Ernst family was Sarah Otis Ernst, who was one of the most effective of the radical abolitionists in the West. Sarah organized the Cincinnati Anti-Slavery Sewing Circle. Their fairs were a major source of support for the Western Anti-Slavery Society.

◇

◇ Carved cherubs found on the Gano monument.

Chapter One

○ Pictured above and at right: Gano family monument.

protocol in Spring Grove to get permission from the family to have anything like pruning large shrubbery done on private lots. Turns out the brother of the descendant I spoke with was going to be in town the following week and fortunately visited the site, then gave permission to trim the shrubbery to make the iconography visible.

Daniel Gano commissioned the monument in memory of his father, Major General John S. Gano. Daniel brought a stone carver from England, John Arey, to Cincinnati in the 1820s to create the family monument. The sandstone monument was erected in 1827, but not in Spring Grove. It originally was in the old Baptist Burying Ground. Daniel ordered it relocated to Spring Grove in 1866. Along with the monument and his father's remains, many other Gano family members were also moved to Spring Grove as well.

Stories in the Grove

The monument is fascinating and includes a great deal of Masonic imagery. The fluted sandstone column once was topped by an urn with an eternal flame. There are four triumphal arches that frame figure groups representing Grief (personified on two faces), Hope, a resurrection from the tomb, and an angelic transport of the deceased to heaven.

Daniel, like many people back then, was involved in many businesses, including building and operating canal boats, animal husbandry, the arts, agriculture, and horticulture. Most likely, the carved sheep heads on the monument symbolize the animal husbandry interest. At one time, Daniel was Clerk of the Court of Common Pleas of Hamilton County. He operated three farms at the same time, one of which was a stock farm along the river in present day Saylor Park called Home Farm. At the farm, he built a racetrack around a prehistoric mound and used it to view horses in Saylor Park. Distinguished guests were transported "uptown" by carriage and bay horses to his home near Cumminsville where his orchard was reported as being "brightly illuminated." It was a busy and social family indeed.

Quite often it's difficult, sometimes seemingly impossible, to track down living descendants of the most ancient monuments and markers. The Gano's rate as one of the most historically and artistically significant not only for Spring Grove Cemetery & Arboretum, but for the entire area. Were it not for that chance phone call to Swampscott, Massachusetts, over ten years ago, we may never have been exposed to a lot of the art and iconography that was hidden from view for so many years. When describing the Gano monument, the term "a museum without walls" truly personifies Spring Grove Cemetery and Arboretum.

Fencing and Walls

∘ ◇ ∘

"OH GIVE ME LAND, LOTS OF LAND, under starry skies above…" a great lyric to a great song that involves fencing, "Don't Fence Me In." The physical boundaries of Spring Grove have an interesting story that started with various types of actual fencing. Years ago private lots were fenced in with not just actual fencing but with additional and extraneous clutter.

The practices of fencing in areas around private family lots were a common occurrence in the late 1800s and played a crucial part in making Spring Grove appear as it does today. Imagine the 52 private parcels of farmland that were on this property prior to Spring Grove's founding in 1845. Keep in mind that many of the farms had to use fencing to contain the farm animals. Even so, many animals continued to roam the area when the cemetery began. It wasn't appropriate to have a cow sitting on someone's grave! So how did the Victorians combat the issue? With fencing. They be-

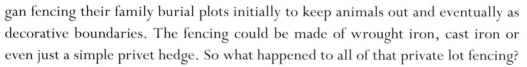

Wall and fencing bordering Winton Road.

gan fencing their family burial plots initially to keep animals out and eventually as decorative boundaries. The fencing could be made of wrought iron, cast iron or even just a simple privet hedge. So what happened to all of that private lot fencing?

When master landscaper Adolph Strauch first toured the cemetery, he knew right away that there was something awry with the overall appearance. It was his groundbreaking (no pun intended) landscaped lawn plan that first called for the removal of lot fencing, as well as other extraneous visuals. When Strauch arrived, a quarter of the private lots were fenced. If that wasn't enough clutter, lot owners at that time were allowed to place trellises, urns, cast iron animals, wire settees, etc., on their lots. I refer to this as "visual clutter," which Victorians were notorious for in the decoration of their homes. They not only cluttered their homes, they also cluttered their burial lots. From *The Commercial* April 14, 1867: "For some time, as we have already said, the beauty of the landscape was materially marred by the iron fences and hedges,

The Jacob Hoffner temple.

Although there is no lot fencing to be found in Spring Grove, there are some impressive walls that surround the perimeter. On the Winton Road perimeter, there now is an impressive stone wall that was erected in 1908 by Elzner and Anderson with stone possibly from Portsmouth, Ohio. The wall was known as the "longest straight wall in the West. It is massive and beautiful being mellowed with time and covered with mosses, fungi, and ivy." But what kind of boundaries preceded the stone wall?

H. A. Rattermann wrote in his book, *Spring Grove Cemetery: It's History and Improvements*, "Enclosures around burial lots, wooden trellises and head-boards of any description whatsoever, are considered useless encumbrances, and are therefore prohibited."

which enclosed lots. Some persons cannot be persuaded that their lot really belongs to them, unless they surround it by a fence or a low stone wall. Many lots have been purchased by persons who have enclosed them and subsequently been removed by the city, and because the fences, when neglected, become rusty and broken, and finally most unsightly things. The officers feel a delicacy in removing them and we are not authorized to incur the expense necessary to keep them in repair so they may remain, growing worse every year. The Superintendent has at length convinced lot-holders that fences are very inappropriate and they are now gradually disappearing. Lots may have, instead, neat corner stones to designate their boundaries, but these should be of the most modest dimensions. A wall of flowers or beautiful shrubs is the only appropriate work that good taste will fully approve."

A wooden fence was first erected around 1881, according to Issac A. Anderson's archives from November 2, 1881, regarding a contract for the fence. The posts were made of black walnut and the railing of white oak. The fence was six feet high and the total length was 2,316 feet. The contract stated that the cost would be $3.94 per linear foot. The rail fences were eventually replaced with an iron picket fence and then Osage orange hedges. There is a letter in the Spring Grove archives, dated May 21, 1881, from H. Belmer regarding a proposition for a wire fence and an excerpt from the *Daily Court* 1878, states: "Further, Superintendent Strauch and 17 families of the employees live in or around the cemetery, and finally the whole is surrounded with a high and thick hedge, inside of which is a wire fence or a close paling fence 8 feet high."

It took Adolph Strauch over five years to rid the cemetery of all lot fencing and I imagine many of the lot owners were not happy about having their expensive fencing removed. But somehow, the cemetery Board of Directors managed to convince them that it was in the best interest of the cemetery's appearance to take down all lot fencing.

Today, you will not find one piece of original lot fencing in the entire cemetery. This was a major accomplishment and has made Spring Grove an international model of the beautiful landscaped lawn plan of design for cemeteries. So with the story of lot fencing and its removal in Spring Grove, Adolph Strauch no doubt would have considered "Don't Fence Me In" as his theme song.

The Gate House

◦ ◇ ◦

THE GATE HOUSE IS A CHARMING LITTLE BUILDING with a big history. Historic cemeteries often greet you with period architecture. One of the first buildings to greet visitors when they enter the main gates of Spring Grove is a smaller building to the left. The story of this charming Victorian-era stone building involves a history of law-abiding visitors, unkempt Victorian ladies, and criminals.

Prior to the present stone structure designed by James K. Wilson, a simple wood building was in use as a gate house. The first reference to any sort of gatekeeper was in the board minutes from May 7, 1857: "The propriety of employing a man as a gatekeeper was referred to the business committee with power to act." The Sheriff of Hamilton County was then requested to deputize the cemetery watchmen. Cemetery records recorded that there were 619 two-horse carriages, 1,540 one-horse buggies or carriages, 424 persons on foot, and 204 "strangers without tickets" that visited the cemetery that year.

On November 7, 1861, a committee was appointed for the procurement of plans for the entrance buildings and a gateway to the cemetery to be built of blue limestone and freestone facing. James K. Wilson was hired in 1863 to design what was initially called the Gate Lodge. It was to be built at a cost of $15,000.

In the late 1800s, Spring Grove was a very popular destination on the weekends. It was so popular, visitors had to present a "proprietor's ticket" to gain entrance. Weekends found hundreds of Victorians dressed in their finest, promenading throughout the grounds to visit loved ones' gravesites, converse with friends, and enjoy the landscape, wildlife, and funerary art. This led to various improvements made to the cemetery. The Gate Lodge was changed to a "Ladies Waiting and Toilet Room." One of the reasons for the change was that female Victorian-era visitors often arrived disheveled from their carriage rides on dusty roads. The building was the perfect venue to refresh themselves before promenading throughout the grounds. No proper Victorian lady would visit a cemetery disheveled!

The Gate House has been the site of some rather bizarre incidences over the years. One involved a signal bell that was rung to alert cemetery personnel when a funeral procession was entering the cemetery. The bell was referred to by hundreds of displeased patrons as "a severe shock" when it was sounded. The bell was replaced in 1912 with a compressed air whistle. *The Cincinnati Enquirer* referred to a report describing the gatekeeper pressing a button, "which opens a whistle at the pumping station, three quarters of a mile distant, using a code for the particular man he wishes to call." Nowadays, with modern technology, direct-connect cell devices are used.

Patrons of the cemetery learned early on that you don't mess with the gatekeeper! A complaint was waged on May 16, 1874, against the gatekeeper for not admitting an allegedly drunk visitor from Indianapolis to attend a friend's burial. The gatekeeper's response to the complaint was that he, "might admit respect-

In 1868, acting as the chairman of the newly formed Building Committee, William Resor presented proposals from Michael Clements and J.P. Walton to furnish material, construct, and erect the new gates at the entrance, according to the plans and specifications of architect James K. Wilson. The photographs and drawings used for the design were brought back by Henry Probasco from Europe, where he had inspected numerous palace and cathedral gateways. His favorite was the gate at the Sandringham estate of the Prince of Wales (later Edward VII), which served as the prototype for Norman Chapel's gate.

◇

◇ The Gate House

Stories in the Grove

able strangers whenever the circumstances would justify the act." Rules for Spring Grove included:

• *Persons on foot will be admitted on odd days, except Sundays and holidays, from sunrise till sunset.*

• *The gates will be closed on Sundays and holidays except to proprietors of lots and their families; and they only on foot.*

• *No children will be admitted unless attended by some person who will be responsible for their conduct.*

• *No riding will be allowed faster than a walk.* (Bicycles were not permitted to go faster than four miles per hour!)

The Jail

◦ ◇ ◦

YOU NEVER KNOW WHAT MIGHT BE LURKING IN A CEMETERY. For example, did you know Spring Grove has a jail? It's true, and the story of the jail is one of my favorite from Spring Grove. It involves a mysterious room in the basement of the Norman Chapel that once housed a holding cell for incarcerated guests.

The front entrance to the cemetery is off Spring Grove Avenue, which was once flanked by beautiful elm trees. The wide expanse once appealed to adventurous carriage drivers who raced back and forth in the mid-1800s, while horse-traders bought and sold outside the main entrance to the cemetery, much to the dismay of area residents.

The carriage racing led to a public outcry, as residents declared the city's authorities were "turning the city into a race track." The government responded and drivers were forbidden to race on the avenue.

Historical rail road bridge

◇ A horse and buggy used for carriage racing.

After the authorities shut down the Spring Grove Avenue carriage racing, racers brought their horse and carriages into the cemetery. Spring Grove responded with hired guards to stop the racers.

So where were all these racers imprisoned in Spring Grove? In 1878, The *Commercial Tribune* reported a tramp had been locked up for a short time in, "the cell at the cemetery entrance," reportedly to "show him how well prepared the cemetery authorities were for such visitors." At that time, the jail cell was in a simple wooden outbuilding. According to the report, the vagrant assumed the cemetery superintendent's home, at the corner of Winton and Gray roads, was that of a "rich man" who might have been able to offer him work. After his one-night incarceration in the jail cell, a stern warning was given to not try coming onto the grounds again, or he would "bring up in the Work-house."

The jail was soon replaced. The report of the building committee on Thursday, January 6, 1880, by Henry Probasco states, "The jail at the lodge being needed for tools and other purposes, a new one has been made beneath the north receiving tomb, in the cellar of the chapel, the iron work being made by M.(Michael) Clements."

Paved roads brought a new sort of racing trouble to Spring Grove. In 1890, Spring Grove Avenue was paved with compacted gravel, creating an exciting new opportunity for racers. Problems with racing weren't limited to horse and carriages. Automobiles were not permitted into the cemetery until 1911, and especially not on Sunday afternoons. Like the horse and carriages, automobile drivers had a penchant for speed. Speeding close to the cemetery was deemed irreverent and irresponsible. In fact, automobile drivers were required to have a ticket issued by J.C. Spear, Secretary of the Cemetery Association, to gain entry to Spring Grove. Nineteen years later, the Cincinnati Auto Club filed a protest against the Sunday afternoon automobile ban, claiming it was "old fashioned, narrow and impractical." The cemetery responded by saying, "It is humane and necessary to protect life."

Today, the iron bars on the east side of the cell window are still intact, as is the built-in concrete sleeping bench. The iron cell gate was removed years ago, but the hinges remain. I always get a chill when I view the cell, thinking about the guests that stayed in this mysterious room, and the stories they brought. Many of those guests were locked up by armed guards for driving no more than six miles per hour! For those considering a race in Spring Grove, beware! The jail cell door can always be re-installed!

The Maintenance Barn

◦ ◇ ◦

THE MAINTENANCE BARN IS ONE of the most significant locations in the cemetery. Being a bit off the beaten path, most visitors don't see it, and if they do, they don't quite know what to make of it. Barns are typically a place where animals are housed and farming chores take place, but, as with many of the locations in Spring Grove, nothing is ever as simple as it seems. Today, the barn is the headquarters for cemetery maintenance and horticulture activities. As a beehive of activity, the barn houses the personnel and equipment which keeps Spring Grove in tip-top shape.

On August 1, 1872, there was a proposition by the Spring Grove Board to purchase three "horse sprinkling wagons." The wagons were likely used to keep the dust at bay on the unpaved roads in the cemetery, especially on Spring Grove Avenue. The concept for the barn was suggested on December 4, 1884, by Superintendent William Salway at a Spring Grove Board meeting. He recommended a barn be built near the "Superintendent's new house." Eventually, the barn was built

Three night watchmen, armed with revolvers, were hired in the late 1860s and told to shoot on sight if trespassers in the cemetery didn't immediately explain themselves.

north of the Superintendent's house at the corner of Winton and Gray roads. The original maintenance barn was built by Charles Farnau and Herman Heinemann, with plans by Samuel Hannaford. It was an impressive structure built with red brick. On March 12, 1885, a contract for a new barn was awarded to Farnau & Heinemann at a cost of $9,989. Oddly enough, on April Fool's Day the following month, another contract was signed with a cost of $9,260. Three months later, board members were reported to be driving through the grounds to examine the new barn.

Wagons weren't the only items kept in the barn. It accommodates a surprising number of items and guests. The maintenance barn has multiple cupolas and two wings which link two smaller buildings to the barn. The smaller buildings have two stories with small rooms on the second floor which served as apartments for employees. Much like rural farms, employees had animals to feed and groom, in addition to the usual duties required at a cemetery, so living on the premises was convenient. At the time the barn was built, Spring Grove used cows and sheep to cut the grass. The barn housed the grass-cutting animals in addition to other barnyard animals. A small community grew up in Spring Grove. Working gardens supplied produce for the workers and greenhouses provided for the horticulture needs throughout the cemetery grounds.

You might be wondering why there are no longer cows, sheep or other farm animals at Spring Grove. On March 2, 1854, "It was voted that hereafter no cows should be allowed to be kept in the cemetery." It seems it was difficult to fully remove the cows from Spring Grove, because on July 9, 1870, "The application of Anton Kesselman for privileges of pastur-

The maintenance barn.

ing cows in a portion of Cemetery Grounds north of Groesbeck Road was declined." On May 4, 1876, "On Motion of Mr. Thomas, the Superintendent, is hereby instructed to prohibit all persons from pasturing their cattle on any of the Grounds of the Cemetery or in any manner trespassing thereon under penalty of the law." Who knew cows were such a concern for the cemetery? In fact, it was reported that cows were still being pastured in Spring Grove as late as 1890.

On the afternoon of August 29, 1900, the barn was nearly destroyed by fire. Wagons used in conveying remains from the railway stations were destroyed in the fire and I imagine some of the animals perished. Apparently, much of the original structure was destroyed in the fire, and a major renovation was needed to repair the damage. An entry in the October 5, 1900, board minutes mentions bids for building a new barn, which is the magnificent structure standing today. The bids were received by the Superintendent and Samuel Hannaford & Sons. Bids were re-

◇ Fred Wimmer, grounds man

Chapter One

ceived from a number of contractors, including: Jas. Griffith & Sons ($12,000); Wm. Stewart & Sons ($11,944); The Cotteral Building Co. ($10,832); Putthoff & Frey Iron Co. for iron work ($1,252); The I. Schreiber & Sons Co. for iron work ($1,302); and Stewart Iron Works ($1,265).

The bids for The Cotteral Building Co. and Putthoff & Frey Iron Co. were accepted. On March 1, 1901, "The Committee on new barn reported the barn all completed and that it was as fine as any building of the kind in the country." Three years later, the Superintendent noted the only lights used in the stable and barns were coal oil lamps and asked the Board to consider replacing them with electric lights. Since then, the maintenance barn has been an important part of Spring Grove.

Today, the maintenance barn is the headquarters for numerous personnel and functions which make Spring Grove Cemetery & Arboretum operate like a well-oiled machine. On any given day in the warmer months, you can see teams of lawn mowers, string trimmers, trucks, gardening equipment, etc. buzzing in and out of the facility like a busy bee hive—much like the official Spring Grove bee hives and beekeeper, which the cemetery has had on hand for more than one hundred years. Sometimes, an old barn is much more than just a barn.

Old Man and Spring Grove Pets

◦ ◇ ◦

SPRING GROVE HAS NEVER ALLOWED PET BURIALS, and you'd be hard pressed to find any stories about animals buried in Spring Grove. However, I know a story of at least one animal that was "snuck" into the cemetery by a good friend of the Superintendent.

Newspaper reports stated that on December 7, 1905, the widow of George Turner arrived by carriage one morning with her daughter, Kitty. George Turner was a bacteriologist for the City Health Department and good friend of Spring Grove Superintendent William Salway. His daughter, Kitty, was a well-known artist with a studio in the Neave Building downtown Cincinnati. The two ladies carried a small casket covered with flowers. Superintendent Salway met the

Man's best friend 'til the end.

ladies at the front entrance and comforted them while they mourned before leading them into the cemetery to the Turner family lot.

Salway was skeptical as to the contents of the mysterious little casket and ordered the cemetery Sexton, or supervisor of burials, to open it. "There is no record of this, and I must see what it contains," remarked Salway according to the records. The lid was opened to reveal the body of a dead dog called "Old Man" with an old slipper folded in its paws. A teary-eyed Salway remembered a promise he made to the widow of his life-long friend seven years earlier. Mr. Turner had been extremely attached to Old Man, and his widow wanted to memorialize the beloved canine with an appropriate burial. Poor Old Man had to be chloroformed when paralysis of his throat incapacitated his body.

According to the reports, Old Man was well known in the Cincinnati area, and supposedly could count change up to a dollar with its paws. The method involved his master putting a pile of change on the floor. Old Man would then separate the change into any sum he called for. No quarter available? No problem. Old Man would push two dimes and a nickel or five nickels to his master. You could consider him a canine calculator! And, according to local stories, if anyone questioned Old Man's patriotism by calling him a Spaniard, he would respond with a savage attack.

Rumor has it that Tillie, the elephant from Robinson's Circus is buried in Spring Grove. But I have to tell visitors when asked about it that it's just a legend. Tillie is supposedly buried near the grounds of the old Robinson estate in Terrace Park, in a cistern near the area where John Robinson kept his circus animals.

Although there are no memorials for pets, there is a marble sculpture of a young boy's dog on the lot of William Coon Redman in Section 46. Little William died from brain congestion at age seven in 1854. The dog sculpture brings tears to the eyes of visitors as it is depicted laying with its head down toward William's monument, holding a broken chain in one of its paws, symbolic of its master breaking away from life.

Dogs are also depicted in some ghost stories of Spring Grove. A local website, *www.ohioexploration.com* reports that, "two ghostly white dogs are said to haunt the area around the Mitchell memorial near the front of the cemetery. Anyone who is not respectful while visiting the cemetery is said to have a streak of bad luck." Another story reports a white dog running by the Dexter mausoleum when the sun goes down. The dogs' eyes will turn red.

While many guests are surprised to learn that Spring Grove doesn't allow pet burials, it hasn't stopped the stories of beloved pets making their way into the cemetery lore.

Bertha Bertram (1840-1912)

◦ ◇ ◦

OK, CINCINNATI REDS FANS, THIS STORY IS FOR YOU! I had never heard the name Bertha Bertram before, or of her sartorial contribution to the baseball world, but I often wondered where the name "Redlegs" and "Reds" originated. Bertha Bertram, a Czech immigrant now buried in Spring Grove, played a key role in helping shape baseball and the Cincinnati Reds.

Bertram was born Bertha Wenzlick in 1840 in the western part of the Czech Republic, called Bohemia. She immigrated to the United States in 1850, and lived near Findlay Market and Music Hall in downtown Cincinnati. Her husband Charles, a bookkeeper, died in 1878. To make ends meet, Bertram operated a day nursery for children in her home on Race Street. Operating a day care was likely an easy transition for Bertram, since she and Charles had eight children.

Eventually, a sporting-goods store owner named George Ellard hired Bertram to make the first Red's uniforms. From *Base Ball in Cincinnati: A History*, written in 1913 by George's son Harry Ellard: "The orders for the first manufacture of the uniforms for the nines of 1867, '68, '69, '70 were given by Mr. Ellard to Mrs. Bertha Bertram, who conducted a tailoring establishment on Elm Street, near Elder." Ellard decided to make baseball uniforms consisting of white caps, white shirts with a crimson old-English "C" on their jerseys, short pants, and spiked Oxford shoes, but the real eye-catcher was the revolutionary foot-wear; bright red "stockings" worn from the ankle to the knee. He was quoted as saying, "As the long red stockings were necessarily made to order, they were quite expensive. For they were up to that time unknown."

The new uniforms with their red stockings got noticed. A newspaper reporter from a local paper was among the first to refer to the team as the "Red Stockings." However, comments such as, "Say, Harry, you've got whiskers like a man and pants like a boy," could be heard from the stands, showing disapproval of the unfamiliar new look. But others embraced the revolutionary new style. When the Red Stockings were playing on the West Coast in San Francisco, the uniforms impressed their competition. A writer for the *San Francisco Chronicle* referred to the Red Stockings as, "the invincible nine," when they conquered teams in the east, and mentioned that the long red stockings, "show their calves in all their magnitude and rotundity." Since then, teams have become synonymous with their uniforms, and vice versa, all because of George Ellard's vision and Bertram's skill with the needle.

The origin of the beloved Cincinnati Reds' moniker can be attributed to a talented lady who previously had no connection to the sport. Her contribution was humorously referred to in a quote from a banquet host in San Francisco in 1869, following the Red

◇ An old Cincinnati Red Stockings baseball card.

Chapter One

Stockings success: "To the Red Stockings—may they never meet the wash in which they are bleached."

George Brabazon Ellard (1829-1916)
Harry Ellard (1864-1913)

◦ ◇ ◦

THE FATHER AND SON TEAM of George and Harry Ellard were destined to become involved in sports. Their stories involve bicycles, baseballs, and even a little poetry. Left behind after their passing was a notable collection of heirlooms making their story all the more intriguing.

The patriarch, George B. Ellard, is known for his organization of the Cincinnati Red Stockings, along with professional cricket bowler Harry Wright and local attorney, Aaron Champion. After Wright played cricket in New

George B. Ellard

York, Ellard lured him to Cincinnati in 1865 to play for the Union Cricket Club at $1,500 a year. Cricket and baseball had some similarities and some of the English cricket customs were applied to baseball. Most chartered clubs at that time used both cricket and baseball in their names, such as "The Cricket and Baseball Association." In 1866, as baseball became more popular, Ellard, Wright, and Champion started the Resolute Baseball Club of Cincinnati with the financial and organizational support of Cincinnati's high society, including William A. Procter, James N. Gamble, Nicholas Longworth, and the son of Cincinnati zoo founder, C. M. Erkenbrecher. The Resolutes' name was short-lived however when Alfred Goshorn became president around 1867 and it was changed to the Cincinnati Baseball Club. The club was successful in 1868 but times were changing in baseball.

Many clubs had been paying their players under the table, but for the 1869 season Cincinnati became the first team to openly pay players. Thus, America's first professional baseball team was formed. The Red Stocking's second president, Aaron Champion, wanted only the best players the game could offer so he appointed George Ellard, Johnny Joyce, and Harry Wright to scout and recruit the players for the 1869 season. The star player was Wright's brother, George, who was an accomplished shortstop recruited from another team. Harry was also playing in center field at the time. Obtaining the best players resulted in an undefeated season (57-0) and it put Cincinnati on the map as the center of baseball. Financial troubles plagued the organization throughout the next few seasons and it wasn't until 1890 that the team was a permanent fixture in the National League.

Like George Wright, George Ellard also had a family member named Harry but in his case, it was his son. Harry Ellard was a baseball writer in Cincinnati and

In 1869, Ellard's sporting-goods company once again made history by manufacturing what was called the "Ellard (base)ball." Noted Cincinnati Reds historian, Greg Rhodes, states that the first baseball may have been made somewhere in New York; either homemade or by someone who worked with leather. Prior to Ellard's creation, the ball was much smaller and handmade of yarn or string surrounded with a single piece of stitched leather. The actual origin of the game itself has been debated for more than a century but most claim the sport emanated from an old English game called "rounders." Abner Doubleday's attribution to creating the game has also been greatly disputed.

◇

◇ George Ellard scouted players for the Red Stockings in 1869.

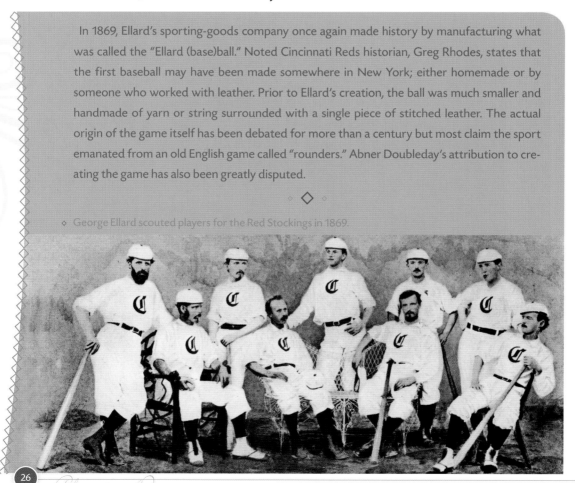

Chapter One

an avid bicyclist winning many races. In fact, in 1878 he started the first of many bicycle clubs in Cincinnati, known as the Brighton Bicycle Club. Sadly, after contracting tuberculosis in 1895, he was sent to Denver, Colorado, by his parents to recover. It was there that he published a collection of poems called *Ranch Tales of the Rockies* about life on the frontier. He was fascinated with western lore, so much so that the literary world knew him as the "Cowboy Poet" and humorously, as the "Poet Lariat."

In 1907, Harry felt that baseball had been overlooked in local history books and wrote *Base Ball in Cincinnati*. His book has impressed baseball experts for years and appears in the bibliographies of many new books on the sport. Even fellow Spring Grove resident Ren Mulford (see Ren Mulford story), local editor and famous correspondent for *Sporting Life* magazine, contributed two chapters on Cincinnati baseball after 1876 and the establishment of the National League. It's interesting to note that "base ball" is in the title of the book as two words; but throughout the text, it's written as the familiar one word "baseball."

Harry died not long after he completed his book in 1913 at the young age of forty-nine while George outlived his son by three years before he died in 1916 at the age of fifty-four. After their deaths, there was an estate auction of rare bats, balls, caps, score books, and George and Harry Wright's uniforms from the 1869 Red Stockings team. The items were believed to be those of Harry Ellard, who gathered them in 1870 and held on to them until he died. In 1917, sports writer and poet William A. Phelon reported in *Baseball Magazine* that the lot was sold on October 25, 1917, at Stacy Auctions on Gilbert Avenue in Cincinnati. Ellard's family gave the collection up for auction a few months after he died. Previous Red's owner, August "Garry" Herrmann, reportedly told an employee to "go get these things and bring them to my office, no matter what the cost." The ultimatum was in vain though as former team president, William C. Kennett, Jr., outbid Herrmann.

Harry Ellard, bicycle enthusiast

I wonder what became of those relics that were considered "one of baseball's most treasured heirlooms?" And although I've never seen the entire list of contents from the auction, I can't help but to wonder if any of the Ellard's bicycles or poetry were thrown in for good measure?

Carl Dannenfelser (1854-1916)

◦ ◇ ◦

SOMETIMES, THE ACTUAL MONUMENT OR MARKER can tell the story of the deceased. When you pass the Dannenfelser family lot on the eastern edge of Section 73, you can't help but to stop in amazement at the site of a beautifully carved female sculpture, kneeling in mourning by a granite, Victorian chair. You might think the story is told by the female statue, but in Dannenfelser's case, their story revolves around the chair.

Carl Dannenfelser was a German-born furniture maker, artist, and founder of the Cincinnati Joinery (a joiner is a type of carpenter who makes things without nails, screws, or other metal fasteners). I've admired Dannenfelser's walnut veneer, maple, bird's eye maple, poplar, and glass secretary-bookcase for many years in The Cincinnati Art Museum. His woodwork at the Butterfield Senior Center building (formerly the Marcus Fechheimer home and men's club on Garfield Place) and the library in the former Taft Home (now the Taft Museum of Art) is stellar. He's also listed as working on oak carvings in the Mother of God Church in Covington, Kentucky.

This quote from the promotional book called *Leading Manufacturers and Merchants of Cincinnati and Environs*, mentions Dannenfelser and his woodworking cohorts: "Messrs. Dannenfelser, Timmich & Biemann, all of whom are skilled wood-carvers and cabinet-makers of year's experience, united their energies and ability during the past year and founded one of the few art-joinery establishments in Cincinnati. The firm makes to order all kinds of carved antique and modern furniture, and also carving for decorative purposes, make designs and execute them in the most artistic manner, and their genius and skill have been abundantly attested in every kind of work in their line. Their carving is all made by hand, and evidences the touch of

The profession of "Art Cabinet Dealer" was attributed to Dannenfelser in the 1900 Census, and his son, Leopold, was listed as a woodcarver in the 1910 Census. Another son, Caesar, was listed in the 1930 Census as a "designer" in the furniture industry.

◇ A pensive pose on the Dannenfelser chair monument.

the artist in accuracy, beauty of detail, and general excellence, and the encouragement the firm has received and the patronage they have enjoyed is a just tribute to their ability, energy, and business integrity. Messrs. Dannenfelser and Timmich are Germans by birth, and Mr. Biemann was born in Cincinnati."

A kneeling female at the foot of a beautiful Victorian chair makes perfect sense in memorializing a family so gifted in the art of furniture making. The Dannenfelser monument stands out among many others, and shows that even a piece of furniture can serve as a memorial to a remarkably storied past in furniture making.

Emma Lucy Braun (1889-1971)
Annette Francis Braun (1884-1978)

◇ ◇ ◇

THE SONG "Sisters," from the classic movie, *White Christmas,* came to mind when I discovered the story of two sisters who were successful in the field of botany, ecology, and entomology. Their story is one of accomplishments and, perhaps, a secret desire for one-upmanship.

Emma Lucy Braun, who preferred to be called Lucy, was a pioneer in Ohio's ecological history and known as, "one of the truly dedicated pioneer ecologists of the first half of the twentieth century." She was highly influenced by her parents' appreciation of the natural world, particularly her mother's collection of dried, pressed plants. Lucy was educated in Cincinnati Public Schools and at the University of Cincinnati, where she earned her Bachelor's degree in 1910, a Masters in geology in 1912, and a PhD in botany in 1914. In addition to her impressive education, Lucy wrote four books and contributed to more than 180 publications. She became a Professor Emeritus of Plant Ecology at the University of Cincinnati and president of the Ecological Society of America in 1950.

Lucy was able to retire early from teaching and she took full advantage of it by conducting research and fieldwork in many areas of special interest, contributing to publications until she passed away. After twenty-five years of field study and traveling more than 65,000 miles, she wrote in 1950 the famous book,

Deciduous Forests of Eastern North America. Locally, she catalogued the flora in the Cincinnati region, comparing it to the flora collected one hundred years earlier. It was the first study of its kind in America and is considered a model for flora study everywhere. In 1951, Lucy was involved with the Ohio Academy of Science and organized an Ohio Flora Committee that created a comprehensive study of the vascular flora of Ohio. This resulted in two books on woody plants in Ohio (1961) and one on "Cat-tails to Orchids" (1967).

Lucy Braun

Lucy was elected as the first woman president of the Ohio Academy of Science (1933–1934) and the Ecological Society of America in 1950. She received the Mary Soper award for achievement in the field of botany in 1952, a Certificate of Merit from the Botanical Society of America in 1956, and the Eloise Payne Luquer Medal in 1966 from the Garden Club of America.

Lucy's sister, Annette Braun, had a career that was nearly as impressive as her sister's. Accompanying and assisting her sister in her field studies, she became an internationally known authority on butterflies and moths. Annette was the first woman to receive a PhD from U.C. in 1911 and was affiliated with the university for five years before pursuing private research. In 1926, she was elected vice-president of the Entomological Society of America. Annette became her sister's lifelong assistant. Annette's notes and vast collection of slides were donated to the Smithsonian Institution and her collection of over 30,000 specimens of moths was given to the Philadelphia Academy of Science.

The two sisters were very close, even living together in the Cincinnati suburb of Mount Washington where they considered their mostly natural and undisturbed garden sanctuary a laboratory, calling it "the science wing." Their garden was used to study the unusual plants that they transplanted. Although they lived together and had a seemingly good relationship, there was a family issue that seemed to rustle Annette's feathers.

When the girls were young, their parents supposedly favored Lucy and always dressed her in pink. Sister Annette was always dressed in blue. But, despite academic accolades and world renown, when Annette died from congestive heart failure in 1978, seven years after Lucy had passed, Annette made sure her "final" outfit was completely pink!

Caledonian Society of Cincinnati

◦ ◇ ◦

THERE IS AN INTERESTING MONUMENT in the center of section 32. It intrigues visitors with its color and thistle carvings. The thistle usually signifies the national emblem of Scotland, and the light pink color of the large rectangular monument is indicative of stone from Aberdeen, Scotland. The only inscription on the monument is "The Caledonian Society of Cincinnati–1892." The story of the monument and its connection to many Spring Grove inhabitants is filled with the music, poetry, and history of Scottish Cincinnatians.

Although most thistle iconography in cemeteries is representative of Scottish heritage, it can also mean such things as bravery, courage, and loyalty. Many of the Cincinnatians in Spring Grove with Scottish roots exemplified those traits. The Caledonian Society of Cincinnati was founded in 1827. One of the founders was the Kilgour family, who were responsible for the development of Cincinnati's street railway, and the founding of the city's Bell Telephone system. Andrew and William McAlpin, of the famed department store family; the latter who wrote an original song, "Bonnie Scotland," in 1869 for a St. Andrew's celebration, were also founders of the

◦ Caledonian
Society headstone

Chapter One

Caledonian Society. Other founders include Bellamy Storrer, the first Judge of the Superior Court of Cincinnati, and Salmon P. Chase, Chief Justice of the Supreme Court and Secretary of the Treasury under President Lincoln. The Society's website states it is the oldest Caledonian Society in existence in the United States.

The objective of the Caledonian Society was, "to relieve such of our countrymen as many arrive among us in distressed circumstances, and to give them information and advice for locating themselves in the western country." Cincinnati was part of the western country at the time. Scots traveled from Virginia to Kentucky, following the flow of the Ohio River. Many ended up in Cincinnati, such as General Arthur St. Clair, who eventually became the first Governor of the Northwest Territory.

The Constitution of the Caledonian Society offers insight into events and concerns of the members at the time. For example: "all discussions relative to the politics of America are strictly prohibited at our meetings; and no political toasts will be permitted to be drank (sic) at our celebration of St. Andrew's Day." If a member attended a meeting drunk, he was fined a whopping one dollar for the first offense, two for the second, and for the third, his name would have been erased from the records forever!

The St. Andrew's Day celebration is one of great history and revelry in Cincinnati. Literature and music is a large part of the annual event and usually involves the recitation of poetry and the singing of "Annie Laurie" and similar Scottish tunes. When the songs begin, bagpipers and drummers enter, followed by speeches and toasts, and then traditional Highland dancing. I was surprised to learn that the origin of those awkward grade school square dances was in the Scottish reels from hundreds of years ago. In 1958, The Scottish Dance Society was formed in Cincinnati to teach and preserve those Scottish folk dances. At the time, you could take a class at the YWCA. The Cincinnati Pipe Band was formed in 1959 and played for the first time at the St. Andrew's Night celebration.

And when Caledonians sung their last song and danced their last reel, many were buried in Spring Grove. Originally, they were interred in a plot of an old settlement area of Cincinnati known as Vernonville. In 1858, a plot was acquired in Spring Grove, along with the Aberdeen granite monument purchased for more than $800. The Society's bylaws require an application and approval to be buried in any remaining space of the plot.

Did you know there are more than 200 types of thistles? The common thistle of Scotland is the most well-known and celebrated. There's an ancient order in Scotland known as "The Order of the Thistle."

◇

As you wander the grounds of Spring Grove and come across the rectangular monument for the Caledonian Society, remember the story of the Scotsmen who came to America, and how important their tale is to our nation!

Albert Day (1814-1849)
Timothy Day (1819-1869)
Elias Harvey Day (1828-1850)

◦ ◇ ◦

IF YOU WALK BY THE DAY FAMILY MONUMENTS IN SECTION 45, your eyes will most likely be drawn to the graceful marble temple with a standing female statue. What many visitors miss is the large marble octagonal column north of the temple, and the monument is not something you should miss! It contains an impressive number of carved symbols; a sail ship, bow and crossed arrows, an hourglass with a hole, a harp, an anchor, a downturned torch, and three carved chains. I was always so fascinated by the iconography, I'd neglected to research the stories behind the Day family—the brothers Timothy Day, Elias Day, and Albert Day.

Timothy C. Day was a judge and abolitionist, known for his work to end slavery. He was considered, "one of the most militant figures in the political history of Cincinnati." He started as a printer, and when his brother Elias died in 1850, he inherited partial ownership of the *Cincinnati Enquirer*.

While working at the *Enquirer*, Timothy Day railed against the extension of slavery into the Territories. He had a reputation as a nuisance in the Democratic Party, even though he represented the Party in Congress in 1854. When the Civil War broke out, he supported Abraham Lincoln and when the city was threatened by Confederate

troops he served as a colonel with the local "Black Brigade." It was said that his views were, "steeped in abolition, nativism, and everyday orneriness."

In addition to their work in politics, soldiering, and as abolitionists, the Days believed in the power of libraries and endowed the Ohio Mechanics Institute $50,000 to fund its permanent library. Factoring inflation, the value of his endowment today would be more than one million dollars. Today, Timothy Day is the namesake of the Technical Library at the University of Cincinnati.

The inscription on Albert G. Day's epitaph reads: "erected by (his) two surviving brothers of the two who sleep beneath." In addition to being in the printing business, Albert held the office of Grand Patriarch of the International Order of Odd Fellows—which explains the imagery carved into the column. When Albert died, the Odd Fellows were devastated by losing a leader and friend. After his death, it was decreed: "that as a mark of respect and fraternal regard, the members of this Grand Encampment wear the usual badge of mourning for

◊ Day family monument

◇

thirty days. Also, the Charter and Emblems of this Grand Encampment be clothed in mourning for six months."

The Day family lot is a fascinating place to stop when touring Spring Grove. It includes multiple upright markers in addition to the large column and temple. Although the markers are highly decorative and tasteful, when placed beside the column with iconography and a temple, the site appears "cluttered," in a manner outlawed by Adolph Strauch during his tenure at Spring Grove.

But what Strauch saw as "clutter" had a deeper meaning to the Day family as they were book lovers, Odd Fellows, and abolitionists! Like most of the monuments in Spring Grove, there is a hidden story behind each if you are willing to dig a little deeper.

The Emery Angel

◇

ONE OF SPRING GROVE'S MOST MAGNIFICENT MONUMENTS is actually hidden from view near the center of an idyllic amphitheater-like setting in section 22. It's a beautiful bronzed angel kneeling on a tufted pillow with her arms outstretched, as if cradling a large object. The angel is not visible until you walk around an assortment of trees and shrubs, and then, voilà, there she is in all her glory. But there's an air of mystery around a missing piece on the sculpture and visitors always want to know what the story is. What was in her hands? A vase? A cross? And where did it go? The only other hint, other than the position of the angel's outstretched arms, is two holes with missing bolts. The ex-director of the Cincinnati Art Museum, Millard Rogers, was the first to enlighten me as to the whereabouts of the missing piece.

The history of the Emery angel sculpture can be traced to the Thomas and Mary Emery family. Thomas, Jr.'s father left a London bank job in the 1830s to come to America, where he opened up a real estate and money agent office in Cincinnati.

Later, he made a fortune in the candle business. Thomas, Jr. accumulated his own fortune and left twenty million shares of family real estate to his wife, Mary. Known as "Lady Bountiful," her philanthropic generosity made her a Cincinnati icon and she become known as the namesake of one of America's first planned communities, Mariemont, on the eastside of the city.

Two of Thomas, Jr. and Mary Emery's sons, Albert and Sheldon, died at young ages. The parents wanted to memorialize the boys with a piece of artwork. The Emery angel was commissioned and given to Christ Church in memory of Albert and Sheldon in 1892 by the Emery family. No information on the sculptor of the work has been found to date, but during a renovation of the church in the 1950s, the angel was removed and placed as the centerpiece of the Episcopalian lot in Spring Grove, again, courtesy of the Emerys. Up until the time it was placed in the cemetery, the angel was holding something in her hands but since the 1950s, not many knew what the missing piece was.

Emery Angel with clamshell font

The mystery was solved when I was giving a tour for Millard Rogers on one of my first tours. Rogers had asked me at the onset of the tour if I knew where the "Emery angel" was located as he had never seen the sculpture in person. I proudly replied, "I sure do. Follow me." But before we approached the angel, Rogers asked if I knew what the sculpture was originally used for. Little did I know that the angel was actually a functional piece of art and acted as the original baptismal font for Christ Church Cathedral in downtown Cincinnati. The missing piece on the angel was a beautiful clamshell font on her outstretched hands. One mystery solved; another to go! What happened to the clamshell font since it was intact on the sculpture at that time?

Further research led me to a book on the church and a photograph from the 1950s which shows the angel intact, with the clamshell font, after the sculpture was first placed on the Episcopal lot in Spring Grove. Whereabouts today, unknown.

Stories in the Grove

The mystery of the Emery Angel sculptor remains, as well as the whereabouts of the clamshell font, but the mystery of the angel's original function is solved, resulting in a happy ending to the story. And let's face it, we all love a happy ending.

Fritz Tree Stone

◦ ◇ ◦

I LOVE TREE STONE MONUMENTS, and Spring Grove has more than forty of these mysterious pieces of art. One of the finest examples is the fourteen-foot high tree stone memorial to the Jacob Fritz family. I often describe the monument as a piece of Folk Art, with its own story behind the monument, its maker, and the family it memorializes.

The tree stone was inspired by German immigrants and their tradition of planting a live tree on burial sites. In America, the immigrants carved memorials to look like trees, but these trees were depicted with branches cut to symbolize a life cut short. Indiana has numerous smaller versions of the tree stone, in the form of logs. Many of the tree stones and logs are carved with the W.O.A. logo of the Woodmen of America insurance company.

A majority of the tree stones and log markers in Spring Grove have interesting iconography carved into them, such as flowers, ivy, animals, bibles, and more. The Fritz tree stone epitomizes funerary iconography. You can see carvings of: a broken padlock to represent opening the door to heaven, an open bible, hands with index fingers pointing to date of death, a serpent (evil) wrapped around an anchor (good). My favorite depicts a dove biting the tail of a beaver. It took more than five years, but I discovered it is another symbol representing good (the dove) commanding evil (the beaver) to stop cutting down trees (or ending lives). I have yet to see this in any other funerary art amongst the hundreds of American and European cemeteries I have visited.

I searched for background information on the family and their magnificent monument with no luck, until I received a handwritten letter from Fred Suhre, grandson of the tree stone monument maker, Herman Suhre. Mr. Suhre asked if I knew of any other monuments his grandfather had carved for Spring Grove. I found a few generic markers, but no tree stones. Fortunately for this story, Mr. Suhre was

Fritz tree stone

able to share a biography of the Suhre family and photos of their masterpiece tree stone monument soon after it was placed on the Fritz family lot in Spring Grove.

Suhre's tree stone was made for Jacob Fritz and his family. Fritz was a butcher with the Salisman Sausage Company, before he died at age 50. Herman Suhre, the monument maker, was referred to as, "one of the prominent Hoosiers living in Franklin County, Indiana." He was born in Germany in 1856 and he worked on his father's farm. Suhre also made wooden shoes since many of his father's customers were Dutch. In 1879, Suhre and his family came to America and settled in Cincinnati.

At age seventeen, Suhre studied free-hand drawing in the evenings, then served a four-year apprenticeship in stone carving and cutting. In 1877, he went to Germany to study for six months. When he returned to Cincinnati, he opened a monument business with Henry Oberhelman on Colerain Avenue, near Spring Grove Cemetery. He carved the Fritz tree stone there.

His son, Rudolph Suhre, also owned a monument business, Rudolph Suhre Sons Co. Thirteen years after carving the Fritz tree stone, Suhre retired, due to ill health, to a farm in Ripley County, Indiana. When he recovered, he came back to Cincinnati, but that time he worked in the newspaper business before purchasing a large tract of land in Brookville, Indiana, where he raised honey bees. He owned five bee yards with two hundred and thirty-five colonies.

Herman Suhre died in 1907 and is buried in Madison County, Illinois. His art, however, lives on in Spring Grove, continuing to fascinate visitors. The Fritz tree stone is no doubt among the most fascinating of Spring Grove's iconic monuments.

Herman Suhre made the Fritz tree stone.

Garden Sanctuary Lawn Crypt Sculptures (circa 1976)

◇ ◇ ◇

UPON OCCASION, TOURS ARE LED PAST four outdoor sculptures in a raised grassy area known as the Lawn Crypt. The Lawn Crypt contains more than 900 pre-fabricated in-ground crypts in a flat area previously used to cultivate sod for the cemetery. It's an attractive and expansive lawn with hundreds of low, flat memorial headstones. The Lawn Crypt is visually appealing, but it is the outdoor sculptures that attract attention, with tour visitors offering reactions such as, "So what's the story with those?" They are diverse and interesting sculptures. Some comment, "Those are so ugly!" and others remark, "I love those! What are they?"

The four modern sculptures were chosen by the former director of the Cincinnati Art Museum, Philip Adams. They provide focal points for the four quadrants, and symbolize the four stages of life, the four elements (earth, air, fire, and water), and the four seasons. The sculptures were designed by the famous Willet Studios of Philadelphia. Beside the sculpture is a large fountain, completed in 1982 and referred to as, "The fountain of faith."

Crypt Sculpture

The first sculpture represents the season of summer—air and youthful energy. The eternal reminder of birth and new life can be seen in burnished bronze birds that dangle gracefully from a mobile that rises fourteen feet into the air.

The second sculpture represents fall, fire, and maturity. In this sculpture, you see a tree-like shape containing bare branches of brass, with red, orange, and yellow faceted glass leaves glistening with light.

The third sculpture represents the beauty of winter. This is the tallest of the sculptures, and "reflects (the) serenity of old age, with "ice-like laminated crystal and glass prisms portraying water in its solid state."

The final sculpture symbolizes spring season, birth, and earth. The sculpture reminds us of new life, and the abstract sculpture that reminds the viewer of tulips, May apples, Jack-in-the-Pulpits, and other plants that bloom in the spring. The green acrylic and fiberglass materials in the sculpture are reminiscent of earth.

Love them or hate them, these iconic contemporary sculptures certainly elicit a reaction. Understanding the symbols and meaning of the sculpture only deepens visitor's appreciation of the art and how it memorializes those interred in Spring Grove.

Thomas Heatherington Graydon (1881-1949)

◦ ◇ ◦

I LOVE TO FIND HIDDEN GEMS IN THE FORM OF GRAVE MARKERS from old cemeteries. The one I found a few years ago in Spring Grove ranks among my favorites. The story of what seems to be a simple piece of stone is filled with intrigue, mystery, and one of my favorite places in the world, Ireland!

Sitting on the family lot of Captain Thomas Heatherington Graydon in Section 13 is a curious upright piece of stone with no iconography, no epitaphs, and no names. So who made it and why is it there? Before I address that mystery, let me tell you a little about Graydon's story.

Thomas H. Graydon was born in Cincinnati to Dr. Thomas W. and Anne Graydon in 1881. While attending Harvard, he played fullback on the football team and was selected All-American in 1901 and 1902. He gained additional notoriety in 1902 by his participation in a charity performance with the Barnum & Bailey Circus. While his classmates performed in a burlesque polo match, it was Graydon who was garnering attention by tumbling in "resplendent pink tights."

Graydon got more national attention when, in 1903, he married Helen Beryl Whitney the daughter of millionaire J. Parker Whitney to whom he had been engaged since she was fifteen. Their elopement was called a "Romeo and Juliet romance" when Graydon helped the bride escape from a New York Boarding school.

After Harvard, he and Helen returned to Cincinnati. Thomas worked for the Donald Kelly Company, manufacturers of men's shoes. When WWI broke out, he enlisted and as part of the occupation and force found himself reaching the Rhine River with the first combat troops, the first Harvard grad to do so. He returned to the United States in 1919, receiving an honorable discharge. Upon return, Graydon entered the insurance business with Colonel I. H. Dube.

The Graydon's marriage didn't endure and he married again, two more times. Sadly, it was his third wife, Marian, who he was riding with in their automobile, when it collided with a passenger bus near Westfield, Indiana, in 1949, unfortunately killing them both. They were en route to their home in New York from Santa Monica, California.

After such an eventful life, it stands to reason that Graydon would end up with a piece of historical significance on his family's lot in the cemetery. Thanks to the great granddaughter, Annie Naberhaus, a rumor was recently dismissed. The memorial came from Ireland and for years, it was rumored to be a piece of the famous Blarney Stone. Not the case. According to Naberhaus, the dark brownish-red stone

The Giant's Causeway is a rare geological area of 40,000 hexagonal columns on and around a "giant" causeway. According to the website for the Causeway, the stone columns are actually made from the results of three episodes of lava outflows over sixty million years ago! A mythical version stems from the legend by Finn MacCool, who said that it was humans who made the stones.

◇

Chapter One

column was brought to Cincinnati by ship from the renowned Giant's Causeway in the North Antrim area of Ireland. Prior to its placement on the family lot in Spring Grove, it was kept at her grandmother's home.

I was curious as to why such a significant piece of ancient history ended up on the Graydon family lot. Quite serendipitously, I came across a biography of Graydon Jr. and Sr. in *Memoirs of the Miami Valley*. In the information on Captain Graydon's studies at Harvard, it says: "Here he took up a scientific course of study, specializing in geology." That's one connection to the monument. And the other? It turns out that his father was from where else? Ireland! Yet another Spring Grove mystery is solved.

Thomas and his Harvard football teammates.

Florence Groff (1880-1948)

○ ◇ ○

THE SONG "WALK LIKE AN EGYPTIAN" was popular in the 1980s. The Groff story is about a woman who not only walked like one, but is buried like one in Spring Grove. After an illustrious life as an archeologist and writer, Florence Groff's life ended in poverty and squalor. Her story, however, is filled with mystery and intrigue befitting an archaeologist who studied the ancient Egyptians.

Groff's father, William, was born in Philadelphia in 1813. William graduated from the University of France and served as a translator with the Egyptian government, speaking more than 32 languages. He also wrote history and antiquarian works in the Oriental languages and French. His books included one that identified the mummy of the Pharaoh featured in Exodus, books about Egypt and the Bible, the origin of Christianity in Egypt, and school books used in both Europe and Egypt. William was the only American member of the Royal Egyptian Institute.

Florence followed in her father's footsteps, reportedly speaking between 22 and 36 languages! She was a graduate of Oriental Languages in Paris and a notable writer. She authored *Guide to Cairo* and catalogues of Egyptian and Arab antiquities.

A successful career did not shield Florence from tragedy. Her father died and was buried in Athens in 1900, followed by her mother, Sarah E. Talbott, who was buried in Ghizeh, near the pyramids. A year later, her brother, William N., died and was buried near the Acropolis. The sudden loss of family was difficult for Florence, causing her to withdraw from the outside world. Reportedly she was living alone in Mobile, Alabama, in 1907, before she returned to her archeological research in the Middle East.

Eventually she returned to her hometown, Cincinnati, where she had inherited the family home. Florence continued her mysterious ways, living a solitary life away from the public eye. In 1919, she left Cincinnati and built a home in New York where she lived in seclusion with a friend, the accomplished artist Miss Jennie Brookbank. According to reports, they shunned the outside world in their shuttered and unkempt home. They allowed their collection of cats to roam day and night. Only an occasional lantern could be seen in the house, devoid of electricity. Groff was often seen wearing black Arabian robes with a long black veil and carried an umbrella, rain or shine, in her hand. An eccentric turban only further fueled the mysterious persona she had created for herself.

On January 21, 1948, Brookbank, who had not been seen for days, was discovered dead when the police broke into the ramshackle house. The ninety-year-old artist was frozen amongst the debris of the home she shared with Groff. Two months later, Groff was also found freezing inside the home. She insisted on being admitted to Grasslands Hospital in Eastview, N.Y. as a "charity patient" before she died. This time, the police went through the debris in the house and found stocks, bonds, French coins, Egyptian relics and oil paintings. Authorities also discovered that Groff had five bank accounts! But no one had expected that the eccentric woman, who lived as a pauper, would have left an estate estimated at $50,000, most of which was dedicated to the erection of a grandiose monument for her burial in Spring Grove.

◇ Florence Groff's
unusual headstone

Groff first wrote her will in Athens, Greece, in 1902. Four years later, it was rewritten, and the modified will was found in the Groff family home in Cincinnati. It included one of the strangest memorial requests I've ever seen in Spring Grove: a pyramid.

Groff's will stated: "The monument is to be in the form of a pyramid, the base of the pyramid to be the size of lot (425 square feet). On the front of the entrance door of the pyramid tomb is to be the name of Groff, on one side written in modern Egyptian and on the side in Greek..." The will continued, as Groff included her own rough sketches and instructions for her burial. The pyramid was completed in 1957 by the Goodall Monument Works, Inc. after almost nine years of litigation and argument from Groff's family. A compromise was agreed upon and only $10,000 of the original $40,000 was allotted for the pyramid. The monstrous size did not conform to the cemetery's regulations, so it was scaled down significantly when finally erected on the Groff family lot. However, the Groff family name was indeed engraved in both Egyptian and Greek.

Today you can find a modest-sized granite pyramid on the burial lot of the Groff family in section 46. It is six feet tall and six feet wide. A nice size, but not what Groff had wanted. After all, the Victorians preceded her family monument with hundreds, if not thousands, of tall obelisks that reach to the heavens in the cemetery. Florence wanted something different and unique to not only symbolize the tomb of the Pharaohs but to also represent her family's association with archeology.

Groff spent her life studying pyramids so it was befitting of her to choose one for her memorial. Florence Groff was buried like an Egyptian, just like the daughter of a Pharaoh would have wanted.

Belinda Groshon (1788-1822)
◦ ◇ ◦

I'VE ALWAYS BEEN FASCINATED WITH FIGURATIVE STATUES in cemeteries. They always make me curious about the stories of the people they represent. Belinda Poole Groshon's full-sized statue stands elegantly and dramatically near her burial spot; surely her story must be equally dramatic. With mysterious name changes, missing children, and the intrigue of early American theatre, Groshon had more than enough drama for her monument.

Belinda Groshon did indeed have a life filled with drama. As an English-born actress, she was lauded as "elevating the character of the American stage" after coming to New York from England in 1813. *Odell's History of The New York Theater* referred to her as "a newcomer of importance to the New York Stage." In 1813–1816, then going by the name of Goldson she was a key figure in bringing dueling actors and managers together before she received a range of reviews from "we cannot withhold our commendation," of her Lady Macbeth, to "it was happily soon over," of her Constance in "Marmion."

Suddenly, on June 26, 1816, Goldson was introduced as "Mrs. Groshon, late Mrs. Goldson" before a benefit performance, but no reason was ever given for the name change. From then on, she went by Belinda Groshon. She had a son from her first marriage, and her monument in Spring Grove contains

◇ Belinda Groshon's monument.

Chapter One

a poem that could have been written by her son as it begins with "Oft mother as I knelt beside thy knee."

Groshon's New York stint ended in 1818 when she came to Cincinnati and performed at the only theater in town at the time, The Cincinnati Theater, on Second Street between Main and Sycamore. She was known for her Lady Macbeth, which many considered to be the tour de force of the characters she portrayed on stage. One admirer said she took "precedence in rank of all other actresses of the West."

Some say that Groshon died while performing Lady Macbeth on stage but to the contrary, she was performing as Imogene in a "celebrated tragedy" called "Bertram" on Wednesday, January 9, 1822, and died twenty-two days later. Friends and acquaintances were invited to attend her funeral two days later at the home of a Miss Junge. On February 4, a fellow actor by the name of Henderson recited a long poem that was carved onto the base of her monument. *The Inquisitor and General Advertiser* included this comment in their lengthy obit: "The tragic muse has seldom possessed a more powerful votary west of the Atlantic than in the person of this interesting woman." Henderson, the actor, was to give a benefit in Columbus the following day, but it was postponed three days "by reason of this sad event." Groshon was obviously revered in the theater world.

Initially, Groshon was laid to rest in the Episcopal Grounds cemetery, which Washington Park now occupies. But it wasn't until 1852 that her casket was removed and reinterred in Spring Grove. The lot was not owned by anyone from the Goldson or Groshon families, but by Mrs. Eliza Dupuy and J.L. Morris. Dupuy was a member of Cincinnati's elite literary circle, along with such notables as Harriet Beecher Stowe and William Henry Harrison. Groshon lies to the right of the monument, leaving an empty space on the opposite side. Elsewhere on the lot are Dupuy's husband, William D. Dupuy, and two members connected with the Longworth family: John Longworth (infant son of Thomas and Appia Longworth) and Nicholas Longworth Morris (son of John and Elizabeth Morris). Turns out that William D. Dupuy died a year after Groshon. Could he have been an illegitimate son of Groshon? But what about Groshon's former husband and their son? Samuel Goldson is listed in the cemetery records as the son of Samuel and Melinda Goldson. Melinda? Mighty close to Belinda, wouldn't you say?

The final resting places for Mrs. Dupuy, and John and Elizabeth Morris, are unknown, as is their connection with Groshon. The drama of Belinda Groshon's life is beautifully memorialized by her marble statue in Spring Grove, but her drama did not end on the stage. It continues at her gravesite, with the mysterious folks along side her.

Charles R. Hall (1878-1945)

◦ ◇ ◦

THERE IS NO OTHER WAY TO SAY IT—Charles R. Hall loved flowers. A lumberman by trade, he made a fortune during his life. In death, he was very generous to friends and family, but his generosity didn't stop his indulgence in flowers even after his death! In his will, he left $20,000 for cut flowers to be left on his gravesite.

In 1909, Hall was listed in a trade book as building a $12,000 "duplex dwelling on the east side of Burnet Avenue." There's not much else to report about Hall's career. His vocation may have been simple, but he amassed a fortune that he left in a large trust fund.

Hall was a generous soul, leaving his jewelry to his niece, Belle Armstrong; $5,000 to a sister, Cora L. Faught; and $7,000 to various nieces and nephews. He even left the Cincinnati Zoo $1,000 and requested a tree (he preferred an oak) be planted in his memory there. The estate was divided among the Salvation Army, the Mystic Shrine Home for Crippled Children, the General Protestant Orphan Home, the Scottish Rite, to Mooseheart, Illinois (an unincorporated village home for children run by the Loyal Order of Moose, near Aurora, Illinois) and Moosehaven (a retirement village, also founded by the Loyal Order of Moose in Orange Park, Florida). Hall even left his clothing to the Cincinnati Altenheim, another retirement home and Cincinnati charity.

After Hall's benevolent trust fund provided for his friends and family, he designated the First National Bank to execute the trust and that money be taken to pay for having the monument and four markers at his gravesite cleaned every April. $20,000 was to be allotted for flowers at the gravesite. His sister, Ruth Hall, and

⋄ Charles R. Hall's footstone.

◇

Barbara Kaufman, his housekeeper, was mentioned in the will and given Hall's home on Hearne Avenue, household goods, and $7,500.

housekeeper Barbara Kaufman, were to buy the cut flowers. It was stipulated that the flowers be put on his marker at various times during the year. Hall specified in his will that, "cut flowers, in vases, be placed at the head of graves on lot 286 in Spring Grove Cemetery every Sunday from May 1 to November 30," as well as on holidays. But in the end, $8,600 was actually allotted to the floral placements. Five years worth of cleaning of a monument and four markers on his lot was also included in the price.

Spring Grove encourages only environmentally and maintenance friendly items on grave sites, especially cut flowers. But I have witnessed some interesting items placed on gravesites, in addition to flowers, such as beer cans, stuffed animals, a pair of dice, stones, and even candy bars. Encouraging fresh cut flowers is in keeping with Adolph Strauch's original plan to keep Spring Grove uncluttered and free from extraneous visual distractions. He no doubt would have been pleased with Mr. Hall's will.

Independent Order of the Odd Fellows Monument

◇

ONE OF THE LARGEST MONUMENTS IN THE CEMETERY belongs to a national fraternity known as The Independent Order of the Odd Fellows (I.O.O.F.); it is anything *but* odd. The organization is dedicated to social and personal improvement, to aid those in need, and to the eradication of vice. A tragic event in 1881 changed the story of this magnificent monument, memorializing the dedicated members of more than ten lodges associated with the Odd Fellows, and forever connected this monument to the rich tapestry of American history.

The history of the monument began when the I.O.O.F. Grand Lodge of Ohio purchased a lot in an area of Spring Grove known as "The Old Burying Ground." When the beautiful knoll the monument sits on became available, the Odd Fellows took full advantage by erecting their memorial. At a height of thirty-four feet, it's an imposing sight in section 15. Constructed of gray granite and bronze, it consists of three parts: a massive base, a cluster of three columns, and a ten-foot statue of Moses that stands stoically on top. In one hand, he holds the tablets of the law on which the commandments are written in Hebrew. The other holds the rod, or emblem, of the Royal Blue Degree of the Order. Three broad steps lead up to a triangular base with three vertical faces ornamented with bronze bas-relief panels that represent Jonathan and David after the covenant, Rebekah at the well with attendant personages about her, and a patriarchal scene showing an elderly man welcoming a stranger into an "Oriental" tent while an armed guard stands in the foreground.

The Odd Fellows allowed no lodge to contribute towards the monument project for fear that their contributions to widows and orphans would be sacrificed. The money was raised through events that they referred to as "entertainments," which included festivals, fairs, etc. It took ten years to secure funding ($20,000), which was then put into bonds.

The monument was created by two other Spring Grove residents, Louis Rebisso and August Mundhenk. Their work could be seen at their foundry on Hunt and Main streets in downtown Cincinnati before being placed on the monument in the cemetery.

Local Odd Fellows, as well as those from across the nation, excitedly anticipated the grand unveiling on September 20, 1881. One account of the day estimated more than 50,000 members of the order were expected to attend. But before the unveiling, tragedy struck America when President Garfield was shot at a Washington railroad depot by attorney and shunned political office-seeker, Charles Guiteau, on July 2. Sixteen doctors went to Washington to aid in Garfield's recovery and Americans held tight to the belief Garfield would recover. Unfortunately, on September 19, Garfield suffered a massive heart attack and died.

America was grief-stricken, and the I.O.O.F. monument's grand unveiling, scheduled for the following day, became nothing like the celebration planned. The nation was grieving the loss of their president, and no one felt very joyous. As a result, the parade that was planned was abandoned, and the elaborate ceremony became a simple, introspective, affair. A reunion and concert at the famed Highland House and a banquet at the Burnet House were cancelled.

◇ Odd Fellows monument created by Louis Rebisso and August Mundhenk.

Stories in the Grove

Many citizens involved with the ceremony wanted to hold a large, solemn, funeral cortege, "with muffled drums and regalia draped in mourning." Those in attendance, particularly Odd Fellows, were instructed to wear badges of mourning. After uncertainty about the purpose of the event and the appropriateness of holding a celebration so soon after a tragedy, only one thousand were estimated to attend the unveiling.

At the unveiling, the monument was enclosed in a wooden structure, and inside was a tier of seats for the Sovereign Grand Lodge and other invited guests. A platform for spectators stood outside the structure. The entire monument was covered in white linen, which was dropped with pulleys for the dramatic unveiling. The Honorable S. S. Davis, Chairman of the Monument Committee, delivered a formal address that included a brief history of the project. There was applause after the unveiling, but it was brief and somber in light of the President's death.

While the unveiling turned out to be like nothing that had been planned, those in attendance were left with memories of a day that forever changed American history. The Odd Fellows monument isn't only a significant work of art or a landmark in Spring Grove, but is emotionally connected to a significant event in our nation's past.

The Sphinx

◦ ◇ ◦

ONE LOOK AT THIS MYSTERIOUS MONUMENT and you know there has to be a story behind it!

Half woman, half animal, the Egyptian sphinx is made of a rare blue marble, said to be quarried in Murphy, North Carolina, and rests on a Columbus limestone base. Visitors who come across the Sphinx wonder how it got there, and what it means. Mysteriously hidden in the middle of section 45, this mystical monument was erected by Davis B. Lawler in 1854 as a memorial to his parents, Mathew and Ann, of Philadelphia, who died in the 1830s, and his two infant brothers.

Davis B. Lawler (1786–1869) was born in Philadelphia to Mathew and Ann Lawler. He passed away in 1869 in downtown Cincinnati. His father, Mathew

(1755–1831), fought in the Revolutionary War as a privateer and was the mayor of Philadelphia from 1801 to 1804. Lawler was a prosperous businessman and one of the original founders of the cemetery, which might be why he was permitted to erect such an interesting monument. Lawler was known for his generosity. He donated the beautiful marble statue, titled "Silence," to the Cincinnati Mercantile Library. Lawler's parents were agnostic, which may have been another reason for the somewhat pagan monument. A message on the Sphinx states: "the future is unknowable," adding to the mystery of the monument.

The sphinx monument, made of rare blue marble.

The Spring Grove cemetery report of 1857 mentions a Spring Grove director objecting to the monument's symbolism as heathen and offensive in a Christian nation. However, others praised its colors as sober and somber, more to, "suit the taste of some who complain of the too great prevalence of white marble in our Cemeteries." The report goes on to say, "It does not accord with the prevailing taste, but it helps to relieve the monotony of which some persons complain, caused by the too frequent recurrence of obelisks, columns, and Oothic (sic.) pinnacles; and its colors, sober and somber, suit the taste of some…"

The truth behind the Sphinx and its meanings may never be known. Before his death, Lawler lost his faculties and ability to write. He had a fall and a concussion, followed by "loss of memory of written language (aphasia)." There was a legal contest over his will, which included an estate valued over $500,000. The Sphinx was largely forgotten in the legal dispute and Lawler's incapacitation.

So many mysteries surround this unusual but impressive monument. Did Lawler decide on a sphinx to symbolize a treacherous and merciless monster as was believed by the Greeks? Or perhaps he believed in the more benevolent view of the Egyptians. Whether Lawler's symbolic intent of the sphinx was malevolence or benevolence, the answer is as mysterious and inscrutable as the Sphinx itself.

D.B. Lawler wrote to the cemetery board on February 7, 1850, asking permission for an "avenue" to be cut through the family lot but the request was eventually denied, even though he stated that he would pay for the project.

One of the largest sphinxes in the U.S. is in Mount Auburn Cemetery in Cambridge, Massachusetts. It is 15-feet long. In comparison, the Lawler sphinx is about half the size.

The Unknown Painter

◦ ◇ ◦

HERE'S A GREAT STORY OF MISTAKEN IDENTITY THAT, in 1943, pitted coroner against coroner from two different states. As the story goes, according to Dr. Vincent Stabile, the Coroner of Jefferson County, Kentucky, said that Hamilton County's Coroner, Frank M. Coppock, made a mistake and an unidentified painter was reportedly given an expensive casket and buried in Spring Grove.

The unidentified painter was found dead in a "tourist cabin" in the area of Louisville, Kentucky. According to a selective service card found with his body, the painter's name was Herbert Ralph Scollon and he was from Cincinnati. The Busse and Borgman Funeral Home directors and the city funeral director purchased an "expensive casket" and had the body shipped to Cincinnati. It was interred, and because the body was in such poor condition, nobody opened the casket before it was buried.

In the meantime, Mr. Scollon's mother wrote to Dr. Stabile to ask how they identified her son. While she was writing the inquiry, Mrs. Scollon received the shock of her life when her son walked into her home after traveling from Atlanta! He told his mother that he had lost his selective service card and wallet the year before. Upon hearing that Scollon was not dead, the Kentucky coroner had the unknown body exhumed and fingerprints were taken. When Coppock agreed to the procedure, Dr. Stabile said that he had telephoned Spring Grove, at his expense, and agreed to pay for the interment ($20.00). According to reports, before he sent the money, Spring Grove's secretary called and told Dr. Stabile that Coppock would not give authorization because, "it was out of his jurisdiction."

Dr. Stabile was not pleased with the refusal and later declared that, "It now develops that the man may be a fugitive from a Georgia chain gang. But we will probably never know now, because we were unable to get fingerprints. The body is probably decomposed and it would do no good to try for the prints now." He went on to say, "I am through trying to identify the man. I got no assistance and I can't do it all alone."

The saga continued when B.J. Bax, Cincinnati's city funeral director, respond-ed to a lack of agreement on who would pay for the casket and lot by saying, "It looks like the Busse and Borgman Company is stuck with it. I did it on their order. All I'm out is the gasoline to go after the body and haul it to the train." The mystery of the unknown painter is one that will likely never be solved!

John Vonderheid (1858-1944)

◦ ◇ ◦

HIDDEN IN THE MONUMENTS AND MEMORIALS OF SPRING GROVE are fascinating stories and vignettes that illuminate human nature. Here's the story of the Vonderheid mausoleum—a story filled with mystery and intrigue. It involves an art-loving janitor who seemed to have little wealth when he was alive, but man-aged to have the last laugh on his family when he had a costly granite mausoleum built on his Spring Grove lot in 1944.

John Vonderheid lived a simple life, working as a janitor at the illustrious Cincin-nati Art Museum for thirty years, and then the Baldwin Piano Company for fifteen years. Known to possess sculptor's tools at one time, his love of fine art was most likely inspired by the time he spent at the Art Muse-um. But the salary for janitors in the early 1900s wasn't known to be very large, leaving Von-derheid little income to purchase fine art.

The story gets more interesting after Vonderheid's death. His apart-ment on Elm Street was mysteriously ransacked after his death. Appar-ently, his heirs had heard rumors of Vonderheid accumulating $100,000 in securities, and they wanted to find it, illegally if necessary! According to reports, two nephews and two nieces had opened trunks in Vonderheid's apartment and

A granite mausoleum fit for a janitor.

scattered the contents on the floor. They gained entrance to the apartment through a door that had been broken days before by the police, just before they discovered Vonderheid's body.

The relatives didn't realize their search was unnecessary. An attorney for the estate, Edward Lillie, had summoned the police to investigate the apartment, and despite the break-in, the "fortune hunt" had been authorized by the court because nephew Frank L. Vonderheid was named the administrator of the estate. After Lillie and Frank spoke, a van moved the contents of the apartment to an undisclosed area.

Captain George Eutle of Cincinnati police wasn't sure if he should declare the illegal search as a burglary or a house break-in. Miss Minnie Henderson, who lived on the third floor of Vonderheid's apartment building, said there were "unidentified visitors" seen days before. A Chinese laundry owner on Central Avenue reported visitors to the apartment when he delivered laundry on the same day. But as administrator of the estate, Frank Vonderheid was placed on a $6,200 bond signed by his relatives.

There was some discrepancy about the actual worth of Vonderheid's estate. Some said, "$3,100 in personal property." Others said no real estate was listed. One thing for sure though: Vonderheid had accumulated enough money to build a private mausoleum in Spring Grove. Some newspaper reports alluded to Vonderheid building it only for himself, but members of the family have been entombed inside the structure since his death.

Vonderheid may not have owned fine art in life, but he did purchase fine art for the afterlife—an elegant granite mausoleum for $18,000.

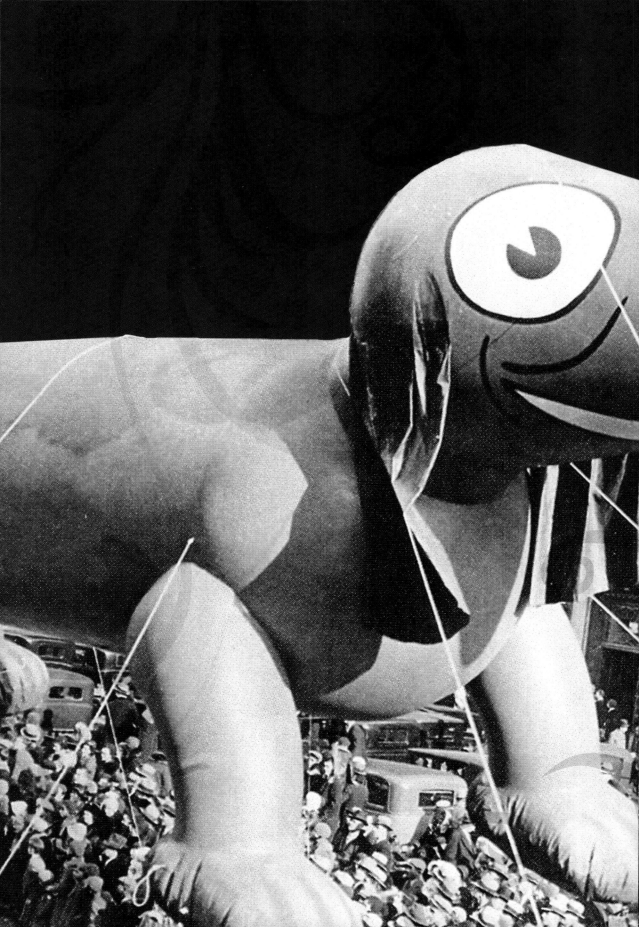

GENIUS AND VIRTUOSO

Dr. Leland C. Clark (1918-2005)

◦ ◇ ◦

SOMETIMES WE TAKE THE SIMPLE ACT of breathing for granted. Dr. Leland C. Clark's contributions to improving the quality of our lives are inspirational! They involve innovations that have improved the breathing of millions of people, as well as advancements to molecular genetics, aviation and space flight, and cell culture. Even advances in wine and beer production have been attributed to Dr. Clark. Combine those contributions, plus over two dozen U.S. patents, and you have a brilliant man with an inspirational story.

Dr. Clark was known as "The Father of Biosensors" due to his impressive contributions in the medical field. He was born in Rochester, New York, and graduated from the Rochester School of Medicine and Dentistry. He was a graduate of Antioch College and it was there, at the Fels Research Institute, he helped invent the bubble oxygenator in 1949. He was known for his passion for learning science, and was once quoted as saying, "It was like discovering that you could get a grade for eating chocolate ice cream."

Dr. Clark helped develop perfluorocarbon-based artificial blood and also invented the first practical heart-lung machine. Famed area cardiologist, Dr. Samuel Kaplan, helped Dr. Clark work on it at Cincinnati's Children's Hospital. In 1966, Dr. Clark used a mouse in a famous experiment involving the breathing of liquid fluorocarbon. As a result, clinical trials with premature infants were a success.

Clark developed a device to determine the level of glucose in the blood, permitting millions of diabetics to monitor their own blood-sugar levels. That's not all! He developed the Clark Oxygen Electrode, which measures blood oxygen levels and is regarded as one of the most "revolutionary

Dr. Leland Clark. "The Father of Biosensors" and king of mutton chops.

devices" in medicine over the past 50 years. It's amazing to think that it has saved the sight of many premature babies who otherwise would have gone blind from excess oxygen while being treated for respiratory distress syndrome.

Without Dr. Clark's oxygen electrode, doctors would not be able to perform over 750,000 open-heart surgeries every year. And I love that it is used to measure oxygen levels in rivers and oceans to protect wildlife populations. In addition to the lives of hundreds of humans, other species have been saved by Dr. Clark's inventive mind.

Dr. Clark was an incredible man. He had around 80 inventions, and held 25 U.S. patents before he passed away. Biosensors, bubble oxygenators, heart-lung machines, artificial blood, and the oxygen electrode were all unknown to me before I discovered the story of this genius who made millions of people with respiratory problems more comfortable in their daily lives. Dr. Clark's last breath was taken at his daughter's home in 2005. His legacy lives on in our healthier society.

Alfred Oscar Elzner (1862-1933)
George Mendenhall Anderson (1869-1916)

◦ ◇ ◦

ANYBODY WHO TRAVERSES THE EASTERN boundary of the cemetery usually comments on the massive and lengthy stone wall that gracefully meanders up Winton Road. I told the story of the stone wall, but the stories of the men who designed the wall as well as the shelter houses in the cemetery, are equally as interesting.

The architectural firm of Elzner & Anderson, formed by Spring Grove residents A.O. Elzner and George M. Anderson, was responsible for the design of the wall, as well as many of Cincinnati's finest buildings, including schools, the Baldwin Piano Company on Mitchell Avenue, the old Longview Mental Hospital, the Ingalls Building, Christ Church Cathedral, the American Book Company, and the Cincinnati Country Club. Elzner & Anderson were well known among elite Cincinnatians, such as the Emery, Procter, and Taft families, who valued their superior design and construction. Not all Elzner & Anderson projects were local.

THE STUDIOS OF "BEAU BRUMMELL" CINCINNATI
MAKERS OF GENUINE PALM BEACH CRAVATS . . . BURTON'S POPLIN TIES . . . 4FOLD SPORTOWN WOOLS

○ Another example of Elzner and Anderson's signature architecture.

The historical and famous Homestead Hotel in Hot Springs, Virginia, was an Elzner & Anderson commission.

A.O. Elzner's background is impressive. Early in his career, he studied with artist Frank Duveneck and attended the prestigious Massachusetts Institute of Technology in Boston. Around 1885, he worked with the famed architect H.H. Richardson and then two years later, he left Boston to set up his office in Cincinnati. Fame came to him when he designed the first reinforced concrete building in the world (the Ingalls Building) at Fourth and Vine streets in Cincinnati. As a result, he was considered "a pioneer in reinforced concrete." Few realize that in addition to his penchant for architecture, Elzner was a local music professor.

The prominent Anderson families in Cincinnati spawned quite a few architects in the 1800s and early 1900s. George M. Anderson trained in New York City and studied with Louis B. Tiffany before studying at the *Ecoles des Beaux Arts*

Chapter Two

in Paris. He was the first Cincinnatian to receive a diploma from the *Ecole*. George had aspirations of becoming an architect even before going to Europe and upon his return he worked as a draftsman for Samuel Hannaford in the late 1800s and then partnered with A.O. Elzner. Not unlike Elzner, Anderson had another talent besides architecture. It was said that if he had not become an architect, he would have been a painter because he loved to paint in his spare time, especially water colors. (His mother, Emma Mendenhall, was also a talented artist.) In 1896, his watercolors of Paris, Siena, and Venice were displayed at the Cincinnati Art Museum and the following year at the First Annual Exhibition of the Society of Western Artists. In 1904, George was a delegate to the International Convention of Architects in London and he was the director of Spring Grove from 1906 to 1916.

George was among several Andersons who were directors of Spring Grove at one time or another. Isaac Anderson was the contractor for Samuel Hannaford's beautiful Norman Chapel in Spring Grove, as well as the maintenance sheds used in the cemetery.

Another member of the family, William Pope Anderson, was a financier, industrialist, and founder of the Ferro Concrete Construction Company which built the Ingalls Building. George's brother, Robert, was also vice-president. William was President of the American Concrete Institute in 1922–23 and at one time, worked as a survey engineer for mine and smelting interests in Colorado. At Spring Grove, he followed in George's footsteps and became director of Spring Grove from 1917 to 1951.

Elzner & Anderson designed their own homes, as well as some of Cincinnati's most notable homes, such as Alberly Manor, the home of mattress king, Edward Stearns. In Spring Grove, they made their mark by designing the beautiful stone shelter houses and the Winton Road wall, considered by some to be the longest stone wall in the Midwest.

There you have it, two talented architects who contributed to the beauty of Spring Grove and managed to hone their talent in the areas of art and music. The next time you see a building or stone wall that piques your interest, think about the story of the people who built them. The wall and the buildings may be impressive but the stories of their creators are sometimes even more so.

Stephen Gerrard (1860-1936)

◦ ◇ ◦

THE FIRST OF THE MORE THAN 40 private family mausoleums in the cemetery is the Gerrard family mausoleum, at the southwest corner of Section 22. Its striking 1930, Art Deco-inspired appearance is a show-stopper on every tour. A granite urn with an eternal flame and a base with four ferocious lion heads warding off evil spirits, sits on the pinnacle of the roof. The simplified neoclassical structure with Art Deco lines incorporates many low relief ornaments representing stylized plant life. People marvel at the story behind the impressive monument and the botanical carvings.

The patriarch of the family was Stephen Gerrard, who made his fortune in the produce industry, particularly melons. He began as a truck farmer and produce merchant before literally building an empire with his farms in several states. He became the largest distributor of cantaloupes in the country, thus the nickname "King of Melons."

Gerrard began his business with a wagon. At two in the morning he would wake up, buy produce and fruit from area farmers, and then load it on his wagon before peddling through the streets of Cincinnati. I love the report of him making his bed, "in a stable with a bale of hay for his pillow," and, as he would say, "The good mosquitoes for my alarm clock in the morning."

The Gerrard mausoleum has two eternal flames burning at the entrance.

Stephen married Estella Markley in 1880. Their first home was at Third and Whitaker streets downtown and then on Betula Avenue in North Avondale. The home on Betula Avenue has a rose theme, representing the Gerrard company logo, with an interior design by Charles A. Pedretti, another resident of Spring Grove (Section 103).

Mr. Gerrard was also an inventor. He hybridized the popular sweet, green honeydew melon and popularized

GENIUS AND VIRTUOSO

Chapter Two

In addition to the statues, the interior of the mausoleum contains motifs with Christian references and a beautiful stained glass window at the rear depicting the Last Supper from the Bible. There are more than 13 family members entombed in the mausoleum.

iceberg lettuce. Initially, Gerrard would go to Hormellsville, New York, to buy potatoes and cabbage to ship directly to Cincinnati. In 1885, he opened the Markley & Gerrard shipping business with his brother-in-law at 236 W. Sixth Street in downtown Cincinnati.

So, why is there so much plant life and symbolism incorporated into the family mausoleum? If you look past the mausoleum's stunning bronze gates, you will see four Carrere marble female statues standing in the four corners representing the four seasons of the year. I found a beautiful description on the statue representing spring in the archives: "Spring personifies the refreshing young beauty of the most delightful season of the year. In her arms she bears all the new blossoms of the springtime that has come to awaken the sleeping earth." The statues were carved in Italy, and then brought to Cincinnati to be placed inside the mausoleum.

The Gerrard family reportedly hired the artisans of the statues to also create the interior of the family's Tudor Revival home on Betula Avenue in the Avondale area of Cincinnati. I had the fortune to meet the present owners of the Gerrard home and tour both the exterior and interior. To my great surprise, I saw portrait paintings in the living room of both Stephen Gerrard and his wife, Estella. Also, the interior wood and plaster work was very similar to the botanical relief on the family mausoleum in Spring Grove.

A man who made his fortune in the plant and produce business, hired artisans to forever celebrate his business in the mausoleum!

Ernst Henry Huenefeld (1838-1931)

ANYONE WHO KNOWS ME WELL KNOWS THAT I ENJOY FOOD, so it will come as no surprise that I enjoyed discovering a story involving food and cook-

ing. This is the story of an unusual, impressive, and ingenious invention that made cooking easier for millions of people.

The man behind the invention was Ernst Huenefeld, who immigrated from Ladberegen, Prussia in 1845. He became an orphan at age eight within a year after his arrival in Ohio. Huenefeld grew up on an older brother's farm and by age 17, he was working for a brickyard and then a large coal company. Ernst and his two brothers, William and Herman, started the Huenefeld Greenhouse and Farm Company on the west side of Cincinnati. The Huenefeld farm was reportedly a popular place to buy Halloween pumpkins and Christmas trees. The Huenefelds branched into the world of manufacturing in the late 1800s and early 1900s.

One has to look no further than the bronze Ohio Historical marker at 2701 Spring Grove Avenue to learn about Huenefeld's invention. The marker stands in front of an old manufacturing building and says, "First glass door oven," in bold letters. It goes on to read, "Specially designed and patented sheet metal frames in the door allowed for expansion and contraction of the glass. The large window guaranteed against steaming up or breaking from heat allowed users to view their baking without opening the oven door." Huenefeld's invention now graces kitchens across the world. But the first glass door oven wasn't his only innovation.

In 1872, Ernst and John H. Schroer founded the Schroer & Huenefeld Company and began with the importing and selling of tin plate, metal tools and machines for shaping and cutting the metal. Huenefeld bought Schroer out in 1877 and expanded his knowledge of metals and markets. In the 1880s, he began to manufacture metal products. There was a period of time between 1896 and 1909 when he received around fourteen patents for his inventions. Four of those patents involved a stove oven door with a full-size glass window. 1909 marked the beginning of the first glass door oven for ranges and portable ovens. Prior to Huenefeld's invention, one could only view through dampers or openings with mica or small glass panels.

Huenefeld's company prospered and became a leading manufacturer of stoves, ovens, ranges, heaters, furnaces, refrigerators, washing machines, and other household products. Many countries where electricity, gas, and coal were unobtainable were able to purchase the stoves. Kerosene-fueled stoves from Huenefeld saw strong demand in Latin America, Africa, the Middle and Far East. The Cincinnati Company was one of the nation's largest manufacturers and exporters of kerosene stoves until 1966 when the manufacturing divisions were sold to the U.S. Stove Co. in Chattanooga and the Union Metal Manufacturing Co. in Canton, Ohio. Boss, Royal, Success, and Uneeda were a few of the Huenefeld products trade names which were exported to more than 43 countries.

Ernst died in 1931 at age 92 from pneumonia. The family has a beautiful Greek Doric mausoleum of Vermont granite in section 21 that gracefully sits next to the beautiful Cedar Lake. When it was completed in 1919, Huenefeld paid $2,400 for perpetual care, which included power washing every two years and caulking every twenty years or when needed. It reportedly won an architectural award upon completion.

◇

Stories in the Grove

Giving to others was another trademark of the Huenefeld family. Ernst was a major supporter of German Methodism in Ohio and became incorporator, trustee, and treasurer of Bethesda Hospital and Deaconess Association (now Tri-Health). In 1908, he donated "Scarlet Oaks" mansion to Bethesda for a retirement community. Another notable Cincinnati mansion, Bishop's Place, was owned by Ernst's son, Walter.

Every year, millions of people check on pumpkin pies to see when they are done by peering through glass door ovens. Were it not for Ernst Huenefeld and his standard invention of the glass door oven, many of those holiday meals may have ended with a much different story.

Marion Rombauer Becker (1903-1976)
John William Becker (1902-1974)

◦ ◇ ◦

MARION ROMBAUER BECKER AND HER MOTHER, Irma S. Rombauer, wrote *The Joy of Cooking* cookbook, a mainstay in many American kitchens. I've used my personal copy of the cookbook for years. It was a revelation when I discovered Marion is interred in Spring Grove.

The Joy of Cooking legacy began in 1931 when Marion's mother wrote the original and self-published *The Joy of Cooking: A Compilation of Reliable Recipes with a Casual Culinary Chat.* It was a new style of cookbook and, as said by Mimi Sheraton, "represented a milestone with its wide-ranging assortment of recipes and its down-to-earth explicitness that soon established a new style for cookbook writing." Marion provided paper cuttings for illustrations in the first edition.

It was in 1936, that an expanded edition was published that included 300 more pages. What made this cookbook so unique for the American cook was that for the first time, the reader could review a chronological listing of ingredients and then instruction for preparation. By the end of 1942, the second edition had gone through six printings, and 52,151 copies had been sold. By 2006, the book had gone through over 15 editions and had sold 18 million copies.

Irma Rombauer and Marion Rombauer Becker

When Irma died in 1962, Marion stepped in and became the lone author. She made her mark quickly in the series. She recognized the importance of using line drawings and illustrations instead of photography so as to not date the cookbook over time. Marion understood the importance of art even before she started on the series. She taught art and was a founder and director of the Cincinnati Modern Art Society, and worked on *Women's Wear Daily*.

In addition to her interests in art and cooking, Marion also enjoyed gardening. She wrote a book titled *Wild Wealth* which received the "Oak Leaf" award from the Nature Conservancy, and the Medal of Merit award from the Garden Club of America. With her success, Marion became the first woman to receive the "Great Living Cincinnatian" award. Marion died in 1976 and her connection to nature was memorialized with boxwood, appropriately named, *Buxus sempervirens Joy.* It means, Evergreen boxwood Joy.

Marion was married to John Becker, who had an impressive career as an architect. Becker's love of architecture and design can be seen on the family lot, which has a brushed aluminum "wing" sculpture on a black granite base, created by Michael Bigger. Marion and her son, Ethan, consulted with Bigger on the design of the monument after John's death. They already owned some of his pieces, and had struck up a friendship with the artist.

The monument in Spring Grove is not the first placed on John's gravesite. The first was a solid block of polished black granite with a slot for the wing. When the monument was delivered to Cincinnati, the temperature was around 40 degrees, but it had originally been stored in Vermont at temperatures below freezing and the stainless wing hadn't been installed. After the monument installers from Vermont arrived in Cincinnati to set the block, they poured a setting compound made of sulfur and water and lowered the stainless steel wing in place. The next morning,

Helios Guardians, the large monumental sculpture of a stylized herd of animals at the Cincinnati Zoo, was also created by Bigger. According to Bigger in a letter to Cecie Chewning in 2005, it was purchased by the City of Hamilton with the hopes of placing it in their Pyramid Hill Sculpture Park. Bigger also did a bronze low-relief realistic bust on a large granite boulder in southern Minnesota.

The Becker monument is a stunning visual tribute to an artistic and creative family and it serves as a memorial to their art, architecture, horticulture, and culinary genius for future generations.

◇

Bigger discovered the water based grout around the wing had frozen, expanded, and put a severe crack in the granite.

It was agreed that the monument couldn't be used, so a new one was made with the same design, but utilizing a different construction method. The present monument is similar in construction to a contemporary office building in that the granite exterior is ¾ of an inch thick over an interior structure of stainless steel designed by a structural engineer.

Charles Hanauer (1860-1948)

◇ ◇ ◇

YOU DON'T NORMALLY associate bicycling history with Cincinnati, but the story of the city is filled with icons of bicycling, including Charles Hanauer. Similar to Harry Ellard's story, Hanauer made a name for himself with sporting goods and bicycles, but Hanauer expanded as a manufacturer of automobiles. Hanauer's story closely mirrors the growing pains of America, moving from the idyllic pastime of bicycles to the frantic world of automobiles.

Hanauer was born in Maysville, Kentucky, in 1860 and received his education

A Hanauer fire engine

in Covington public schools. At an early age, he learned the skills of his mechanic father, who specialized in the manufacture and repair of machinery. When he was sixteen, Charles became an apprentice with the J.A. Fay Company, a company that made machinery for woodworking. Nine years later, in 1883, he founded a new company, the Charles Hanauer Cycle Company, manufacturing bicycles.

Bicycles were suited for Hanauer and his penchant for manufacturing. His company was known for having the most complete line of "Wheels in the West," and produced built-to-order bicycles with a choice of saddles, handle bars, and enamel colors. An advertisement in the *Cincinnati Illustrated Business Directory* touted the company as offering a "Riding school on premises," and "Instructions free to all purchases." Hanauer was an agent for American and English bicycle manufacturers and offered cycling accessories, such as riding clothes, lamps, polish, and tires. In addition to bicycles, the advertisement promoted other athletic goods including fire-arms and ammunition! Hanauer's company was located on Walnut Street in Cincinnati, and included a branch on Madison Avenue in Covington, Kentucky.

Hanauer's wife, Dr. Stella Hunt, was also actively involved in promoting her husband's business. Stella was the president of the Queen City Cycling Club that catered only to female bicyclists and met on the second floor of her husband's store on Walnut Street. Her father, Marcus Hunt, was also a manufacturer, building spring beds. Another family member, Hanauer's brother Andrew, assisted in the operation of the company.

After fifteen years as a bicycle manufacturer, Hanauer decided to branch out into the automobile industry. With the decline of cycling's popularity, the auto business had been growing by leaps and bounds; the timing was conducive for Hanauer's new venture. He was referred to as one of the best salesmen in America, and quickly added the title of President of the Hanauer Automobile Company to his resume. Initially, he only sold Pierce Arrow autos, but eventually added Packards and Cadillacs.

In 1902, the world's first gas-powered fire engine was invented by Charles A. Fox and his son-in-law, Chris Ahrens. It was created from a salvage car on a Winton automobile chassis, but the body was built at the Hanauer Bicycle Shop for local fire insurance companies, known as the Underwriters Salvage Corps of Cincinnati. The body was made of wood with wicker equipment lockers—quite fancy for those days!

After he ventured into the auto industry, he participated in the first automobile races in the Midwest during the fall of 1901. One of his competitors was a 10-horsepower auto built locally by the Lunkenheimer Company. *The Cincinnati Enquirer* hinted that Hanauer might have won the race had he not stopped several times to adjust the fuel mixture.

Hanauer embodied that critical moment in the history of America, when the automobile went from a promising technology to a critical component of modern life, and he did it with style, ingenuity, vision, and an occasional stop to adjust fuel!

Emerson Kemsies (1905-1970)

◦ ◇ ◦

AN UNUSUAL AND MYSTERIOUS MARKER STANDS OUT from its surroundings in section 14. Your eyes are drawn to the dark color of the stone. Look closer though and you will see a bas-relief of a bird. It seems obvious to the viewer that the story behind the deceased must involve a love of birds. Another tip off is the word "ornithologist" inscribed at the bottom. For years I had wondered about the story behind this very cool monument and like others, the story came from an unexpected source.

While interviewing John Ruthven one day, he offered an enlightening account of the "story behind the stone." The marker is a memorial to Emerson Kemsies who was a nationally known ornithologist and good friend of Ruthven's. Kemsies often accompanied Ruthven on field trips, in search of bird specimens. Kemsies was a ranger naturalist in Yellowstone National Park in 1929 and again in 1933. Many of his published articles were on birds in that area. Kemsies and Worth Randle wrote *The Birds of Southwestern Ohio* in 1953. Another "feather" in Kemsies' hat was when he became the head of the Ornithology Laboratory of the University of Cincinnati's Department of Biological Sciences, a perfect gig for a devoted bird collector.

Kemsies had few friends but as one of his best, Ruthven prevented Kemsies' prize bird collection at the University of Cincinnati from being sold. Much of it was successfully transferred to the Cincinnati Museum of Natural History and is

Robert McNesky
created "The Megalith"
memorial in section
135 in 1970. It consists
of two slabs of Ohio
limestone set in the
ground. Although
it has engravings
of faces, flowers,
and animals, it was
actually designed as a
memorial to people as a
whole. The memorial's
limestone is of the
Ordovician period (500
to 700 million years old)
and commonly found in
the Cincinnati area.

◇ Emerson Kernsies' grave stone.

now under the auspices of the Cincinnati Museum Center's Geier Center. I was astounded when Ruthven told me that the collection consists of around 75,000 birds!

So what about the bas-relief of the bird carved on Kemsies' marker? I'm pleased to say that it isn't a generic bird relief but one of Kemsies' favorite species, a Smith's Longspur. The artist responsible for the bas-relief turned out to be another friend and fellow artist of Ruthven's, Robert McNesky. Another homage to Kemsies' love of birds can be found in McNesky's bronze passenger pigeon at the passenger pigeon museum at the Cincinnati Zoo.

It amazes me to think how many times I viewed Kemsies' charming stone marker without knowing the man's story. Knowing exactly what kind of bird the marker depicts, the Smith's Longspur, and who Ruthven's best friend was, makes Kemsies' story even more amazing.

◇

Emerson Kemsies, by John A. Ruthven

I first met Emerson in 1958. A good friend and well known naturalist, Mr. Karl Maslowski, told me about Emerson. At that time, Emerson was a curator of birds at the University of Cincinnati. I was working on a bird identification book on ducks and geese of North America and I needed to see some of the specimens in the collection. It was a very fortunate meeting as we hit it off very well. He took the time to listen to my story and show me specimens I wanted to see. This collection is one of the finest in the country, and contains some 75,000 different "bird skins" from around the world. This meeting was doubly important because on the same day that I met Emerson, another wildlife artist, Mr. Bill Zimmerman, was there to see Mr. Kemsies as well. Over the years, both Emerson and Bill became my very good friends and we had a chance to spend many hours in the field studying birds.

The collection was called the Herbert W. Brant Collection, after its founder. Brant was a wealthy meat packer from Cleveland, Ohio, and his life-long hobby was writing about and collecting bird skins and eggs from all over the world. He wrote two volumes of stories about his adventures with birds. Both volumes are now collectors' items and very hard to find. The names of these are "Alaskan Game Trails- Volume I and II." After Mr. Brant passed away, the entire collection was sent to the University of Cincinnati until it was eventually sold. While at the University it was curated by Emerson Kemsies.

Because of the importance of the collection, many people called on Emerson for information about birds. I felt very fortunate to have had him as my teacher. Almost every

Chapter Two

weekend for ten years or so, we would drive up to Lake St. Mary's in central Ohio and collect specimens that we didn't have in order to augment the collection. If we succeeded in collecting birds, they would be cataloged, frozen, and then later, "skinned out" and preserved. Over the years, many fine and unusual specimens were obtained. Some were first records for Ohio.

Emerson spent a lot of time with a fellow birder, Worth Randal, studying the life histories of birds called "Longspurs," particularly the Smith's Longspur. Emerson was credited with naming a new sub-species of that bird. Being a founding member of the Cincinnati Bird Club, he had the chance to influence a lot of students and people in general on the life history of birds.

Since Emerson was, "An old time collector of birds," he was not well understood or liked. In the early days before fine binoculars, people who wanted to identify a species would have to shoot the bird. Since Emerson was curator of one of the finest collections in the country, he felt that he had every right to enhance the collection by shooting a specimen that he thought was needed. He had a federal collecting permit to do this. Emerson was not a well man and one of his maladies was Parkinson's disease and had difficulty handling a shot gun. He designated me to shoot for him and as a consequence, I had a collector's permit as well. In all of the years that I knew him, I learned a heck of a lot about birds, inside and out.

On one of the last trips to Lake St. Mary's, Emerson said to me that he was dying and was naming me as the executor of his estate. I immediately said, "Emerson, don't say that! You're in good shape." He said that, "That was a fact!" For the rest of the day, no more was said about it except when I dropped him off at his apartment, he said to me, "After I go, I want you to use the whole of my estate to save the Brant collection of birds at the University." I didn't think about that until he passed away two weeks later. His lawyer contacted me about the burial and said Emerson had a family lot in Spring Grove Cemetery. For years, we would bird watch through the Grove. On one of the outings we saw a Red Crossbill and a White-Winged Crossbill, birds that you never see. In those outings, he never mentioned anything about his family plot. After making the arrangements, I was notified by the cemetery officials that there were no grave markers on the plot. I checked with the office to see if I could get permission to design a monument for Emerson and they said yes but it had to conform to the regulations of the cemetery. My design was a "Ba-relief" (bas-relief) sculpture of a Smith's Longspur, Emerson's favorite bird. It was carved in a depressed oval on a stone of green serpentine. A friend of mine, Robert McNesky, did the sculpture work. The face of the stone says Emerson Kemsies, the birth and death dates, and the word "Ornithologist" in a circle beneath the Longspur.

About a month after Emerson's passing, I received notice that the university was going to sell the Brant Collection. This wasn't their property to sell. A group of locals had paid the descendants of Herbert W. Brant's estate for the collection. It seems that Emerson knew about the possibility of the university doing this. As a result of this notice, I met with the president of the university and he told me that the collection was theirs to sell and he was going to do it. I said that if he did I would use the entire estate of Emerson's to fight him. About a week after our meeting, the president told me to remove the collection as soon as possible. What a wonderful thing to hear. So I contacted the president of the Natural History Museum, Mr. Ralph Dury. He was thrilled to hear the news. I told him that the 75,000 specimens were stored in many wooden and metal cabinets. He said we'll find a space for them. I called Allied Van Lines to do the moving. It took three vans and two weeks to complete the job. As a footnote, I didn't tell the university that Emerson's will only had $10,000! So I paid the moving company with part of it and gave the rest to the museum to curate the collection. The collection remains proudly housed for all to use thanks to Emerson Kemsies.

◇

Otto Luedeking (1864-1939)

THE CLASSIC SETTING FOR MANY CHILDHOOD STORYBOOKS was a castle. This is more of an "adulthood" story that is also set in a castle. Not Cinderella's castle, but the castle of Otto Luedeking and his family in the Cincinnati neighborhood of East Walnut Hills.

Otto Luedeking was born in Detmold, Germany, in 1864, and immigrated to America when he was 14. After leaving his father and brother William in Germany, his wanderlust led him to travel, eventually settling in Cincinnati. According to *Williams' Cincinnati Directory* in 1884, Otto lived at 55 Court Street and was a salesman with the Alms and Doepke's department store. (Both Alms and Doepke are interred in Spring Grove.) By 1867, Luedeking had moved twice and become a salesman for another well-known department store, H. & S. Pogue Co. on Fourth Street.

By the time Luedeking was 27, with the experience he had accumulated as a salesman, he was ready to explore merchandising on his own. He acquired a partner by the name of August Wilhemy and together, they opened the Luedeking and Wilhemy shop on Vine Street. The two lived together on Franklin Street for the next nine years, while operating the shop. But then in 1900, the partners apparently had split and opened separate shops. Luedeking was the proprietor of "The Fashion" shops on Vine Street and Wilhemy opened a shop on Sixth Street. It was during this time that Luedeking began to establish his wealth and all fingers pointed to something akin to a "royal lifestyle."

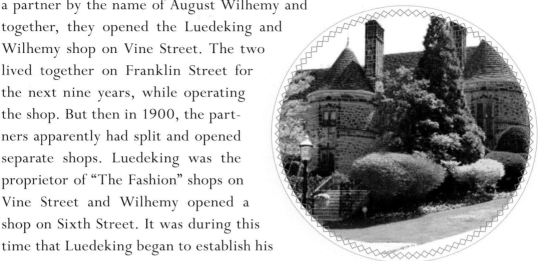

The Luedeking mansion

1907 found Luedeking opening a half-dozen shops, starting with the Luedeking Shirt Tailoring Company on Vine Street. He eventually needed a new business partner so he engaged John H. Shaw, who acted as the secretary and treasurer of the new venture, Luedeking & Shaw.

After an exhaustive series of home relocations around the city, Luedeking was now able to afford the upscale East Walnut Hills area of Cincinnati. Luedeking and his wife, Catherine Holabird, commissioned Cleveland architect, Bloodgood Tuttle, to build a "castle" for them in 1928. Tuttle had just finished an impressive estate in Indian Hill for grocer, William H. Alber. The Luedekings were impressed with Alber's estate and had become very fond of French chateaus from their numerous trips to the Loire Valley in France. They fancied one of their own, so much so that they actually took Tuttle with them to France to show him exactly what they had in mind for their chateau in Cincinnati. Once some design elements and features were chosen from their top three chateaus, Amboise, Bloise, and Chambord, the Luedekings gave Tuttle carte blanche to create their dream castle at home. Perched on a hilltop, overlooking the picturesque Ohio River, the Luedekings managed to create their beloved French chateau on their own turf. Originally called "Les Tours," or "The Towers," the locals quickly began referring to the home as "the castle." Rightfully so, as it had such features as library windows depicting the great books of the world and a conservatory with walls, floors, a fountain, and a fireplace made of Rookwood tile. This was not an ordinary home by any means.

Over the years, I have had the pleasure of attending functions at the "the castle" and one of my favorite features is the amazing lighting system built into the 20-foot high leaded glass ceiling. Operated with a button, the system creates patterns of light that emulate morning sun through a starlit sky. Lady Guinevere would have felt right at home!

So, it seems appropriate that a man who made his life as a leading haberdasher, making men look and feel like a king, would use his own wealth to live in a home that was built for a king, the king of haberdashers in Cincinnati. He put the "king" in Luedeking.

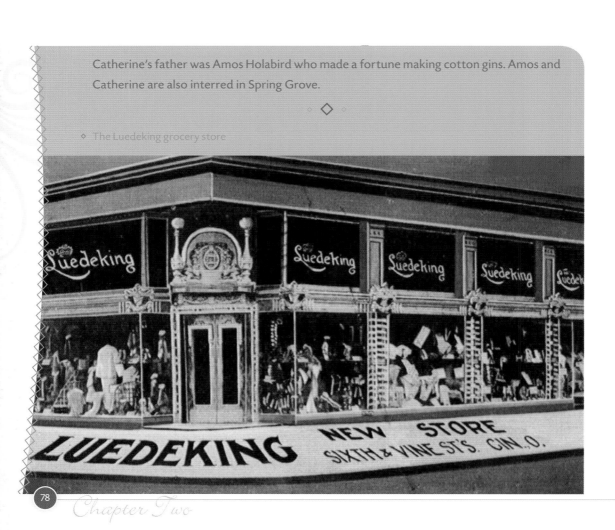

Catherine's father was Amos Holabird who made a fortune making cotton gins. Amos and Catherine are also interred in Spring Grove.

◇

◇ The Luedeking grocery store

Chapter Two

Harold Edwin McClure (1922-2004)

◦ ◇ ◦

I LOVE SURPRISE STORIES THAT MAKE YOU ASK, "Why didn't I know about this?" The life of Harold Edwin McClure is certainly one of those stories.

In McClure's obituary by Karen Andrew, he is referred to as "a man of extraordinary accomplishments who remained humble throughout his life." McClure was indeed extraordinary. I had the good fortune of meeting his sister, niece, and nephew during their photo shoot for *Beauty in the Grove* and formed a treasured friendship with them.

McClure graduated from Withrow High School and went to Paris to study at the Conservatoire Nationale. While there, he became an accomplished classical pianist and earned extra money as an accompanist for the effervescent femme fatale, Josephine Baker, who affectionately called him "Sonny."

After returning from France, McClure joined the famed Tuskegee Airmen and served in World War II. Thanks to the G.I. Bill, after the war he earned a bachelor's degree from the University of Cincinnati and a master's degree in business administration from Xavier University. McClure began a career with the United States Postal Service, eventually becoming the first African-American supervisor of a branch office. In addition, he founded the first African-American-owned travel company in the Midwest, Harold's Tours.

In 1961, the former Belgian Congo was still fighting for independence. McClure was asked to serve as a negotiator for the conflict. A year later he returned to Cincinnati, then went to Washington, D.C. to work at the postal headquarters as a financial systems analyst. McClure was transferred to the Office of Special Assistant to the Postmaster General for International Postal Affairs where he worked as director of technical relations. His success led to a position with the United Nations' Universal Postal Union in Berne, Switzerland.

Another of McClure's contributions was assisting in the development of the U.S. Postal ZIP code system, which revolutionized the delivery of mail in the United States. A Philadelphia post office employee, Robert Moon, is considered, "the father of the ZIP code." He was aptly named "Mr. ZIP Code" after develop-

McClure had a vast and impressive collection of eight-millimeter home movies chronicling his life. The movies were donated to the National Underground Railroad Freedom Center in Cincinnati.

◇

Harold McClure with other Tuskegee Airmen

ing the idea that was refined by others including McClure.

Despite these accomplishments, McClure still found the time and energy to give back to his community. McClure and his wife, Marybelle, were philanthropists, assisting many students with funding for schooling. McClure remained humble, never asking for recognition or accolades for the charitable work he and his wife did for area children.

When someone tells me that they have family buried in Spring Grove, I perk up and listen. You never know when an unknown and fascinating story may surface. Had I not listened to Judy McClure when I first met her, I may never have known the story of her humble, yet accomplished uncle, Harold Edwin McClure.

Emma Bepler (1864-1947)
Augustus Bepler (1828-1890)

◇ ◇ ◇

SOMETIMES I FIND fascinating connections between stories that deepen my appreciation for the intricate web of tales in Spring Grove. Emma Bepler and her father, Augustus, are not only connected as family, but by trees!

In 1854, Augustus emigrated from Prussia to the United States. He first worked as a banker with his brother, Edward.

◇ A chair carved by the crafty Emma Bepler.

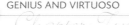

Emma's death in the original records is listed as "broken hip pneumonia," an ailment I've never come across before.

◇

But he later found his fortune in the manufacturing of paper bags. Augustus was nothing if not inventive, and devised a number of machines to aid in the manufacturing of paper bags. He sold his factory in Lockland, Ohio, along with machines and patents, to the Chatfield and Woods Company.

After leaving the paper bag business, Augustus and his brother became famous as detectives of counterfeit money. Counterfeit money was common at the time, and a detective was often used to ensure money was genuine, making Augustus and his brother very influential!

Augustus' daughter, Emma, became a carver for the famous Ben Pitman & Frye woodcarvers. Emma's career in woodcarving began when she attended the School of Design at the age of seventeen. One of her signature pieces was a mantel she carved for the parlor in her home. She based her design on the sitting room in Ben Pitman's home, which was known for showcasing the best of Cincinnati art carving. He and a famed art joiner, John H. Frye, mentored the young Emma as she carved the mantel from black walnut. Emma added her own unique touches to the mantel by incorporating carved American plants, such as sunflowers and marigolds.

The mantel can still be seen in the Cincinnati Art Museum's Cincinnati Wing, home to Emma Bepler's carved easel of mahogany and brass, as well as the famed fireplace mantel of black walnut and glass.

Stories of a father and daughter finding success is always interesting, but their connection to trees, carved, counterfeited, or paper bagged, make the story of the Bepler's even more intriguing!

Thomson Marble Relief

◇

THE THOMSON MARBLE RELIEF ON THE PETER G. THOMSON (founder of the Champion Paper Company) family monument is a classical stele (an upright stone tablet) with a haunting bas-relief of an allegorical female, lifting a veil that represents the separation of life from death, or "the mysterious unknown." A quote by famed poet, Robert Browning, is inscribed on the monument, as well as the signature "E.B. Longman" and the date of 1914. It is one of the most haunting, and beautiful, sculptures in Spring Grove, and the story behind the work adds depth and life to the artwork.

The marble relief is a memorial to Peter's wife, Laura Gamble Thomson. Laura died in 1913 on Sanibel Island in Florida. Her husband had Laura's body brought back to Cincinnati and embalmed before having her photographed in bed at their stately home, Laurel Court. The rather morbid photograph was included in a slide presentation that I attended while researching the family history. It was a sight I will never forget, even though it was meant as a loving tribute.

Award-winning sculptress and Ohio native, Evelyn Beatrice Longman Batchelder (1874–1954), carved the Thomson memorial to Peter's wife, Laura. During an opportune vis-

◇ The Thomson marble relief is a stele which is an upright marble tablet.

Chapter Two

it to the College Hill Presbyterian Church with a descendant of Thomson, I was able to see a bronze version of the Thomson's marble monument found in Spring Grove. This copy was discovered in the bell tower of the church a few years prior to my visit. It was originally placed at the front of the church sanctuary. Both were given to the church by Peter Thomson in memory of Laura.

Evelyn B. Longman is a fascinating woman. She was born into poverty on a farm in Adams County, Ohio. At the Chicago World's Colombian Exposition of 1893, she was inspired to become a sculptor. She studied under Daniel Chester French and contributed to the creation of the Lincoln Memorial. Her career blossomed, and she has been called, "one of the most respected and honored sculptors in American history." Evelyn's impressive list of awards and commissions included the bronze library doors at Wellesley College in Massachusetts, the bronze chapel doors at the U.S. Naval Academy in Annapolis, Maryland, and collections at the Metropolitan Museum of Modern Art in New York, The Chicago Arts Institute, and the Cincinnati Art Museum. Perhaps my favorite Longman commission was *Genius of Electricity:* the twenty-four foot high, forty ton bronze statue that stood atop the AT&T building on Broadway in Manhattan. The piece was covered with forty thousand pieces of gold leaf, thus inspiring Evelyn to nickname it "Golden Boy." The image of "Golden Boy" was widely recognized as it appeared on most telephone books at the time.

The Thomson Marble Relief is a beautiful example of the art found in Spring Grove by one of the greatest American sculptors. Knowing the story behind the work and the artist adds to the allure. The unexpected discovery of an additional piece of artwork that had been hidden for years has added another chapter to the story. Longman would no doubt be pleased her bronzed version was not done in vain.

Charles Pedretti (1864-1891)
Francis Pedretti (1829-1891)

◦ ◇ ◦

MY FIRST GLIMPSE AT FRANCIS PEDRETTI AND HIS SONS' WORK was on a tour of the magnificent European-inspired Cathedral Basilica of the Assump-

○ Grand Stair Hall, located in the Ohio Senate Building, includes detailed murals by Pedretti and Sons.

tion in Covington, Kentucky. Those Cincinnatians familiar with the west side will recognize the Pedretti name from Pedretti Road and Pedretti Avenue, but the Pedretti story is much more than simply artwork, even as beautiful as it is.

Francis, the patriarch of this talented family, was born in Chiavenna, Italy, in 1829, and studied under the auspices of Luigi Scrosati at the Brera Academy of Fine Arts in Milan. Some sources say that Francis was a follower of Guiseppe Garabaldi and was a soldier in the failed Italian Revolution. He left for America around 1854 to work in New York City where he worked for a dry-goods magnate as well as the inventor of the telegraph and painter, Samuel Morse.

Notable architect Isaiah Rogers (also buried in Spring Grove) hired Francis to decorate the Astor Hotel. He earned commissions in Buffalo and Montreal before following Rogers to Cincinnati in 1854 to fresco the Burnett House. Mural artists were in short supply, and Pedretti's career blossomed. He earned commissions to decorate Pike's Opera House, Robinson's Opera House, and other buildings in the city.

Francis and his wife had two sons, Charles and Raphael, who became well-known portrait, figure, landscape, and fresco artists. They had followed in their father's footsteps by receiving their training in Milan, Italy.

Francis joined his sons to open the F. Pedretti's Sons business in 1886. They created masterpiece frescoes in many notable homes, such as those of George B. ("Boss") Cox, "Parkview" or "Park View," and Charles Wiedemann, "Cote Brillante," in Newport, Kentucky.

In addition, they painted numerous works in the region, including in municipal buildings such as Cincinnati City Hall, Memorial Hall, the re-stenciled interiors of K.K. Bnai Yeshurun Isaac Mayer Wise Plum St. Temple in Downtown Cincinnati, and the four allegorical murals in the annex of the Ohio State House in Columbus.

They even painted the Montana State Capitol in Helena. They brought experienced workmen with them from Ohio, for that project, which included fourteen paintings and stained-glass. But, not everyone liked the windows. Local newspapers reported frequently on the work, referring to it as, "the absurdly inappropriate clothing, pose, and lodging of Sacagawea in *Lewis and Clark at Three Forks* in the original House of Representatives." Others were more impressed, such as E.B. Kennedy at the dedication in 1902. He stated that, "The harmony of the colors effects…is wonderful and the building has been given by (the Pedrettis) a character and beauty not surpassed by any building in the land."

Art will never please everyone, but most would agree that Cincinnati (and perhaps Helena) wouldn't be the same without the talented Pedrettis.

Louis T. Rebisso (1837-1899)

◦ ◇ ◦

Rebisso's statue of William Henry Harrison on his horse.

I LOVE STATUES! I ALWAYS HAVE, so when I started exploring Spring Grove for the first time, I was overwhelmed with the variety and styles of statuary I viewed throughout the grounds. I surmised each one must have a story of its own, as well as its maker, so the story of famed sculptor, Louis T. Rebisso, was of particular interest to me.

Rebisso was born in Genoa, Italy in 1837, where his family had lived for many generations. He studied with Professor Varini at the Academy of Fine Arts in Italy, and like area muralist and stencilist Francis Pedretti, Rebisso became involved in the political upheaval surrounding the Italian War of Independence. In order to escape twenty years of hard labor in prison, Rebisso left Italy for America on June 16, 1857. He escaped in the middle of the night and stowed away on the *Osmauli,* an American steamer based in Boston. Rebisso arrived at Long Wharf in Boston on September 15. He ignored the letters of reference his father gave him and immediately applied to monument makers, convincing them that he was an expert with the chisel. He quickly found employment with the best monument companies in the city.

In 1859, Rebisso's father pleaded for his son to return to Italy after a pardon was extended to all political prisoners, whether they were in Italy or elsewhere. However, Rebisso had found his niche in America and decided to remain and find fame and fortune as a sculptor.

In the early 1860s, Louis moved to Cincinnati, and under the tutelage of sculptor T. D. Jones, he created a number of significant sculptures for over twenty years. Through public subscription, Rebisso was commissioned to create the impressive statue of William Henry Harrison, mounted on a horse, in Cincinnati's urban Piatt Park. The sculpture itself was stored in the basement of the National Guard Armory for nearly five years before it was finally placed in the park and dedicated in 1896. After gaining a reputation for his expertise in equestrian sculpture, Rebisso competed with 15 other artists a year later to sculpt the equestrian statue of General U.S. Grant that now stands in Chicago's Lincoln Park. It pleases me greatly, when I travel, to come upon a statue that was made by a Cincinnati area artisan.

Rebisso's work in Spring Grove can be seen in the mammoth monument to the I.O.O.F. (Independent Order of Odd Fellows) in section 15. With the assistance of another local sculptor, August Mundhenk, Rebisso created the colossal bronze statues and bas-relief plaques that adorn the granite monument. Rebisso's bronze statue of Moses that stands atop the monument reportedly weighs three thousand pounds.

Often times we get caught up in the beauty and creativity of statues and other works of art without knowing the story of the people who made them, like Rebisso. Knowing the makers' story gives us a greater appreciation for both the artwork and the creator. In Rebisso's case, that appreciation is enhanced now that I know of the political turmoil he fled from in his homeland to create beautiful works of art like the one in Spring Grove.

Kitaro Shirayamadani (1865-1948)

◦ ◇ ◦

YOU WOULDN'T THINK A JAPANESE ARTIST would play such a large role in the story of Cincinnati, or become such an important part of Spring Grove's story, but Kitaro Shirayamadani is just such an artist.

In the late 1880s, America became obsessed with all things Japanese. Maria Longworth exposed Cincinnati to Japanese pottery after receiving a little Japanese book of designs from a friend who brought it back from a trip to London in 1875. Five years later, Maria founded Rookwood Pottery, where the first pottery to be fired was more than likely Japanese-influenced. Her favorite potter was Kitaro Shirayamadani, who became one of Rookwood's principal decorators.

In 1865, Kitaro was born in Ishikawa, Japan, a city famous for ceramic and laquerware. He immigrated to Boston in the early 1880s, and later moved to Cincinnati in 1883 or 1884.

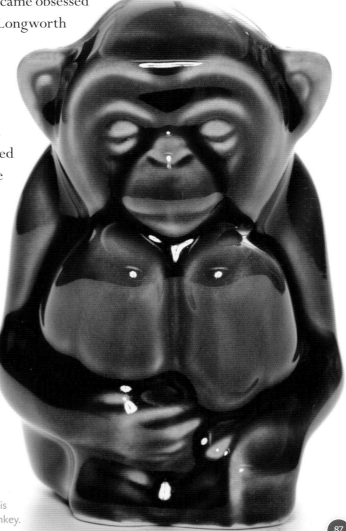

◇ Kitaro's pottery has sold for more than $36,000 at auction. Here is one of his more whimsical creations, a ceramic monkey.

Stories in the Grove

Kitaro seemed destined for the life of an artist. His name, Kitaro, means "son who designs," appropriate for the man who created some of Rookwood's finest pieces of pottery.

Some sources claim Kitaro was the first Japanese national to live in Cincinnati. He arrived in Cincinnati in 1887, as part of a tour that show-cased the latest in Japanese industrial design. He and other Japanese artists demonstrated their skills for visitors as the exhibit traveled to different cities across America. In 1887, Kitaro was hired as a decora-tor by the Rookwood Pottery and Maria Longworth Storer. William Watts Taylor wrote the next day, "Mrs. Storer and the writer are quite pleased with his appearance and manners and the experiment seems quite worthwhile to make."

Candlestick's created by Kitaro.

In 1893, Rookwood sent Kitaro to Japan for an immersion in Japanese art. The following year, Kitaro returned to Cincinnati and created a number of pieces with Japanese motifs. In 1900, Rookwood participated in the Paris Universal Exposi-tion, with Kitaro and his fellow artists winning major awards for the "High Japa-nist" art inspired by Kitaro.

Later in his life, Kitaro incorporated silver and copper into his works through the new process called the "electro-deposit technique," which was the basis for his famous *Black Iris* vase. *Black Iris* is an iconic example of Rookwood pottery, and includes six flying herons, three electroplated lotus leaves, an unopened blossom, and according to Elizabeth Fowler, "a 'fruiting receptacle' or seed pod in profile at the bottom of the vessel."

In 1912, Kitaro travelled back to Japan and lived in Tokyo until 1921. He shared his work from Rookwood, bringing new found awareness and interest in the art. Fowler called Kitaro "an artistic ambassador." But Kitaro had become "disillu-sioned" with Japan and returned to Cincinnati and Rookwood, living there until his death in 1948.

Kitaro's foot stone in Spring Grove appears simple, although his life was anything but simple. The Japan America Society of Greater Cincinnati recently held a memorial at his gravesite, followed by a visit to the Cincinnati Art Museum to view his creations. The story of Kitaro Shirayamadani continues to inspire and delight patrons of the arts and is closely connected to the enduring legacy of Rookwood pottery. In fact, a rare 1909 Rookwood vase created by Kitaro sold at auction in 2010 for more than $36,000.

Leon Van Loo (1841-1907)

◦ ◇ ◦

SOMETIMES, SMALL CLUES TO A PERSON'S STORY LEAD ME on a quest of discovery. Most likely, I would never have known anything about Leon Van Loo had it not been for a simple bas-relief carving on his pedestal monument depicting an artist's palette, quill, and paint brush. Above the pedestal is an empty space, where a mysterious, missing piece of art once sat. The bas-relief is a rather obvious clue to Van Loo's professions as a portrait artist, photographer, art critic, and collector and so began my quest.

Leon Van Loo, photographer and bohemian king.

VAN LOO'S PATENT 1865

Van Loo was born on August 12, 1841, in Ghent, Belgium, to Eulalie and Peter Van Loo. As a young man, and prior to the start of the Civil War, Leon travelled to Cincinnati and started a photography business as well as other business ventures. His southern cotton trading business brought him a small fortune in the late 1860s.

Van Loo was a perfectionist. Legend has it, Van Loo didn't care about his photography client's opinions, and he didn't allow a photograph to leave his shop unless he was satisfied. Leon photographed generals, five presidents, many governors, and other famous men. Most of them visited Van Loo in his Cincinnati studio. The studio was deemed the unofficial headquarters of General Joseph Hooker for the amount of time the General spent in Van Loo's studio.

Although Van Loo enjoyed a prestigious career in photography and art, he was known as more than just an artist. He was equally famous as a host and patron of the arts. Fellow members of the Cincinnati Art Club reveled in his "entertainments" during their meetings. Those "entertainments" included Leon's proclivity as a gourmand and his wine cellar filled with rare vintages, making him quite popular in the club. He proudly provided $250 in his will for a posthumous banquet for his "little group of bohemians," which included fellow artists. One hundred and twenty five of them attended, with William F. Behrens residing as president. Behrens was described as "the genial host type."

Van Loo was also vain. Two years before his death, Van Loo commissioned famed Belgium sculptor, Do Van Den Bossche, to create his bronze portrait bust.

The first photograph taken of the Cincinnati Red Stocking baseball team was in 1868 by Van Loo. Four of its members were retained on the following year's more famous team.

◇

◇ The bronze bust of Van Loo that is supposed to rest atop this podium has gone missing and nobody knows where it is.

LEON VAN LOO
1841 ~ 1907

Chapter Two

Van Loo was strong-willed and demanded perfection of Van Den Bossche, to the point of directing artistic touches on the bust. Van Loo's demands perhaps explain why the bust depicted the Burgomeister outfit Van Loo was known to wear. Six months before his death, the bust was placed on his lot in section 77.

Leon designed the pedestal base for the bust and commissioned G.A. Douglass to create it. No doubt, Van Loo was also responsible for the bas-relief of his paint palette, brush, and quill pen on the monument base that led me to learn his story. Although we know where Van Loo rests in eternity, unfortunately for guests of Spring Grove, the bronze portrait bust is missing, and we may never learn its final resting place.

Paul Briol (1889-1969)

◦ ◇ ◦

ANYONE FAMILIAR WITH FAMOUS PHOTOGRAPHERS from Cincinnati knows the name of Paul Briol. His marvelous black and white prints from the late 1900s are still admired today, but an unexpected find in the Spring Grove archives brought a new twist to Briol's story.

Briol was born in Spencer, Massachusetts, in 1890 to French-Swiss immigrants (though there is some dispute as to the exact date of his birth). His mother was an artist, teacher, and musician, and his father a teacher, scholar, and ordained Presbyterian minister who spoke seven languages. While living in New Orleans with his parents, Briol met a scholar from China who taught Briol to write numbers using Chinese characters. During his career, Briol used Chinese characters, much like hieroglyphics, to date and identify his photography.

After high school, Briol moved to Cincinnati and worked at the *Cincinnati Commercial Tribune* as a journalist and photographer. While there, he photographed Leopold Stokowski conducting the Cincinnati Symphony Orchestra in rehearsal. It was to be Briol's first professionally credited work.

A year later, Briol joined the staff at the *Cincinnati Enquirer* as a staff photographer, where he also wrote a column, 'Old World Chit-Chat.' After leaving the *Enquirer*, Briol managed The Book Shelf bookstore on Garfield Place in Cincinnati. The store became a center for literary discussions before closing in 1930. Briol supplemented his income through photographic journaling of his beloved Cincinnati, producing his most famous work by exploring the city and using his photographic skills to his advantage. Briol gained a reputation as a portrait photographer in the 1930s, and was also commissioned to photograph the facilities of Cincinnati area corporations and private gardens.

A very handsome Paul Briol.

After a debilitating car accident in 1950, left Briol in a partial coma, he never fully recovered from his injuries and closed his business in 1955. In 1962, he moved to Katonah, New York, to live with his daughter. In 1969, a year and a half after his wife passed away, Paul Briol died.

But, as I said, this isn't the end of the story. I recently discovered Briol was commissioned by James A. Green to do a series of photographs of Spring Grove for *A Centennial History of Spring Grove Cemetery*, but the book was never published. The photographs disappeared until a set of 46 were discovered in the Spring Grove archives a few years ago. Amazingly, they were still in their original brown paper wrapping tied with yellowed twine. Each photograph is marked with Briol's signature Chinese characters.

The collection remains in the archives as yet another example of "hidden gems" that appear unexpectedly from time to time in The Grove.

James F. "Jimmy" Brown (1933-2006)

◦ ◇ ◦

PEOPLE CONTACT ME ONCE IN A WHILE requesting that a family member or non-related personality, be added to the list of notable Spring Grove burials, but not all of the suggested folks elicit particularly outstanding backgrounds. Reasons for notoriety have included, "She was the lady who put in that beautiful garden at the corner of 8th and Elm" to the one I received from the lovely widow of James "Jimmy" Brown.

I received a phone call from Jennifer Palanci one day, asking if I could include her deceased husband, Jim, on the notables list. His name was rather "generic" and I knew that he wasn't famed soul singer, James Brown. So what *was* Brown's claim to fame, I asked? Not only did Jennifer explain his background, she also sent me a beautifully written biography that highlights an incredible career in photography.

Brown's first exposure to photography came when he was nine years old. A wheelchair-bound gentleman in Canton, Ohio, amazed Jim when he watched the man make a print in his dark room. This promoted Jim to start taking family snap shots. That story is particularly touching since Brown was born with "severe club feet" and did not fully learn to walk until around the age of six.

Brown's professional career actually began when he was around fifteen years old, when his family moved to Dayton, Ohio. He was hired as a staff photographer of school events for the *Dayton Daily News* after he impressed the staff with his photographs of May Flower girls. But the family's residence changed when Brown's mother died unexpectedly. That is when they moved to Cincinnati.

Brown attended Withrow High School and after graduating, he started studying briefly at the University of Cincinnati. But his wanderlust took him to Hollywood to do still photography. He met, lunched, and partied with the likes of Norma Jean Baker (better known as Marilyn Monroe) but he didn't succeed with his business and returned to Cincinnati.

The interim found Brown joining and being kicked out of the U.S. Army Corp. (because of his feet) and a stint in New Orleans as a cook on a mine sweeper. He enjoyed New Orleans and what it had to of-

Jimmy "Quick Draw" Brown

fer but ended up going back to Hollywood when an "admiring lady friend" offered lodging at the Bel-Air Hotel. He couldn't pass that offer up, so he got a gig doing still shots in Hollywood movie studios. This time, he met Clark Gable, among others, but still the work was not plentiful and he once again returned to Cincinnati.

Finally, in the late 1950s and early 60s, Brown got a job as a freelance photographer for *The Cincinnati Post.* While there, Brown claimed to be one of the first photographers to use a 35mm camera in his editorial work. Obviously it paid off as he relished in the occurrence of taking a photograph of a murder scene and beating his cohorts to print. They didn't have a 35mm camera. They were still using more heavy and impractical cameras which slowed them down on the way to print. Jimmy was labeled "Quick Draw" by his co-workers who were amazed by his rapid-fire process.

Brown went on to do freelance for popular magazines, like *Life, Look,* and *Time.* The list of celebrities that he photographed from his biography is staggering. The first page of Roberta J. Torrens article on Jim from 1996, shows a photograph of John F. Kennedy speaking at his inauguration. Who took that photo? A twenty-eight-year-old Jim Brown. But that's just the beginning of the list of photographs that Jimmy took of internationally renowned personalities. Among them were Frank Sinatra, Elizabeth Taylor, Joan Crawford, Vincent Minnelli, Louis Armstrong, Bob Hope, Paul Newman, Doris Day, Queen Elizabeth, and Prince Philip. Velva Sheen commissioned Jim to photograph its clients in Paris and his photos have appeared in catalogues and product packages for corporations such as Procter & Gamble, Kroger, and Nutone. Remember Sam and Samantha, the first two baby gorillas ever born into captivity at the Cincinnati Zoo? Jim photographed those two "celebrities" in the 1970s and he was a noted photographer of other wildlife, especially exotic cats.

The United Press International commercial photography division in New York awarded Jim "best photo of the month" for six consecutive months, prompting them to kindly ask him to refrain from entering "so other photographers could have a chance to win." They also rated Jim as one of the top ten most versatile photographers in the country. He also won an award for the best Public Relations Photograph of the quarter of the century (1945–1970).

So, the moral of this story is to never assume that there's not an interesting history behind a generic name. I would never have known about James F. Brown had

I relied solely on his name. And oh yes, I forgot to mention that James F. "Jimmy" Brown actually did photograph famed soul singer, James Brown!

William Southgate Porter (1822-1889)

◦ ◇ ◦

WILLIAM SOUTHGATE PORTER WAS NOT A TYPICAL PAINTER or sculptor but considered an artist. He was actually a photographer, whose signature photograph was known as the "Mona Lisa" of daguerreotype photographs (an image captured on a silver coated plate in the 1800s). With a reference to one of the most famous pieces of art in the world, I knew there had to be a story behind Porter's career and his tour de force photograph.

In the Public Library of Cincinnati and Hamilton County main library's Cincinnati Room, the panoramic daguerreotype of Cincinnati's riverfront is back on display. Local historian, John Fleischman, humorously refers to the panoramic daguerreotype as the "Dag." Taken in September of 1848 by Porter and Charles Fontayne, (only three years after Spring Grove was founded) it is a 120 degree image of the Cincinnati riverfront. Some claim Porter was the sole photographer. I'm not so sure because both of their names appear on the original brass nameplate that was affixed to the panoramic.

◦ This daguerreotype of the Cincinnati riverfront is said to be the earliest surviving photograph of any city on record.

Stories in the Grove

Porter and Fontayne were partners in Baltimore until Fontayne left for Cincinnati in 1846, around the same time that Porter had a studio in Pittsburgh. Two years later, Porter reconnected with Fontayne in Cincinnati, shortly before the famous riverfront photograph was taken from a rooftop across the Ohio River in Porter's hometown of Newport, Kentucky. Porter opened his own studio in 1848 on Fourth Street, and it must have impressed a lot of art enthusiasts when a few years later, it was referred to as the "Art Palace."

The panorama has an astounding background story itself. Not one, but eight full-plate daguerreotypes were put together to create this masterpiece that has been brought back to life following a restoration project. And although it is the first photograph ever taken of the bustling 1848 Cincinnati waterfront, it's also the earliest surviving photograph of any city in America. Add the earliest image of steamboats, a railroad terminal, and likely the first candid image of free African-Americans and you have one of the most significant and rare photographs in the nation.

The panorama gained fame in the Great Exhibition of 1851, at the Crystal Palace in London. It was not publicly displayed again, most likely remaining in the possession of Porter until in 1887, it was briefly on exhibit in the Fourth Street photo gallery of James Landy. After Porter died in 1889, and Fontayne in 1901, the panorama was on loan to the old Main Library on Vine Street where it was hung on a wall. Forward ahead to 1946, and the arrival of a new librarian, Carl Vitz, from Minneapolis. Impressed with the panorama and perhaps in need of more fodder for the campaign to replace the old Main Library, Vitz purchased the panorama from Porter's son. The original was kept in a bank vault, after being copied on film.

Remaining out of public view for another 51 years, the panorama traveled to the Cincinnati Art Museum for an exhibit in 1985. However, by the twenty-first century, the deterioration and the slippage of the eight plates was evident. It was time to revive the panorama! In 2007, the Daguerreotype View of Cincinnati Panorama was sent to the prestigious George Eastman House in Rochester, New York, for painstaking conservation and preservation work. It was resealed in inert argon gas, as well as digitally scanned. An unexpected result occurred. For the first time, minute visual details could be seen. It was flabbergasting. Details such as the time on the Second Presbyterian Church (it was 1:55p.m.) and signage on riverfront businesses could be seen which was a major accomplishment and a miraculous discovery for historians and art scholars as they could now record the history of buildings and culture from Cincinnati's riverfront in 1848.

I often wonder, perhaps even fantasize, if William S. Porter photographed Spring Grove Cemetery in his lifetime. Perhaps not, however, it's rather awesome to be able to say we have the "painter" of a "Mona Lisa" resting in eternity in the cemetery.

Anthony Frederick Sarg (1880-1942)

◦ ◇ ◦

SOMETIMES SPRING GROVE STORIES HAVE A SIMPLE BEGINNING and then blossom into something both surprising and wonderful. In the case of Tony Sarg, the story begins with a message I received from a colleague at the Woodlawn Cemetery in the Bronx, New York. The cemetery's director of historical services, Susan Olsen, gave me the name Tony Sarg, the artist who designed the early balloons for Macy's Thanksgiving Day Parade. His burial in Spring Grove in 1942, gathered little attention, but I was intrigued and wanted to know Sarg's story.

Guatemalan-born in 1880, he was the product of an artistic family—his father was an artist, his grandfather a woodcarver, and his grandmother a painter. It was perhaps his grandmother's collection of dolls, animals, mechanical toys, and tiny houses that interested him most, for when he was only six, he made his first invention. He attached a line to pulleys that ran from his bedroom window to the door of the family chicken coop. He spread grain the evening before, and then completed his morning chores by pulling the line and releasing the chickens to be fed.

The family moved to Germany when he was seven, where he finished schooling in a military academy. Most of his time when out of uniform, however, was spent presenting his drawings to editors and publishers. He met an American tourist, Bertha McGowan, from Cincinnati, and they were married in 1909. They moved to England where his career began. He followed a marionette troupe of English puppet master Thomas Holden and posed as a stagehand to learn the secrets of puppetry.

Inspired by Holden, Sarg set up a stage and gave parties where he entertained audiences with marionettes. Puppets were still an avocation. However, his vocation was commercial art, at which he excelled. With the outbreak of WWI, Sarg, his wife, and daughter left the continent and arrived in New York. By 1917, his marionette hobby had become his profession.

Sarg's creative aptitude spilled in all directions. He designed jigsaw puzzles, musical blocks, children's story books with moveable parts, and animated movies. In the 1920s, his puppet company performed across the country. Sarg's "charming, elaborate entertainments" captured the attention of even adults. He was known as, "the man who revived the marionette theater in America," and, "the father of modern puppetry in North America." He ignored the craft's traditional secrecy and taught its techniques through classes, articles, and his books, guiding a new generation of puppeteers.

In 1927, came the innovation for which he is best known—the animal balloons for Macy's Thanksgiving Day Parade. One of Sarg's protégés, Bill Baird, supervised the work, calling the balloons "giant, upside-down marionettes" because the strings were below, rather than above. The largest one, a rubber dragon, was 125 feet long and required fifty handlers to operate it. When the parade reached Macy's, one set of balloons was accidentally released, and some of them were found one hundred miles away. The balloons became an annual holiday fixture, and Sarg became famous.

In the mid-1930s, Sarg made Macy's first elaborate, mechanized Christmas window. He's credited with the invention of animated window displays. He did illustrations for books and periodicals such as *The Saturday Evening Post*, designed a fabric line for children's clothes, wallpaper, and decals for nursery decorations (his designs decorated my childhood bedroom).

His work made him rich and famous. At one point he earned $80,000 a year (which would be almost $1.3 million in today's economy). But in the late 1930s,

A remarkable volume by Sarg, *Up & Down, New York*, is filled with isometric bird's-eye views of madly lively slices of the twenties boom city, packed with tiny, scurrying urbanites. Subtract all the hats, swap the Model-T Fords for Honda Civics, and many of these scenes could be yesterday. Sarg's work has been compared to that of Red Grooms, but these not-just-for-kids illustrations also evoke those wonderfully busy Richard Scarry books, or even the *Where's Waldo?* series–the kind of images that keep one staring at each page for far longer than ought to be possible.

Chapter Two

"If I were asked for a simple prescription for joy, it would be this: A boy, say of twelve, with an attic at his disposal, busy on a half-finished marionette show. Let him have two assistants, one other boy somewhat younger, whom he can 'boss,' and the other a girl, preferably one who admires him intensely and who is deft with the needle. He must have a supply of discarded boys, the scrap-bag of an adoring aunt, perhaps, and a tool-chest all his own—and I'd rather be that boy than the President."

—Tony Sarg

◇ The puppetmaster from South America, Tony Sarg.

In the summer of 1937—with his experience designing balloons for the Macy's parade—Sarg built a huge serpent that he and his friends launched off Coatue, on the tip of Nantucket, where he was living. They had already begun rumors of sightings, and then footprints were found. The serpent appeared on South Beach, to the delight of children (and from the pictures, adults as well). The "Nantucket Sea Monster" may be found in a vintage film clip from the Nantucket Historical Association. You can watch it on YouTube.

◇

there were new performers and new competition. Demand for his work declined, and Sarg filed for bankruptcy in 1939. His sense of humor helped him survive. He listed his assets as: "four suits, a couple of overcoats, an evening suit, several pairs of socks, and several shirts, ties, and collars, worth about $200. Also a few reference books, an easel, and a chair of no value." Despite the setback, Sarg had made a financial comeback by the time he passed away on February 17, 1942, of complications from an emergency surgery for a ruptured appendix. He was brought back to Cincinnati, his wife's home, for burial in Spring Grove.

So just think, had I not received that simple message from Susan Olsen, I may not have learned Tony Sarg's colorful story and his connection to Spring Grove. Watching the Macy's Thanksgiving Day parade has new meaning now that I know more about the man who created the first balloon and that he is buried in Spring Grove.

Chapter Two

Clara Baur (1835-1912)
Bertha Baur (1861-1940)

◦ ◇ ◦

CINCINNATI'S MUSICAL HISTORY IS ILLUSTRIOUS, but the story of the two women who contributed so much to it is seldom told. The Baurs were pioneers, beginning with their role in a rented downtown room at Miss Nourse's School for Young Ladies. Through its many transformations over time, it became one of America's leading music conservatories—the University of Cincinnati College-Conservatory of Music.

Clara Baur was born in the German state of Württenberg, and studied piano in Stuttgart before following her older brother, Theodore, a banker, to Cincinnati where she worked as his housekeeper and gave private lessons in voice and piano. There was nothing here to presage her remarkable career except her dream of a music school to be built in the style of the European conservatories.

Her single room, called Clara Baur's Conservatory of Music, was in 1867, one of the first conservatories of music in America. She made housing arrangements for students from outside the city and began one of the first summer music programs in the country. Her belief that music should be taught within a broader educational context—she required courses in Italian, French, and German, for instance—found opposition in the 1878 appearance of a competing school, the College of Music of Cincinnati.

The new school, adjacent to Music Hall, siphoned away some of Clara's instructors and damaged it financially. But Clara began outreach programs for young children, recruited new faculty from Europe, gave Sunday afternoon musicals, and began a department to train prospective teachers. Her con-

The tireless teacher, Clara Baur.

Bertha Baur, Clara's successor.

servatory regained its former prominence. It also survived the disastrous 1884 flood and a smallpox epidemic. It was apparent that her business acumen matched her artistry. By the end of the century, Clara had nearly a thousand students from every state in the union.

She was described by one writer as "a serious-minded matron who wore a large crucifix around her neck and dedicated the school to 'the praise of God and the study of music.'" She was also attractive, slight, and energetic. At one point she taught over one hundred classes a week. She began her day by reading Bible passages to her girls after breakfast, stopped before lunch for a set of breathing exercises to which she credited her health, and then carried on, usually through the evening hours. She lived modestly, without a salary, drawing only the barest minimum from her school's cash flow.

What began as Miss Baur's one-room music school has today some 1,500 students. In giving nearly a thousand performances and presentations each year, it is the largest single source of performing arts presentations in Ohio. Its graduates have ranged from trumpeter Al Hirt and diva Kathleen Battle to Lisa Howard, the Broadway actress who also played vampire Siobhan in *The Twilight Saga* finale.

◇

Her life and the life of her school were inseparable, and therein lay the secret to her institution. The school had been wholly her creation, owned, designed, and run by her. "There are not many that live to see their dreams come true," she told the *Cincinnati Times-Star*. "There are not many that worked and see the work come out as they have planned. But it was so with me, that as I dreamed, the hopes of my life came true one bright, bright day."

When she died in 1912, her niece, Bertha, known as "temperamental but shrewd," assumed control of the conservatory—after a thirty-four year apprentice-ship with Aunt Clara—but the environment was changing. There was increased competition, and demands for higher salaries and scholarships. Under Bertha's stewardship, the school was granted authority by the state to award degrees in music, rather than diplomas, and it continued on much as before. The year before her retirement in 1931, she transferred the school's stock to the nonprofit Cincinnati Institute of Fine Arts.

The conservancy managed through the Depression and the war, but by the early 1950s, both it and the College of Music were struggling. And so in 1955, after nearly two decades of discussion and two failed attempts, the two old competitors became the Cincinnati College-Conservatory of Music. There was one more incarnation. In 1962, it became the fourteenth college of the University of Cincinnati, gaining for itself what one biographer called "the ungainly label" of the University of Cincinnati College-Conservatory of Music.

The Queen City's musical environment had been transformed by Miss Clara's single-minded passion. For half a century, she was the personal face of music education in Cincinnati, and her dream—a century after her death—has not only remained intact, it has been shared with an entire city.

William Howard Doane (1832-1915)

∘ ◇ ∘

OLD HOMES HAVE THEIR OWN STORIES OF THE PEOPLE WHO BUILT and lived in them. In the case of William Howard Doane, carvings from his home and monument give hints about his story. I discovered both when I first visited his

Italian red-brick villa on Auburn Avenue and noticed "Sunnyside" and the initials "WHD" carved on two marble fence posts on either side of the driveway entrance. I had previously been mystified by the carved bas-relief of a feather quill pen on the Doane monument in Spring Grove.

"Sunnyside" was built for William Howard Doane, a notable businessman and musician. William became interested in music as a boy growing up in Connecticut. At age 12, he had already mastered the flute. The next year, the double bass viola, and two years later, he learned to play what was called the "cabinet organ." At age 15, William started mastering musical composition and three years later, he wrote his first composition for his future wife, Fanny Treat. It just so happened, that Fanny was the daughter of his father's business partner, James S. Treat, at Doane & Treat, Cotton Manufactures. Doane wrote his first Sunday school hymnal, "Sabbath Gems," in 1861, and received an honorary degree of doctor of music from Denison University in 1875. He went on to write more than 600 songs for Sunday schools, 150 church and "prayer-meeting" hymns, and 250 various songs, ballads, anthems, and cantatas. He made the Christmas cantata business popular with one of his cantatas titled "Santa Claus." William wrote a lot of his music in the evenings and it has been told that the neighbors always knew when he was writing when they saw the light on in the tower. He carried a notebook with him at all times in the event that inspiration would strike.

After three years with his father's company in the counting room, William went to work for Treat. Eventually, William made a foray into the wood-working machinery business at J.A. Fay & Co. When the business moved to Cincinnati, William followed and became president. Doane was credited as being one of the most influential manufacturers in the wood-working machinery industry, resulting in the Grand Prix award and the Cross of the Legion of Honor by the French government in 1889, at the Paris Exposition.

"Sunnyside" was filled with music. A transom window has musical characters from the opening strains of "Home, Sweet Home" and there are frescoes of celebrated musical compositions. Doane's impressive collection of musical instruments was from such places as Egypt, Japan, Turkey, and Syria, some said to be several hundred years old. The collection was donated in three bequests to the Cincinnati Art Museum, starting in 1887 and ending in the 1950s by his daughter, Marguerite.

Most of the instruments from the collection were stored in Doane's music room, which was considered at the time, one of the largest in the country. A grand pipe organ in the room was powered by water and had a fresco of four measures of the "Hallelujah Chorus" above it.

The mysterious carvings of Doane's initials and the word "Sunnyside" both became clear when I learned of his burial in Spring Grove. And now the carved feather quill pen on his monument is no longer a mystery. The story of Doane's contribution to the musical world, and the musical associations connected to his home on his monument have provided yet another fascinating page to the Spring Grove storybook, or in this case, "songbook."

William Howard Doane

HEROES AND VILLAINS

The Civil War Section

◇

SPRING GROVE IS THE FINAL RESTING PLACE of more than one thousand soldiers who fought and died in the Civil War and visitors are curious as to why there are so many buried there. The answer stems from the numerous hospitals in the area that tended to the injured soldiers. Many of them were sent here with disease and injuries from places like Memphis, New Orleans, Vicksburg and Pittsburgh Landing. Many, if not most, died here. A majority of them were Union soldiers and are interred in Section 21, commonly known as the Civil War Section. There are 40 Union generals buried throughout the cemetery and one lone Confederate Colonel, Philip N. Luckett.

The Civil War section is visually marked by its three large mounded areas, each with a single downturned cannon barrel in the center. The first mound was donated by the Spring Grove Board of Directors and labeled Mound A. Mounds B and C were purchased by Ohio Governor Tod but later became the property of the United States.

Entries from the original cemetery Board minutes provide an interesting progression of the Civil War area in section 21:

The Sentinel Statue stands watch.

In 1861, The Spring Grove Association appropriated "a suitable place in their grounds" for the burial of soldiers "in our army as may die in battle or otherwise during the present war." Originally, they set aside section 34 but the next month substituted it with Section 21. In December, surveyor Joseph Earnshaw provided a drawing of the "Soldiers Lot" and surroundings in a frame. The next year, The U.S. Sanitary Commission wanted to donate a 100-foot diameter circular lot to bury 300 bodies on and

Section 21 depicted in this vintage sketch.

that June, there was a motion to sell Mound B for 20 cents per foot. Earnshaw then provided a map in 1863 with two of the three circular lots on it and asked the Board to designate the location of a third lot (Mound C). Three years later, a request was made to give preference "to parties who have been Soldiers in our Armies, believing that a one armed Soldier can act as Watchmen equally as well as a man with both arms."

Eventually, the State of Ohio took ownership and control of the Soldiers Lot in 1866 and reinterred over 300 deceased soldiers from the cemetery at Camp Dennison on Cincinnati's east side, to Spring Grove. Since the lots belonged to the State of Ohio, it was necessary for a U.S. Government officer to obtain an order for burial from the Governor.

On May 30, 1868, the first ceremony was held to honor the deceased soldiers and it brought thousands of people to the cemetery for the occasion. The graves were "profusely decorated with flowers" but it was noted that "not a shrub, flower or even the grass seemed to be disturbed" by the huge attendance. Initially, the grave sites were reportedly marked with small wooden stakes and ivy. The first mention of head stones to replace the stakes and ivy was made two months later when a Miss E. F. Morris asked if marble head stones with arched tops, five inches thick and 6-8 inches high, would be allowed to be placed at the head of soldiers' graves. The Board recommended the use of granite instead and not over six inches high, set in stone blocks without a foundation. In February of 1871, the Ladies of Cincinnati and Congress proposed to "erect proper monuments" over the graves. Three months later, the Superintendent ordered more simple wooden stakes instead of the proposed head stones. And as late as 1880, a request was made to the U.S. Government to "use such headstones" that would not disfigure the Grounds."

In 1882, the board minutes mention a proposal made to the Quarter Master General in charge of National Cemeteries for purchase of between ten and twenty acres in section 21. There was talk of moving the cannon barrels and disinterring bodies so that the valuable land could be sold to private lot owners. Spring Grove was offering $3,000 per acre, but when Congress denied the funding, everything remained intact.

In the end, marble was chosen as the material for the simple square head stones and in 1905, Fred C. Jones of the Grand Army of the Republic Committee (a fraternal organization of Civil War veterans) requested to have metal markers "with slight iron rods to hold them" placed on each soldiers' grave, in addition to the marble stones already in place. Judge Worthington declined the request, saying that the metal would not have been durable and also conflicted with the rule of permitting only one marker per grave. Today you can view almost one thousand of the marble, square stones in concentric circles on the three mounds. It was most likely a combination of that rule and Adolph Strauch's open lawn landscape plan that prevented Spring Grove from becoming a National Cemetery. At one time, even an elaborate temple monument was proposed for the site by Adolph Strauch.

Today, when a tour winds around the southeastern bend of section 21, the sight of cannon barrels, the American flag, and 999 graves beckons them to learn more about the Civil War history in Spring Grove. But the stories of those brave souls interred in "The Civil War Section" go beyond the grave.

The Cannons

◦ ◇ ◦

MORE OFTEN THAN NOT, the sight of cannons inspires Civil War enthusiasts to discover the stories connected to them. In Spring Grove's case, you don't even have to be a Civil War buff to wonder why there are cannons (or cannon barrels) in the cemetery. Their mere presence evokes questions about their history.

The three upright cannon barrels in the center of the three mounds in Section 21 were most likely made by the John Mason Columbia Foundry in Georgetown, Washington D.C., according to initials on their base. One has the date of 1831, another has 1837, and the third is illegible. The Columbia Foundry was established in 1801, in Georgetown and the original owner was Henry Foxall, who sold the foundry to General Mason in 1815. The foundry was one of the first to produce rifled cannon barrels for the United States Government.

There has been speculation as to whether or not anyone is buried under each of the downturned cannon barrels, but according to Spring Grove burial records, no one is buried in the center of Mound A. Under the cannon barrel on Mound B is the body of Colonel Fredrick Jones and in the center of Mound C is General Thomas Williams. Most of the Cincinnati deceased hospital patients are buried on Mound A and deceased patients from the hospitals at Camp Dennison are buried on Mound B.

There are reports that General Joseph Hooker detested the cannon barrels and called for their removal. He felt they were not in keeping with the peaceful surroundings of a beautiful cemetery, even calling them "uncouth." Hooker's request fell on deaf ears with the federal authorities and the barrels have since remained.

In addition to the upright cannon barrels on the three mounds, there is a full-scale cannon that rests majestically at the foot of the flagpole. The Parrot Cannon

The flagpole near the cannon was dedicated on May 30, 1917, by Frederick H. Alms and the Sons of the Union Veterans Commandery No. 1.

◇

Stories in the Grove

was dedicated to the "Unknown Dead" soldiers buried in Spring Grove. In 1906, a request was granted by Major Jones and the Grand Army of the Republic (GAR), a fraternal organization of veterans, for a monument to the unknown dead in the form of a cannon and gun carriage. They asked that it be placed on or near the soldiers' mounds at a location selected by the Treasurer of the Grand Army of the Republic Committee and Spring Grove Superintendent Salway. The cannon was obtained from the Watervliet Arsenal in New York in 1907, when the War Department authorized the gun be given to Cincinnati as a monument to unknown soldiers. The inscription plaque on the cannon reads: "1861 'Unknown' 1865/ Brave comrades who gave their lives/that our country might live/who sleep in unknown graves./Erected by their friends 1907." The cannon was designed by Robert Parker Parrot, the first Superintendent of the West Point Foundry and patent owner. His Parrot Cannon was the first successful cast iron cannon in America. Before then, large cannons were made mostly from bronze.

The serenity of cannons that once caused so much damage and turmoil now bring hushes to the thousands of visitors who marvel at the beauty and dignity that the Civil War Section in Spring Grove epitomizes today.

The Sentinel Statue

◦ ◇ ◦

CINCINNATI'S FAMED TYLER DAVIDSON FOUNTAIN has graced the center of the city since 1871, but before finding its home, the fountain led a nomadic lifestyle for a sculpture, having moved from several locations. In Spring Grove, there is a piece of sculpture cast in the same foundry as the fountain. Its story also involves travel.

The large bronze statue of "The Soldier of the Line" stands stoically in a circular lot on the main roadway in Spring Grove. It faces the Civil War section as a poignant memorial to the soldiers who fought in the war. Commonly known as "The Sentinel," or "A Galvanized Hero," the bronzed statue depicts a Civil War soldier standing with his bayonet pointed toward the graves where more than one thousand soldiers are interred.

The small mound of bricks and artillery shells behind the Henry House at Manassas has often been referred to as the nation's first monument to Union soldiers, however, "The Sentinel" at Spring Grove predates it by nearly two years.

○ The Sentinel Statue's bayonet points toward the graves of interred Civil War soldiers.

In 1863, Cincinnatians raised $15,000 in gold to erect a memorial to the Civil War dead. The cash value of the gold, $25,000, went towards the creation of "The Sentinel." Randolph Rogers, the artist who created the statue, spent the winter in Cincinnati that year. A year later, the model was completed in Rome by Rogers. It was eventually cast in bronze in the same fashion as the Tyler Davidson Fountain by Ferdinand von Miller's Royal Foundry in Munich, Germany, the same foundry that cast the Fountain. The base of "The Sentinel" was completed by the reputable New England Granite Works of Hartford, Connecticut.

The original Spring Grove board minutes gives a peek at the statue's journey to its present location. At one time, a more traditional monument was proposed by Strauch—a mausoleum. This is noted in an entry from October 3, 1864: "Resolved that we recommend to the favorable consideration of the board, the suggestions of A. Strauch as made in his report in respect to the building of a suitable temple or mausoleum near the Soldiers' graves in which can be inscribed the names of Ohio's Sons who have fallen in the defense of the liberties of their country, and that the board be instructed to subscribe the sum of ten thousand dollars toward the enterprise."

On June 7, 1866: "Board asked to assist the Ladies of Cincinnati in inducing the Ohio Assembly or U.S. Congress to erect a proper monument over the graves of nearly 1,000 Union Soldiers buried at SG." The "proper monument" evolved into the commission of an actual statue. May 14, 1867: "On motion of Mr. Anderson, the foundation for the Soldiers Statue was ordered to be made at the expense of the Association and the location thereof to be fixed by the Supt. Bus. Com. & Mr. Shillito."

When "The Sentinel" was completed and sent from the foundry in Munich, it did not go directly to Spring Grove, but was instead displayed in the Fifth Street Market from January to May of 1866. After the merchants demanded the statue be moved, it was taken to Spring Grove. Originally, the plan was to place it directly in the Civil War section, on Mound A.

Despite the merchants of the Fifth Street Market who ran "The Sentinel" out of town, it found a good and fitting home in Spring Grove where he continues to guard over the souls of the courageous soldiers.

In addition to "The Sentinel" sculpture, Rogers was also commissioned to do two bas-reliefs "of war" for $3,210 but only "The Sentinel" was completed.

Chapter Three

Major General Joseph Hooker (1814-1879)

◇

SOMETIMES, EVENTS OUT OF OUR CONTROL LEAD TO STORIES and nicknames we just can't shake. General Joseph Hooker has forever been branded by nicknames he may not have wanted, but were very much earned.

For years, visitors to Hooker's grave have assumed that the term "hooker" was coined from his last name, and not without reason. He was tall, dignified, and attractive to the ladies. The attraction actually began in Mexico, when he was serving in the military as a staff officer in the Mexican War. The señoritas called him the "Handsome Captain" and his headquarters gained the reputation as being a combination of bar and brothel. This reputation continued throughout his career. John Quincy Adams' grandson, Charles F. Adams, Jr., said that Hooker's headquarters during the Civil War was, "a place where no self-respecting man liked to go, and no decent woman would go." Hooker had a proclivity to fraternize with the ladies in his encampments and red-light districts. Initially, the ladies Hooker had in camp were referred to as "Hooker's girls," the term was eventually shortened to "hookers."

In truth, the slang word "hooker," in reference to a prostitute, was in use fifteen years before the Civil War started. N.E. Eliason claimed it was used in North Carolina at the time Spring Grove was founded in 1845. The 1859 *Dictionary of Americanisms* defined the term as "A resident of the Hook, i.e. a strumpet, a sailor's trull, so called from the number of houses of ill-fame frequented by sailors at the Hook (i.e. Corlear's Hook) in the city of New York." Interesting connection since it

◦ Hooker was a lover and a fighter for he was known for his conquests on and off the battlefields.

was "Hooker's Division," a large red-light district in Washington, which popularized the term.

Hooker's other nickname, "Fighting Joe," was an accident, one of the odd little moments where the consequences dog a man to his grave and beyond. "Fighting-Joe Hooker" was the original tagline on a series of takes sent out during the Seven Days battles, but a typographer inadvertently dropped the hyphen and Hooker had a new surname—forever. He was disgusted because he thought it made him sound like a bandit.

Did the name plague him by setting unnaturally high expectations? Perhaps, but the man could fight. He was "aggressive and inspiring" at Antietam until leaving the field with a foot wound. He claimed the day, the bloodiest single-day battle in American history, would have led to victory for the Union if he could have remained on the field. From the battle, even though it was inconclusive, came Lincoln's opportunity to announce the Emancipation Proclamation, as well as one of the war's singular images, "Fighting Joe" in his fighting stance, a Currier and Ives' etching that boosted support of the Union troops.

It was at Chancellorsville that the legend came undone. Holding all the cards against Lee's vastly outnumbered forces, he inexplicably dithered the battle away. On the third day, he was knocked unconscious by a portico pillar during a shelling. Hooker retreated. His soldiers were stunned, and even Hooker had trouble understanding that he lost the battle. There are enduring rumors that just before Chancellorsville, Hooker had stopped drinking and begun reforming his headquarters, and so he had lost his "edge" in battle.

Hooker's ties to Cincinnati began in 1861, on a visit to Cincinnati, when he met and fell in love with the sister of U.S. Congressman, William Groesbeck. They met at the famed Burnet House hotel during an elegant ball. According to the *New York Times,* they married on October 3, 1865.

Despite his successes (and failures) during the war, Hooker will be known more for his demons rather than his prowess in war. Thus "Fighting Joe" has become one of the enduring psychological mysteries of the war, his psyche as much a battlefield as Antietam. "I was not hurt by a shell and I was not drunk," he said after Chancellorsville. "For once I lost confidence in Hooker, and that is all there was to it."

Perhaps, but the legend of Fighting Joe carries on.

HEROES AND VILLAINS
Chapter Three

The Fighting McCook Family

◦ ◇ ◦

SPRING GROVE is the final resting place for many members of the Civil War's most famous family, The Fighting McCooks. Can you imagine having more than a dozen members of your family fighting in a war? The number of McCook family members who served varies from thirteen to eighteen, but the toll of having even more than one family member in battle at the same time is difficult to imagine.

The Scottish-Irish McCook family had migrated from Pennsylvania to the eastern areas of Ohio in the 1820s when the patriarch of the family, Daniel McCook, enlisted at the age of 63 as a volunteer nurse and obtained the rank of Major at the beginning of the war. He died from wounds received in a fight against Morgan's Raiders at Buffington Island two years after being in the Battle of Bull Run.

Daniel's sons and nephews fought in various capacities on forty-six battlefields. It is said that "no major battle took place in the western theatre of war that did not include at least one of the Fighting McCooks." Sons Dan and John fathered a total of 14 sons which resulted in the naming of two family branches: the "Tribe of Dan" and the "Tribe of John." Among the McCooks were three major generals, three brigadier generals, one naval lieutenant, four surgeons, two colonels, one major, one lieutenant, one private, and one chaplain. They were an educated and ambitious family of doctors, lawyers, politicians, riverboat pilots, and judges.

General Robert Latimer McCook was a lawyer and staunch abolitionist who commanded Cincinnati's all-German unit, the Ninth Ohio Infantry. His dedication to his troops was so great that when he fell ill with dysentery, he didn't allow his illness to hamper his direction and command. He just kept on leading. Stories report that while laying unclothed on a cot in an ambulance in 1862, Confederate rangers found and shot him to death. Much of America was appalled at the brutal assassination.

It's amazing that with all of the battle seen by the legendary McCook family, only four actually lost their lives while serving. The "Fighting McCooks" exemplified the fortitude and strength it must have taken to experience such a personal commitment to the Union army in the Civil War. It is only befitting that the McCook family has one of the most impressive monuments that memorialize the Civil War.

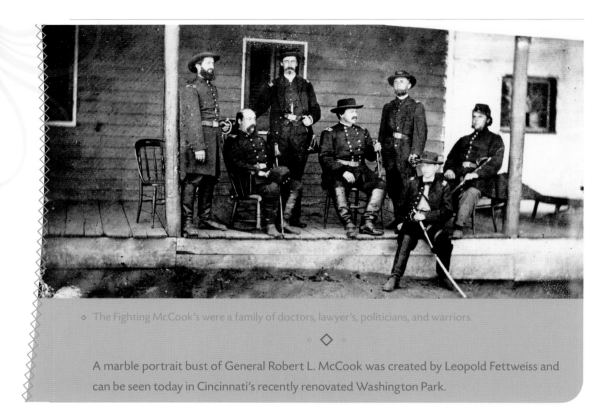

The Fighting McCook's were a family of doctors, lawyer's, politicians, and warriors.

◇

A marble portrait bust of General Robert L. McCook was created by Leopold Fettweiss and can be seen today in Cincinnati's recently renovated Washington Park.

Catherine Coffin (1803-1881)
Levi Coffin (1789-1877)

◇

WITH ALL OF THE REMARKABLE Civil War history attached to Spring Grove, it stands to reason there would also be stories related to abolitionism. Here we have the story of the so-called "President of the Underground Railroad" and his wife.

Levi and Catherine Coffin were instrumental in the region's anti-slavery movement. Levi was an Abolitionist

The tight lipped Catherine, abolitionist and secret keeper.

Quaker who was reported to have helped more than 3,000 slaves escape to freedom. The Western Freedman's Aid Society helped educate and provide for former slaves, and Levi was one of its leaders. In 1867, he served as a delegate to the International Anti-Slavery Conference in Paris, France.

Levi Coffin risked his and his wife's lives to help free slaves.

Levi and Catherine ran real underground railroad depots, and together they staged fake funerals to move slaves out of town. The Coffins purchased a 30-room house at Broadway and Franklin Street in downtown Cincinnati. The house became known as "Grand Central Station" because Catherine rented the rooms to those who belonged to abolitionists and Quakers, and served as a hiding place for runaway slaves. Levi kept the precise movements of the slaves to and from his home secret so slave hunters had difficulty finding out when a search of the Coffin's home might be possible or successful. In addition, he threatened trespassing suits on anyone who might invade his privacy.

One of the most infamous refugees to find shelter in the Coffin's home was later immortalized as the heroine, Eliza, in the book, *Uncle Tom's Cabin*. Levi and Catherine are supposedly inspiration for the characters Simeon and Rachel Halliday in the book!

Levi died in 1877 (interestingly, Spring Grove cemetery records state "vertigo" under the cause of death) and Catherine passed away in 1881 at Cross Street in Avondale from pneumonia. Both were originally buried in the Quaker Burying Grounds. They were reinterred to Spring Grove in 1904 because of, "the splendid underlying bed of sand that had since been entered into the construction of many buildings and walks in the vicinity." The threat of construction to many of the area cemeteries was another reason why the founders of Spring Grove chose the area to create the cemetery. If anyone deserves a "splendid underlying bed of sand" to rest peacefully in eternity, it was Levi and Catherine Coffin!

Henry Boyd (1802-1866)

◇

NOT EVERYONE IN SPRING GROVE HAS AN ELABORATE MEMORIAL, and some have no marker or monument, but it doesn't mean there isn't a story! A good example is the story of Henry Boyd. You won't find a memorial for him, but he was a successful businessman and a maker of beds. He even had his product named after him, "The Boyd Bed."

Henry Boyd was an African-American, born in Kentucky in 1802, who bought his freedom from his master before moving to Cincinnati in 1826. In 1831, he was able to buy the freedom for his brother and sister with the money he had saved. Prior to his move, he trained as a master carpenter and became an expert in furniture making. No carpenter or joiner in the city would hire an African-American at the time.

Fate finally shined favorably on Boyd when the owner of the store where Boyd worked as a porter discovered Boyd was a talented carpenter and joiner. He hired Boyd to build a counter for his shop. His employer was so impressed with the counter that he hired Boyd to build a large frame warehouse. From there, Boyd progressed to building houses and acquiring property in the city.

Boyd saved $9,000, and in 1831 he opened a small furniture factory, Boyd's Manufacturing Company, that made beds at Eighth and Broadway in downtown Cincinnati. The beds made by Boyd were superior to other beds on the market. The "Boyd Bed" was usually made of cherry or maple, and had side rails screwed into the framing, giving them strength and limit hiding places for disease-causing insects and rodents. Hotel owners loved the Boyd Bed. More than 1,000 Boyd Beds were manufactured and shipped up and down the Ohio River in 1844.

In the 1850s, Boyd's shop expanded, according to Census records, and in 1855, a showroom was added displaying the latest, fashionable, parlor furniture. Boyd employed nearly 50 workers, and he became one of the most famous furniture makers in Cincinnati. It is unclear whether Boyd was able to patent his bed, but he did stamp his name on each bed frame made. According to the journal of the Ohio Historical Society: "Many prominent white citizens, even the bitter anti-abolitionist Jacob Burnet, endorsed his product in the local newspapers."

HENRY BOYD,

MANUFACTURER OF

PATENT

Left Wood Screw and Swelled Ra:

EDSTEADS,

CORNER BROADWAY & EIGHTH STF

CINCINNATI.

hing to purchase Bedsteads, would do wel
or themselves, as this Bedstead is warranted ;
ver offered in the West; they can be p·
one fourth of the time usually required, a
o become loose and worthless, and without
rmin.

CERTIFICATES.

d, having used the above-named Patent Bedsteads, feel ι
them to be the best now in use.

D,   Hon. HENRY MORSE,   Hon. RICHAR·
        M. ALLEN,   Rev. L. G. F
        S. B. HUNT,   WM. D. GAI
        ISAIAH WING,   J. B. RUSSEI
ⵏ.   B. TAPPAN,   DANIEL BUF
ⵏEDIEU,   MILTON MCLEAN, Esq. G. W. H. Ev
FORD,   WM. H. HENRIE, Henrie H. JAMES ESH
ES,   J. W. MASON. Fourth st. T. M. Coc
alt House,   House.   Hous
MAN and JOSIAH FOBES, Trustees of the Commerc

CAUTION.

tions of this Bedstead, very much resembling it i
e genuine, which are invariably stamped " F
y manufactory, at the northwest corner of Broad

Although Boyd's business was prosperous throughout the 1850s, his business, as well as others in Cincinnati, declined during the Civil War. In addition, there was a series of fires at his business that were determined to be arson. No insurance would cover rebuilding after the fires. Sadly, Boyd closed his shop in 1863, and he died three years later at age 64.

It's ironic a man who made his fortune in the world by making beds has no monument on his gravesite to mark where he lies in eternal rest, and hopefully, peace.

James "Jimmie" Mussey Johnson (1885-1968) Gertrude "Trudy" Wilson Johnson (1901-1986)

◇

THE WRIGHT BROTHERS are iconic heroes in the field of aviation. Their story began in the city of Dayton, Ohio, a city known as "the

○ Henry Boyd's beds were so popular that at one point he employed over fifty people at his factory.

birthplace of aviation" because of the connection to the Wright brothers, but not many Americans know about the story of two other Daytonians with stories linked closely to aviation history. In fact, I hadn't heard of James and Gertrude Johnson until a co-worker told me their story, and mentioned he was their grandson.

James M. Johnson, better known as "Jimmie," had a remarkable claim to fame. He was one of America's first licensed test pilots. He tested more planes than any other pilot in WWI. Jimmie was one of the first pilots to land on water, one of the first to fly what was the predecessor of the helicopter (called an autogyro at that time), and a founding member of America's first "flight aerobatic" teams.

Jimmie was a 1907 graduate of Purdue University, where he majored in Mechanical Engineering. In 1917, Jimmie was a test pilot for the government at Langley Field, as well as the chief civil test pilot at Dayton's McCook Field. In 1922, he became president of the Johnson Flying Service and vice-president of the Johnson Airplane & Supply Co. He went on to work as an inspector for the Department of Commerce, followed by a stint as chief test pilot and sales manager for Buhl Aircraft Company in Detroit until 1932. Retirement soon followed with a residence in Weslaco, Texas.

Being a fan of vintage movies, I was particularly intrigued by Jimmie's connection to the 1955 MGM movie, "The Court-Martial of Billy Mitchell." Directed by Otto Preminger and starring Gary Cooper, the film centers around the trial of Billy Mitchell for disobeying his commanding officers. Mitchell had criticized his superiors of "negligence" based on their apathy toward airpower after WWI. Mitchell is found guilty and receives a five-year suspension, but the movie ends dramatically with a formation of "flying jennies" flying overhead in his honor as he prepares to exit Washington, D.C.

In real life, Billy Mitchell became Jimmie's most famous student and best friend. When President Wilson declared war on April 6, 1916, Major William (Billy) Mitchell, tasked with building America's airpower, needed instruction on the capability of planes. Jimmie became his instructor, teaching Mitchell what he knew of planes and their possibility in combat. In fact, Mitchell soloed for the first time when Jimmie was ill and unable to teach. They became life-long friends, and Jimmie attended the world premier of the movie in Zanesville, Ohio, with Mitchell's sister. Mitchell himself died in 1936, but not before teaching the American

Natalie Wood and Tabb Hunter were sent to the premier of "The Court-Martial of Billy Mitchell" to drum up business with young people, encouraging them to attend court room dramas. Of course, they did not appear in the film but their appearance together at the premier launched their reputation as a couple to the world.

military the importance of airpower in war, and seeing his (and, perhaps, Jimmie's) vision of combat realized. Today, Billy Mitchell is considered the Father of the American Air Force.

Jimmie wasn't the only member of his family to live for flight and aviation. His wife, Gertrude "Trudy" Wilson, was one of the first female pilots in the world to receive a pilot's license. Jimmie's father and his son were also pilots. The Johnson family has deep and lasting roots in early aviation.

The chapter on Jimmie from John Norberg's book, *Wings of their Dreams-Purdue in Flight*, starts with a quote attributed to Jimmie and Trudy: "Flying wasn't complicated in those days. You just got in and flew." While the quote is short, simple and uncomplicated, Jimmie and Trudy lived a life that was anything but simple and uncomplicated.

Jimmie died on August 20, 1968, only eleven months after fellow Ohioan and Purdue grad, Neil Armstrong, made his history-making first step on the moon.

Captain John L. Beatty (1914-1994)

THIS STORY INVOLVES A BOAT, ITS CAPTAIN, PERILOUS RESCUES, and Cincinnati icons—there's something here for everyone!

Captain John Beatty was born in Ironton, Ohio, in 1914. Before World War I, his father and grandfather worked in marine construction and demolition. After finishing school, Beatty and his father worked on marine salvage operations during World War II. They retrieved sunken boats, barges, pipelines, and removed abandoned bridges. In 1944, Beatty went to work for a very successful marine insurance company, Neare, Gibbs and Company. Eventually he left to start his own company, Beatty Inc. Beatty's skill and reputation in salvage earned him many jobs. The U.S. Army Corps of Engineers called on Beatty for emergency cleanup after accidents on the Ohio River.

Beatty and his wife, Clare, purchased property along the Ohio River for marine ways and facilities, where they built and repaired towboats, barges, pleasure boats, and river ferries. They also operated river-to-rail railroad tracks which ran through their property.

Everything Beatty touched seemed to find success. An old steam towboat, named the *Mike Fink*, was battered, beaten, and ready to be recycled until Beatty remodeled the old boat into a restaurant in 1967. The *Mike Fink* was actually Beatty's gift to his mother and became one of the premier dining destinations in the Cincinnati area. It was a truly unique dining experience in historic surroundings with excellent food.

Before remodeling the *Mike Fink*, Beatty remodeled another steamboat into *Captain Hook's* floating restaurant in 1964 on Cincinnati's public landing. Obviously Beatty found success giving boats a second life!

Beatty named one of his towboats, the *Clare E. Beatty*, after his wife. The boat quickly earned a special place in Beatty's heart. During a blizzard in 1978, one of the worst storms in Cincinnati's history, the *Clare E. Beatty* got trapped in an ice flow above the Markland Dam. Although he assisted in rescuing many other run-away barges during the blizzard, Beatty couldn't save the *Clare E. Beatty* and the boat sank during the storm. Refusing to give up, Beatty and his crew were able to raise the boat out of the icy water and return it to service. John Hartford's song, *In Plain View of the Town*, memorializes the epic struggle between Beatty, his crew, and the elements to save the *Clare E. Beatty*. The struggle is echoed in Hartford's lyrics: "Looks like no matter how hard they push, these barges are still on the ground. Must have been embarrassing for the pilot, here in plain view of the town."

Luck ran out for Captain Beatty in 1994, when he fell from a bunk on that very towboat, the *Clare E. Beatty*. He died from the injuries he sustained in the fall, on the banks of his beloved Ohio River and in the boat he so famously saved.

India Boyer (1907-1998)

◇

INDIA BOYER HAS A FASCINATING STORY THAT NOT ONLY SAW her fight through adversity and into the once exclusively male world of architecture in Ohio, but helped shape the beauty of Spring Grove. Boyer strove to break through the barriers that prevented other females from exercising their creativity in the male-dominated building industry.

Boyer was named after a family friend, India Schoaff, and lived in Sidney, Ohio. Her brothers both succeeded in their careers in mechanical engineering and metal-lurgy and were role models for Boyer. At a young age, Boyer showed talent in art and was interested in architecture, a male-dominated industry. Her family encour-aged her to pursue her dream, but was sidetracked before she made it to college when she chose to work in the office at the Sidney Machine Tool Company for $10 a week.

In 1926, Boyer finally made it to college at The Ohio State University. The Department of Architecture had just opened to women. The initial enrollment

◇ The annex that India Boyer designed is on the left.

was only six ladies and military training was a requirement for enrollment. India was not willing to participate in the training, and saw no reason to march around in circles with the male students. Fortunately, the military requirement was eliminated by her senior year.

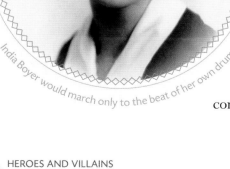

India Boyer would march only to the beat of her own drum.

Marching wasn't the only difficulty the new female students faced in the architecture program. The strict academic requirements proved too arduous for the other female students, and by her second year Boyer was the only one who remained in the program. As the other women left, Boyer had to endure not only the work load, but a chilly reception from the male students. She was excluded from a competitive exam that provided the winner with an invitation to study architecture in France. The committee in charge of the competition told her there were no facilities for women there!

Boyer persevered and eventually won the respect of her classmates. She worked for the University's architect, Joseph Bradford, in the summer before graduation. In 1930, Boyer was the only woman among 1,450 other graduates to receive a degree in architecture.

The Great Depression followed, and Boyer's plans to pursue a graduate degree at Columbia University in New York City dissolved like fortunes in the stock market. She returned to Shelby County and remained jobless until an opportunity came up in the U.S. Army Corps of Engineers. She supervised projects in Cincinnati such as the Beechmont Levy, and was appointed the head of the Architecture Department of the Corps in 1939. In 1945, she resigned her position with the Corps of Engineers and started the firm of Vogt, Ivers and Associates in Cincinnati, finally fulfilling her dream of entering private practice as an architect. She became Ohio's first licensed and practicing female architect, and the first female member of the American Institute of Architects.

In 1955, Boyer was hired to design an addition to the Historic Office in Spring Grove. Her work blended beautifully with the original 1863 Norman gothic building by James Keys Wilson, and included a perfectly matched colored slate tile roof. Boyer's work graced many other buildings in the region, including the Provident Bank and Federal Building in downtown Cincinnati, the Elmwood Place School, Shawnee Park, the original WCPO-TV studios, and even portions of the King's Island amusement park.

After a heart attack in 1975, India was forced into retirement, but she still managed to work as a consultant for the Hamilton County Park District. Watercolors became her hobby, and her paintings were shown at local exhibitions. In 1998, India died at the age of 90, but not before receiving a YWCA Women of Achievement award in 1982 and having the India Boyer Guild of Woman in Architecture named for her in 1994. Boyer's life was filled with challenges, but also success. She described it best, "Looking back, I am reminded that my career presented many challenges and often took precedence over my personal life. However, along with the challenges came many rewards and much fulfillment."

Selina Wetherington Cadwallader
(1836-1886)

◦ ◇ ◦

THIS IS A STORY about a successful dressmaker and boarding house operator who used her husband's early inconsistent work career as incentive to rise above and create a successful life for herself. In the late 1800s, many of the most fashionable women in Cincinnati desired to have a "Cadwallader original" in their wardrobe and there's a reason why.

Selina Wetherington Cadwallader was born in Ireland in 1836. Although the dates of her immigration to America are unknown, Cadwallader did eventually settle in Cincinnati and married Morris Cadwallader in 1862, when she was twenty-six. Morris came to Cincinnati after a shaky work history in his hometown of Henrietta, New York. He worked as an attorney for a post office and abandoned a boot and shoe shop not long after he had purchased

◦ A hog farmer's wife, Selina Cadwallader, was a sought after dress maker. Pictured right, is one of her wedding dresses on a model.

it in 1866. After he and Selina married, his fortune changed when he became a farmer and was successful in raising hogs.

Although her husband seemed to be doing well in the hog farming business, Selina still couldn't rely on his past work history. In 1870, she bravely forged ahead by opening her first business: a boarding house. At the time it was not unusual for well to do women to operate a boarding house and Selina proved that she was up to the task. For sixteen years, she operated her boarding house successfully, in addition to a dressmaking salon. Both establishments were in East Fourth Street's fashionable shopping district, making them accessible for the wealthier citizens of Cincinnati. Her skills as a dressmaker were highlighted with her attention to detail. Selina had a reputation for her fine workmanship and made sure that her well-heeled clients were happy. As a result, she ended up being listed in the *Cincinnati Society Blue Book and Family Directory,* published by Peter G. Thomson in 1879.

Morris died in 1880 and despite his unpredictable career, he provided an inheritance of around $110,000 for his wife and their three children. By then, Selina was already established and successful so the inheritance "feathered the nest," so to speak. Her wealth allowed her the luxury of hiring a servant, which was unusual for a dressmaker in those days. And her clients included the likes of Cincinnati's wealthiest, such as the Emery, Krippendorf, and Thoms families. They were drawn to her ability to make her gowns as fashionable and up-to-date as those in Paris. In fact, she once made a companion piece to match a skirt made in Paris by notable designer Charles Frederick Worth for Mrs. Joseph C. Thoms in Cincinnati. Thoms brought the fabric back from a trip to Paris and asked Cadwallader to make an "evening bodice" to compliment Worth's skirt. No doubt, Thoms was the envy of Cincinnati fashionistas at that time!

Cadwallader did not die penniless when she passed in 1886 on the same street, East Fourth, where she made her fortune. The bulk of the estate went to her daughters, which included personal belongings estimated at $50,000 and real estate around $70,000. Her "dress goods" were appraised at more than $2,300 and the estate also included seventy shares in the Cincinnati, Lebanon, and Northern Railroad Company. Although Cadwallader initially sought to overcome her insecurity with her husband's first lack of success, she ended up becoming her own person simply because she loved what she did. She made dresses. And she did it well.

Alfred Traber Goshorn (1833-1902)

◦ ◇ ◦

ONE OF CINCINNATI'S FIRST BRUSHES WITH ROYALTY occurred in the late 1800s when a gentleman impressed the world with his successful leadership of an international exposition and contributions to the art world. While many of his accomplishments have been greatly documented, I've been most intrigued by his undocumented contributions to Cincinnati pie-eating!

Alfred Goshorn was the president of the National Lead Paint Company. Goshorn organized the Cincinnati Industrial Expositions held between 1870 and 1888. Goshorn traveled to Europe to study exposition methods in London, Paris, and Vienna. For his efforts he was named as Ohio's delegate to the Philadelphia Worlds Fair in 1876. The other delegates named Goshorn to serve as the director-general. Under his guidance the event was such a success, Goshorn was decorated by many nations for his accomplishment. One honor was that Goshorn became the only genuine knight from Cincinnati in the late 1800s after Queen Victoria bestowed the honor upon him. Yes, Queen Victoria, whom I deem responsible for the Victorian "clutter" that existed in the cemetery before Adolph Strauch literally got his hands on it and ordered it removed to open up the views and vistas. In addition,

A. Goshorn: President of the Reds, the Cincinnati Art Museum, and lover of pie.

Another member of the Goshorn family, A.O. Goshorn, was the superintendent of Greenwood Cemetery in Hamilton, Ohio, where many of my family members are buried. His daughter, Sadie, followed her father as superintendent for that cemetery. Greenwood Cemetery also has a connection to Adolph Strauch because of his consultation on its landscape design. Although Strauch helped with the design, the names Millikin, Erwin, and Earhart are associated with the development of Greenwood.

◦ ◦

Goshorn received criticism for his suggestion that local women who organized The Women's Centennial Exposition in 1874, "secure a credible representation of women's work" and, "to bear the expense of its transportation and exposition." Goshorn wanted the women to pay for the Women's Pavillion. They did agree to pay $5,000 after disgruntled members called it "an injustice of putting women on a different footing from other exhibitors."

Goshorn was the first president of the Cincinnati Art Museum. He donated William Sontag's *Landscape* to the museum in 1886. I know him well as the first president of the Cincinnati Ball Club or Red Stockings (now our great Cincinnati Reds).

But in spite of his fame and fortune, A. T. Goshorn never allowed anyone to interview him. Not even after he supposedly introduced the practice of eating pie with a fork to Cincinnati! On April 4, 1877, Goshorn was honored at a dinner at the Grand Hotel in Cincinnati. The menu, speeches, and correspondence have been published by Robert Clarke & Co., but I haven't been able to find verification of the pie-eating claim. And who knows? Maybe it did begin at the Grand Hotel that evening! This is one of those stories that is so intriguing, but maddeningly unsubstantiated!

Thank you, Sir Goshorn, for all you have done! I imagine that no genuine knight should eat pie with his hands.

Charles "Charlie" Grant, Jr. (1875-1932)

IT'S A SHAME THAT SO MANY TALENTED AND WORTHY PEOPLE in this world never receive the recognition or praise they deserve. This is the story of one such talented man who missed his chance to play major league baseball simply because of his skin color.

Charles Grant, Jr. was born in the Cumminsville area of Cincinnati around 1875, to Charles and Mary Grant. He was quite intelligent, and even learned to speak German fluently. When he was old enough, Grant frequented the sandlots in his neighborhood, where he honed his impressive baseball skills. Grant's talent as a second baseman has been compared to legends such as Jackie Robinson, the first African-American to play major league baseball. Grant's nicknames included "Speedy" and "Cincy." Researcher John Holway said Grant, "was rumored to be an inventor of the screwball." Although the rumor is probably not true Grant nearly made the major leagues 46 years before Robinson. So why didn't he make it to the big leagues with skills that reportedly matched those of Robinson's? The story is telling and heartbreaking.

In 1901, Grant was hired as a bellhop at the Eastman Hotel in Hot Springs, Arkansas. The region was known as a place for notable baseball players to relax and rejuvenate before the baseball season. Grant joined a team with other bellhops, and quickly became the star of the team. The manager of the New York Giants, and then the Baltimore Orioles, John J. McGraw, was one of many who watched Grant play in Hot Springs. Almost immediately, McGraw recognized the raw talent of Grant, deeming him capable of becoming a major leaguer. However, at that time, baseball had a traditional ban against African-Americans. McGraw still sought to add Grant to his team in Baltimore.

A simple little creek in the Southwest, called Tokohoma Creek, supposedly inspired McGraw's plan to get Grant into the majors. McGraw had been looking at a map of the southeastern states in the lobby of the hotel where Grant worked and the name of Tokohoma jumped out at him. The very next day, the Baltimore Orioles signed Grant, but McGraw changed his name to "Charlie Tokohoma," and informed the league Grant was a Cherokee Indian from Lawrence, Kansas. Despite the name change, Grant was still a talented baseball player. According to the *Chicago Tribune*, when McGraw asked him where he had learned to play baseball, Grant replied: "I never learned, I already knew how." The *Tribune* also said, "Tokohoma bats right handed, is fleet of foot, and throws with quickness and ease, snapping the ball away with a graceful motion. He will be tried at second base, but will likely be removed to right field."

Unfortunately, the president of the newly organized Chicago White Sox heard of this new "Indian" ball player and immediately protested by saying, "If Muggsy (McGraw) really keeps this Indian, I will get a Chinaman of my acquaintance and put him on third. Somebody said this Cherokee of McGraw's is really Grant, the crack Negro second baseman, fixed up with war paint and a bunch of feathers." The statement was politically incorrect, even at the turn of the century!

Dave Wyatt,
a black Chicago baseball
player and later a sportswriter,
also claimed it was his idea to
pass Charlie off as a native Indian
when he approached McGraw
while working as a "rubdown man"
in a popular bathhouse.

Charlie was not alone in his attempts to gain entry into the big leagues. Brothers Moses and Welday Walker from Ohio, met similar fates. The Walkers were sons of a fugitive slave who traveled via the Underground Railroad to Mt. Pleasant, Ohio. Moses studied law at the University of Michigan after graduating from Oberlin College, and was a catcher in 41 games in Toledo, Ohio. Threatening letters were sent to the Toledo baseball club, and just like Grant, the Walker brothers never made it to the big leagues.

Charlie's father once trained a famous trotting horse, called "Maud S." which appeared frequently in the Cincinnati area. Charlie Jr. acted as a "hostler" or groomsman for the stables.

The *Times Star* reported on May 28, 1901, that Grant denied the allegation he was black and he would be going through Cincinnati on his way to Baltimore to open the baseball season. Sadly, that didn't happen. He received instructions in Cincinnati from McGraw not to report to Baltimore. The manager of the Orioles didn't care for the attention Grant had gathered, and thought it would be impossible to cover up Charlie's true identity, thus ending Grant's dream of making it into the major leagues.

For the remainder of his life, Grant worked in Cincinnati, sometimes as a janitor of an apartment complex at Reading Road and Blair Avenue. When the New York Giants played in Cincinnati, McGraw would always leave a pass at the gate for

The unwritten law that blacks could not play major league baseball came from Adrian (Cap) Anson, manager of the Chicago White Stockings. Not one black player appeared in a major league game until Jackie Robinson joined the Brooklyn Dodgers in 1947, thus breaking the color barrier.

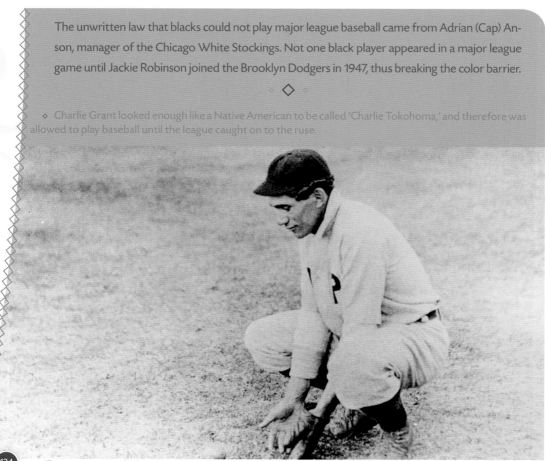

◇ Charlie Grant looked enough like a Native American to be called 'Charlie Tokohoma,' and therefore was allowed to play baseball until the league caught on to the ruse.

Grant. In turn, Grant would often visit the dugout and listen to accolades that Mc-Graw heaped upon him. McGraw always introduced Grant to his players and told them the story of how Grant almost made it into the big leagues.

In his mid-fifties, Grant died unexpectedly and tragically while sitting on the very steps of the apartment complex where he worked and lived with his parents as a janitor and handyman. On a hot afternoon in July of 1932, a car blew a tire, causing it to jump the curb and strike Grant. He was killed immediately.

It is a sad story of a talented athlete and worthy man denied the opportunity to show the world what he was capable of accomplishing, but also a reminder of how important equal rights are, and how easily they can be lost.

Ruth Hooke (1893-1969)

◦ ◇ ◦

A LONE ELEGANT MAUSOLEUM STANDS AT THE SOUTHERN END of section 117. One would think it holds a multitude of family members. Surprisingly, it belongs to one infamous lady, Ruth Hooke, also known as "The Lady on Ice." Her story involves a most interesting and detailed will, and a litigious family that has left her alone in eternity.

After receiving a master's degree from the University of Michigan, Hooke began her career as a shorthand and typing teacher at Norwood High School in Cincinnati in 1918. She spent her career teaching, and from reports I've read, she drew no attention to herself. She wore old-fashioned, unassuming clothes that included holes in the soles of her shoes. She was a miser who distrusted everyone she came into contact with, never owned a car, and lived in a $60 a month apartment. Local Norwood historian, Debbie Simpson, told me about a classmate's father who used to help Miss Hooke carry home groceries. Apparently, Hooke complained when the price was raised on the Apple Brown Betty she bought every day from the school cafeteria, but she reluctantly continued to purchase it at the new price.

Before you think she was destitute, Hooke had saved more than $200,000 in cash when she died. In 1974, Hooke's executor, Leslie Sharp from the Fifth-Third Bank, said that had she invested that money, it would have been worth more than one million dollars. Today, her net value would have been even more!

Most considered Hooke a good teach-er, but also strange, mysterious, and hard to understand. Some co-workers and students called her "Hattie the Witch" because she had a reputation for not be-ing friendly. Another co-worker reported that Hooke lost a man, perhaps a fiancée, in World War I and never recovered from the loss. That, in addition to the death of her father when she was young, may have contributed to her loneliness and solitary ways. The co-worker explained, "It was as though she wanted to get back at everyone who had hurt her." It was a sad situation, but Hooke did have a scheme to get back at everyone in a very interesting way.

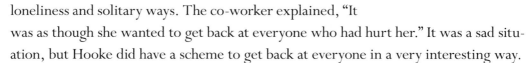
Ruth Hooke's surprisingly elegant mausoleum.

Hooke spent her life as a miser to have a dream funeral and burial. Since she didn't have true love in life, she wanted to make sure she was taken care of in death. She even made all the arrangements.

In Hooke's 1963 will, she asked the executor to spare no expense in carry-ing out her requests. She bequeathed her fortune, except $7,100, to her funeral, memory, and the 'perpetual care' of her burial lot in section 117. The details of her hand-written will were above and beyond normal requests. She wanted a steel casket with an innerspring mattress and beige quilted silk lining (a girl's gotta be comfortable in death, right?). She wanted to look good so she requested "a pale, pink silk dress, nylon hose, undies, slip, and slippers in vogue at the time (not paper-soled variety)." She wanted her hair shampooed, tinted with brown Color Magic, and dressed with a soft wave. She had manicured nails, clear nail polish, diamond rings on her fingers, and organ music at the service.

Hooke's family was not happy when they learned they were left out of her will, and even more upset when they learned Hooke split the remaining money from the estate among her friends. One friend from Norwood was bequeathed $100, "for purchase of a pin in remembrance of me and our fun together at work." Obviously, Hooke had *some* fun in her life!

Of course, family members contested the will when they learned the details and how little they inherited. Hooke went so far as to say, "Anybody mentioned in the will who tries to break, set aside, or change any bequest shall forfeit the bequest mentioned and receive absolutely nothing." Hooke's body was held in the White Pine Chapel of Spring Grove for six years as the will was contested in court, which was the source of her "Lady on Ice" moniker. I don't know if the body was actually kept on ice. It's more likely her coffin was placed inside the holding vault. Finally, the family received nothing and Hooke was given the funeral she wanted.

The requests in her will didn't stop with a remembrance pin and funeral arrangements. I came across a copy of a University of Michigan (Hooke's alma mater) magazine from 1976 that shows a photograph of the $5,000 memorial stained glass window Hooke had commissioned, "to be placed for me, preferably facing the sunset, in a suitable location at the University of Michigan." She also requested a Tiffany window in her private mausoleum. However, it was not installed. Ironically, the modest window that was installed faces the sunset.

After living a simple, but melancholy life spent alone, "The Lady on Ice" seems to have gotten the fame and afterlife she wanted, despite the best efforts of her family.

Edward Maschmeier (1897-1979)

◦ ◇ ◦

THIS PERSONAL REMEMBRANCE WRITTEN BY FORMER Spring Grove employee, Edward Maschmeier, gives us a poignant look into the daily routine of dedicated workers who kept the cemetery and arboretum beautifully groomed back in the early 1900s. Edward shared the following insight in a type-written letter published in the cemetery's monthly bulletin in 1960:

"My home was just below where John Lynn lives today on what is now Spring Grove property. The foundation of the house, long gone, can still be seen if you observe closely. In those days [1900] it was a nine hour day and a six day week. Paid vacations, sick pay, social security, and unemployment relief were unheard of then. We were just as interested in pay day then as workers are today. Mr. Winans came out to the Grove from the City office located on Fourth Street. Accompany-

Footstone of Edward Maschmeier.

ing him was an armed guard in best television tradition. We were paid out-of-doors, in back of the blacksmith shop under a maple tree except in bad weather when we gathered inside the shop. Wages were paid in cash and doled out to each employee according to the hours worked that week.

I remember when all hauling, all transportation, and some of the grass cutting was [sic] done with the aid of horses. Twenty-five to thirty horses were housed, fed, watered, and cared for at the Big Barn near the corner of Gray and Winton roads. Caring for all these animals was a major task in itself. There was hay to be stored, oats and salt to be kept in supply, and a blacksmith shop busy all the time. The horses were cared for round the clock and seven days a week. It's hard to realize now what all that involved.

I can remember what a thrill it was when I was promoted to driving a team of horses. I remember the further thrill when I was given a truck to drive and the years of work spent hauling grave dirt with this truck. We had horse drawn mowers. Of course in those days we didn't have as much territory to cover. Sections 62, 68, 105, 122 and A to the North Gate were still all woods when I came to work at the Grove.

My first duty upon starting to work at Spring Grove was planting ivy and myrtle as a grave groundcover. At that time the ivy and myrtle plants were combined in planting a grave. The effect was pleasing when the plants grew well. But the myrtle was subject to crown rot disease and to blight. Later it was left out of the plantings and the English Ivy used alone.

"Young" Henry Weghorst was foreman of the ivy planting gang at that time. "Tug" Wilson, an Englishman, was in charge of ivy and myrtle propagation and growing it in cold frames. In winter, in addition to glass sash covering the cold frames of potted ivy and myrtle plants, a layer of leaves was placed on chicken wire under the sash. Then boards were placed on top of the glass sash as further protection against the cold. All this involved a tremendous amount of hand labor.

The ivy and soil used in planting the graves was delivered to the site of the grave on wagons drawn by a team of horses. There were twelve or more teams of horses used in the Grove besides those used for passenger service. Hay and oats were used to accomplish the results in transportation that gasoline and oil are expected to accomplish today."

The contrast in methods used today and thirty-five years ago in the Grove are almost unbelievable.

Maschmeier's words epitomize how valuable personal accounts are to the preservation of our history and well-being, and remind us how far Spring Grove has come in a relatively short period of time.

Inez L. Renfro (1885-1965)
St. Julian Renfro (1882-1946)

◦ ◇ ◦

SOME OF MY FAVORITE STORIES COME OUT OF NOWHERE. I learned of this story when I serendipitously ran into Spring Grove's Advanced Planning Advisor, Venita Brown, in an office parking lot. When I told her I was working on another book, she asked I make sure to include notable African-American stories. Up until that point, I had very little information about contributions of the African-American community to the funeral industry, so I jumped at the chance to educate myself with Venita's assistance.

The African-American funeral business in Cincinnati involved Inez and St. Julian Renfro. They met in Louisiana

The Renfro Funeral Home was in a building downtown.

African-American deaths in Cincinnati increased considerably between 1920 and 1923, providing the impetus for many blacks to enter the funeral business. By 1926, there were seventeen black undertakers.

◇

and married in 1904. In 1913, they moved to Cincinnati. Inez had been a school principal, and after their move, St. Julian became a clerk in the Cincinnati Post Office in the registry division. Rampant discrimination prevented him from advancing, but that didn't stop his determination to better himself. He left the post office and enrolled in the Cincinnati College of Embalming. St. Julian completed his training, and together with his wife, opened a funeral business in Cincinnati's West End in 1921.

With the large immigration of blacks and the overall increase in the African-American population, mortality among the community increased greatly in Ohio after 1915. The demand for African-American funeral and undertaking services grew. Many of these new African-American funeral businesses were in the urban areas where most African-Americans lived. William W. Giffen stated in his book, *African Americans and the Color Line in Ohio, 1915-1930* that J. Walter Wills' "House of Wills" in Cleveland, along with nine other black funeral homes, employed 32 other African-American undertakers in 1930. Wills' may have been the most prosperous black funeral home owner in the state of Ohio.

Inez Renfro was a force to be reckoned with, often called "the amazing Inez" because of her involvement in Cincinnati politics. She was a key figure in getting African-Americans appointed to key positions as well as elected to political office. Despite her confidence, her initial involvement in the funeral industry was harrowing. She had to get over a fear of the dead in order to become a licensed funeral director and embalmer. Despite her fear, Inez turned her home into the business and made all of the clothing for burials.

I'm extremely thankful for that unexpected encounter with Venita, which led to the story of the African-American funeral industry and its two pioneers, Inez and St. Julian Renfro. Today, the name Renfro continues to be one of the most recognizable names in Cincinnati's African-American community.

Martha Evelyn Stone (1850-1924)

◦ ◇ ◦

THERE ARE A MULTITUDE OF BEAUTIFUL MONUMENTS in Spring Grove. An obelisk in a small triangular lot of section 56 catches the eye, and is a gorgeous work of art, but the monument truly comes to life when you learn the story of Martha Stone, the amazing woman buried there.

A lovely woman from the American Titanic Society visited Spring Grove a few years ago, and asked where the *Titanic* survivor was buried. I knew nothing about a *Titanic* survivor. She told me the story of Martha Stone, the wife of a prominent Cincinnatian, George N. Stone. Martha was a *Titanic* survivor and a hero of the doomed ship.

Another interesting connection between Cincinnati and the *Titanic* is the engineering firm of Earnshaw & Punshon. Earnshaw & Punshon has done impressive work for Spring Grove Cemetery & Arboretum over the years. In addition, they designed Fairview Lawn Cemetery in Halifax, Nova Scotia, which holds 121 victims of the sinking *Titanic*, the largest number buried in any single cemetery.

◦ ◇ ◦

◦ Life rafts carrying survivors to safety away form the sinking Titanic.

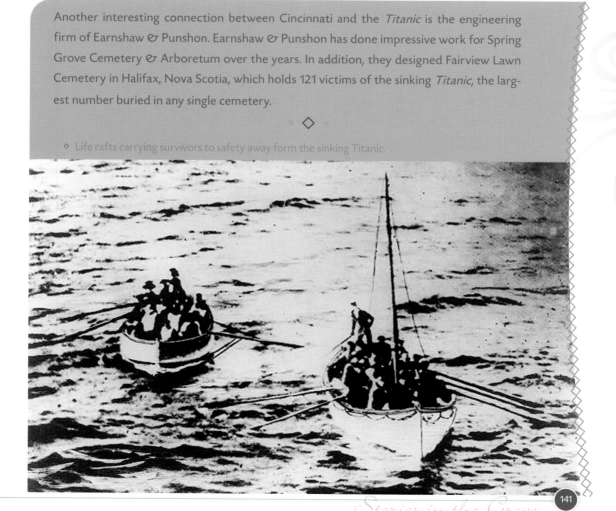

Stories in the Grove

George Stone was a veteran of the Civil War, the manager of the Cincinnati Bell Telephone Company, and director of the Cincinnati Street Railroad. Mr. Stone preceded his wife in death, and was not alive to accompany his wife on the *Titanic*. Her maid, Miss Amelie Icard, did. Martha was in England to attend the coronation of King George V and wanted to get back to Cincinnati in time for the 1912 May Festival. Stone and Miss Icard stayed in the first class cabin B-28 when the ship struck the iceberg. Stone explained she was told several times by the crew to "go back to bed and sleep," after the *Titanic* hit the iceberg, but she knew something was wrong when she heard the steam blowing off the ship.

Crew members confirmed the ship had struck an iceberg. They explained the ship was stopping to assess the damage. Stone returned to her cabin, but the sound of the roaring steam went on and on. She got dressed and stepped outside, and was told by another passenger to don a life jacket and find a life boat. Stone and Miss Icard followed orders and got into boat number 6. There was no order in the loading of the boats. In her recollection, she thought there were perhaps 20 women and two men in her boat. An uncapped plug in the lifeboat caused a leak, and water was seeping into the boat, endangering the lives of everyone onboard. Stone rose to the occasion and stopped the leak by standing on the plug for more than seven hours!

Upon returning to safety, Martha criticized the crew's lack of attention during the sinking. She recalled the sounds of the passengers and crew screaming, while the sad hymn the musicians kept playing continued as the ship slowly went down. Martha claimed that she would never forget those sounds for the rest of her life.

In addition to Stone and Miss Icard, there were four other Cincinnatians on the *Titanic*. After her death, Stone bequeathed a large amount of cash and personal possessions to Miss Icard for her dedication during the *Titanic* tragedy.

Stone returned to New York City after her experience on the *Titanic*. She died on May 12, 1924, and her body was brought back to Cincinnati and buried next to her husband, George. Many gravesites in the cemetery have both small and grandiose stone obelisks. One website I found states that "ancient obelisks were idols of Gods' anger." The tall granite obelisk rising to the heavens on the Stones' gravesite in section 56 is a fitting tribute to Martha's courage and determination to survive the night the *Titanic* sank. I wouldn't argue that the Stones' obelisk may very well be an idol of Gods' anger.

HEROES AND VILLAINS
Chapter Three

Some accounts say that Chester Park (originally a race track and later an amusement park) was named after George Stone's horse, Lady Chester, which frequently ran at the half-mile oval. A 1920 article about early horse racing in Cincinnati states that the name came from Edwin W. Miller, a journalist and secretary of the track. When asked what the name should be Miller quoted a Walter Scott poem, "Charge Chester, Charge; On, Stanley, On!" and Chester became its name. However, when the builder of the track, John Sullivan died, the Post indicated that he named Chester Park. Still all three stories could be true if Miller knowing of Stones' horse quoted Scott and Sullivan agreed to the name in honor his partner's mare.

◇

Lida Scott Howell (1859-1938)

◦ ◇ ◦

RECENTLY, THERE HAS BEEN A RESURGENCE OF HEROINES in Hollywood with skill in archery. My niece dressed as Merida, the lead character from the movie *Brave,* on Halloween. She sees herself as a budding archer. But Lida Scott Howell's story began at a time when women weren't as accepted in sports. However, the sport of archery, which was an event in five of the earliest Olympics, had long been a leisure sport for upper class women.

Howell was young when she became interested in archery. She remarked once that the national interest in archery was greater than the interest in both golf and tennis. Howell described the qualities of a successful female archer as, "Nerve, an eye for distance, a quality of perseverance, and a natural ability inborn for archery." She remarked that archery was a "dead fad" across the nation, but "right here in Cincinnati the true archers who love the graceful old English sport, flourish." In fact, there were three archery clubs in Cincinnati at the time, giving Howell the opportunity to practice.

Howell's husband, Millard C. Howell, was also an accomplished archer. Together, they were referred to as, "Maid Marian and Robin Hood." They both trained on the archery range in their backyard at the corner of Carter and Williams Avenue in Norwood, a suburb in Cincinnati. Millard became the President of the National Archery Association in 1892. After the two were married, Howell won the first of her seventeen National Championships in 1893. Her record setting performance in

1895, stood until 1931. Millard won the USA National Championship in 1899. They were the only husband and wife to have won the USA championship in archery in same year.

Howell conquered the archery world wearing a white ruffled shirtwaist, a black skirt that touched the ground, and lots of petticoats all topped by a proper hat. She became the first woman to win an Olympic gold medal in archery at the 1904 Olympics in St. Louis. She went on to win three gold medals at St. Louis, a feat rarely matched by an American woman. To this day, Lida Scott Howell remains one of the most celebrated female archers of all time.

A newspaper reporter once asked Howell why she preferred archery over other sports. She responded, "Archery is a picturesque game, the range with its smooth green and distant glowing target with its gold and radiating red, blue, black, and white, the white-garbed players, with graceful big bows and flying arrows, makes a beautiful picture." Although petite, Howell was picturesque and graceful.

◇ Swimmer Lenore Wingard, being honored for her accomplishments in the Olympics.

Chapter Three

In 1903, at the height of her fame, Howell still lived in Norwood, Ohio, when she was described as "the best female archer in the United States." Today her story lives on in Hollywood heroines and female athletes across the world.

Lenore Kight Wingard (1911-2000)

◦ ◇ ◦

LIDA SCOTT HOWELL ISN'T THE ONLY FEMALE OLYMPIAN found in Spring Grove. More than thirty years after Howell participated in the Paris Olympics, Lenore Kight Wingard swam in the 1932 and 1936 Olympics and was regarded as "America's Supreme Distance Swimming Star."

Wingard's story starts with her success as a swimmer. At 5' 2" she was a tiny woman compared to her competitors, adding to her allure as a feisty underdog. In the 1932 Los Angeles Olympics, seventeen-year-old Wingard won the silver medal in the 400-meter freestyle. Wingard was out touched by the 5' 10" gold medalist, Helene Madison. It took officials 15 minutes to determine a winner as both swimmers broke the world record.

When Madison retired after the Los Angles games, she was called the "greatest woman swimmer of all time." However, from 1933 to 1936, Wingard broke many of Madison's records setting 25 national and nine world records. At the United States championships in 1933, Wingard won every freestyle event from the 100-meters to the 1500-meters.

Wingard became a celebrity among sports enthusiasts. As a result, her marriage to Cleon Wingard (1907-2005) was kept quiet. She met Cleon in Pennsylvania, and they both lived there until Cleon accepted a job at the University of Cincinnati in 1935. That year they married while en route to Cincinnati. Reporters from all over the world were taken aback by their humble lifestyle. Wingard was quoted as saying about the attention of the reporters, "They were shocked—then they'd ask where my swimming pool was." Cleon then exclaimed, "They heard she'd brought her swimming pool from Pennsylvania to train in."

In 1936, Lenore returned to Pennsylvania to train for the New York Olympic trials, where she won the 400-meter freestyle and a place on the women's team.

The team consisted of Lenore, diver Dorothy Poynton Hill and the U.S. and world backstroke champion Eleanor Holm Jarrett. Jarrett never made it to Berlin. She was kicked off the team when she ignored warnings to "behave" after she was caught coming back tipsy from a late-night party given by actress Helen Hayes. Wingard defended Jarrett, feeling she was dismissed unfairly. Wingard believed a lack of supervision from chaperones and coaches was to blame. This wasn't the end of the challenges facing Wingard at the Berlin Olympics.

Hitler was in power, and the Olympics had become a struggle between fascism and the free world. Wingard explained the male athletes were treated very differently from the female athletes in Berlin. The men were housed in comfort and fed Berlin's best cuisine, but, according to Wingard, women stayed in "an army barracks and the beds were just built-in wooden things with little tiny mattresses on them. The whole thing was a military camp, and there were underground passages all over the place. They allowed us to use one to get to the pool. And there was talk about a concentration camp near there, but I never saw it." She went on to say, "And the food was just awful. Everything was cooked in one big pot, with all the ham, beans and potatoes, all [the] beef and carrots, all thrown in together." The woman who was in charge of Wingard's housing at the Olympics was Baroness von Wangenheim, described as "a humorless Prussian with tiny eyes and great jowls, who, among other things, wouldn't allow heat in the rooms."

Wingard faced more than just poor housing and a humorless Prussian at the Olympics. She had a close call with Hitler on her way to compete one day. Wingard was stopped as Hitler's car approached. She feared she would miss her event as she waited until he passed. She was close enough to touch him and his many guards, which she had no desire to do. She explained that during the Opening Ceremonies, when they passed in front of Hitler, "we didn't give the 'Heil Hitler' salute like most of the other teams did, we just

The tiny and unstoppable Lenore Wingard.

Wingard with one of her many medals.

turned our eyes to the right." That didn't garner the attention the U.S. flag bearer, Al Jochim, did when he refused to dip the U.S. flag, as was tradition, but it does speak to the character and fearlessness of Wingard.

The brief delay with Hitler didn't prevent Wingard from winning a bronze medal in the 400-meter free-style. She returned to America and became a professional swimmer. Wingard's celebrity status introduced her to Hollywood celebrities like Johnny Weissmuller, Will Rogers, and Buster Crabbe. She posed for a Camel cigarette ad, even though she never smoked. Because of her love for Wheaties cereal, she became the first female Wheaties Champion.

In 1937, Lenore stopped swimming competitively and began offering private swimming lessons. Her husband became the principal of the old Sands School in 1948. Cleon became a hero in his own right, devoting his life to helping children and helping found the charity the "Neediest Kids of All" in Cincinnati.

So goes it. A tiny lady from Pennsylvania grew up to be, as *The Literary Digest* called her in 1934, "One of the fastest mermaids in the world." That same year, Paul Gallico in the *Olympic Pool* referred to Wingard as "Lenore the Lioness." Wingard earned her place in several Halls of Fame, including the International Swimming Hall of Fame. Gallico explained Wingard's success, and gave us another view of how female athletes were seen at the time, with this quote, "You know you can say what you want [about] gal athletes and their inability to compete on even terms with men in any sport, but there is one department in which they will match and frequently pass him and that is heart-moxie, courage, the old ticker. How those girls will hang on and fight and get their teeth into a race and shake it like a puppy."

I found it especially interesting that famous Hollywood columnist, Louella Parsons, once compared Lenore to another female sports icon, Babe Didrikson,

America's first female golf celebrity. Here is Louella's account of Lenore's reaction to a defeat by Helene Madison: "Her eyes were still wet when, through the courtesy of one of the officials I had a chance to talk to Miss Kight. Shy, rather shy, rather quiet, but still all a-tremble, she looked like a small boy, her gray shirt and trousers and her shortcut hair made me think of Babe Didrikson, the Texas Terror. But only in her young boyish appearance does she resemble the talkative Babe."

It is remarkable that Wingard and female athletes and heroes like her literally changed the history of, not only the Olympics, but also female sports. Wingard once remarked that, "as late as April 1931, the International Olympic Committee seriously considered eliminating women's events. We young Americans did our part to capture the imagination of spectators and reporters. Through the sports press we catapulted the Olympic Games and women's athletics into the nation's consciousness as never before."

George "Fats" Wrassman (1894-1929)

◇

SITTING DOWN WITH GOOD FRIENDS AND CHATTING over a meal is always fun, but even more so when they share unexpected stories about Spring Grove inhabitants. My friend Owen recently shared the shady past of his grandfather during a casual lunch conversation.

George "Fats" Wrassman was born in Indiana in 1894. It was there that his life as a notorious gang leader during Prohibition began. In 1920, he was arrested in Indianapolis for operating a "blind tiger," a term used for an establishment that sells illegal intoxicants. Police reported seeing Wrassman putting two half-pint bottles of whiskey on the floor of a poolroom as they were raiding an alleged craps game in progress.

From Indianapolis, Wrassman went to Hamilton, Ohio. I grew up in Hamilton, and knew nothing of the city's corrupt past, which earned it the nickname "Little Chicago." With a notorious past (that has since been cleared), the name was well earned. According to local historian and former editor of the *Hamilton Journal News*,

Jim Blount, Wrassman, along with criminals such as John Dillinger, helped earn Hamilton the nickname.

Wrassman was considered a leading bootlegger at one of the many saloons and speakeasies in Hamilton. He was convicted for the murder of "a good beer joint" proprietor, Edward Cocannon. He did manage to elude conviction for the suspected murder of Glenn Hiatt and Jack Parker, at the Superior Fishing Camp on the Little Miami River in 1927. Theses murders were linked to a bootleggers' war. Parker had been shot in the knee while arguing with Wrassman and Hiatt was shot when he grabbed Parker's revolver and attempted to shoot Wrassman. Parker escaped but was found a year later, shot to death and thrown into a ditch. Parker had been sought by authorities for the slaying of a prize fighter at the Garden of Allah roadside inn near Cincinnati during a fight over a woman. Suspicion in the murder focused on a possible revenge killing. A week before his death, Parker had also been implicated in a robbery of a bank in Columbus, Ohio.

A year later, the *Lima News* reported that the Mosler Safe Company in Hamilton decided to pay their employees with checks instead of cash after the "Wrassman Gang," headed by Wrassman and "Wildcat" Reynolds, attempted to rob the company's payroll.

Wrassman's life of crime ended on June 11, 1929, in Cincinnati when he was shot and killed after his parked car was spotted by the chief of detectives, Joseph B. Schaeffer, on a downtown street. Wrassman fired several shots but it was too late—Schaeffer was faster, firing five or six times. After Wrassman's death, it was rumored his gang sought retaliation when an unidentified man called police to say, "They're going to get Schaeffer."

Although Wrassman left quite an indelible legacy in the area's criminal world, his grandson took a different direction. Not only did Owen refuse to follow in his grandfather's footsteps, he's made a reputable life working for a financial advisors group that, "builds upon shared values of honesty, integrity, genuine concern for clients and respect for associates." His moniker of "Superman" for his charitable work in the area fits his character well.

Hamilton, Ohio, wasn't the only city to earn the nickname "Little Chicago" because of its criminal activity. The term was also applied to such cities as Sheffield, England, and Moose Jaw in Saskatchewan, Canada.

Wrassman's first son, George, Jr., tragically died at the age of three when he fell down an elevator shaft in Indiana.

◇

Armstrong Chumley (1822-1880)

◦ ◇ ◦

TELEVISION THESE DAYS IS INUNDATED WITH "COP SHOWS." We're intrigued by the drama and sordid tales of crime and passion that unfold week after week. The story of Armstrong Chumley played out like a cop show, with the sordid drama, passion, and criminal behavior supplied by his children.

Chumley was a special police officer with the Cincinnati Police Department for twenty-three years before he met his untimely death in 1880. The drama began with his family when his oldest daughter, Emma, took work in the world's oldest profession at Frank Hall's house of ill repute. Her sisters soon followed in her footsteps and also found work in the same profession!

Ella and Emma Chumley provided the passion in the Chumley story. Emma became the mistress of Colonel Thomas Snelbaker, the son of a Cincinnati mayor, secretary of the water works, and superintendent of the police department. Snelbaker lost his superintendent job after two years for directing prisoners to favored attorneys. Snelbaker quickly found a new profession in show business as proprietor of the Vine Street Opera House.

Around 1880, after seven years together, Snelbaker's relationship with Emma Chumley soured and he took her sister, Ella, as his mistress. Ella was Snelbaker's ticket-seller at the Opera House. Snelbaker reportedly spent large amounts of money on Ella, prompting some to accuse her of "queening it up." When Virgie Jackson, a beautiful actress who was performing at the opera house, gained the attention of Snelbaker, Ella grew jealous accusing her of trying to steal Snelbaker. Ella began to threaten to injure or kill her rival.

Ella provided her own special flavor of crime in the Chumley story. While Snelbaker was running the Bijou Theater in New Orleans where Jackson was performing, Ella and the opera house treasurer, George Fisher stole a large sum of Snelbaker's money. The two headed south and Ella told friends that she was hunting Virgie Jackson. Ella arrived in New Orleans but Jackson had left town. Ella and Snelbaker then returned by train to Cincinnati. On the trip Snelbaker said, "Frequently, Ella tried to stab me in the sleeping car" but by the time the two arrived in the city, they had reconciled. As for the theft she and Fisher were arrested, but never prosecuted. The reconciliation lasted only a couple of months before Snelbaker, discovering Ella was "bestowing her favors on other men," told her he would no longer support her. By that time Jackson had returned to perform at the opera house and once again Ella blamed the actress.

The Chumley drama came to a fevered pitch on August 8, 1880. After spending an afternoon at the Highland House, Virgie Jackson and Snelbaker returned to the opera house. Switching streetcars at Fifth and Vine they were spotted by Ella and her sister Molly who got on the same car and sat across from the two. As the streetcar started moving, the sisters attacked Jackson. Snelbaker was attempting to separate the women as the car reached Sixth Street where none other than Officer Armstrong Chumley jumped aboard! Intent on arresting the culprits, Chumley boarded the carriage and discovered his own children and Snelbaker involved in the fray. Chumley pulled Snelbaker away and the two sisters resumed their attack on Jackson. At this time James Chumley, Armstrong's son and a man known as "Doc" boarded the car and also began attacking Snelbaker. By now the incident had attracted several hundred people and two other police officers boarded the car. The officers were able to separate the assailants and get Snelbaker and Jackson off the car, however the fighting which had now nearly reached Seventh Street continued as Chumley again went for Snelbaker who stopped him with a blow from his cane. Snelbaker was then struck across the nose by a blow from the younger Chumley's billy club. Finally, order was somewhat restored when the officers arrested Snelbaker.

But the passion, violence, and crime in Chumley's story wasn't over. Snelbaker

◇ Chumley's badge which had no influence over his senseless and troubled daughters.

Lee Chumley who was not in Cincinnati when her father was shot, was a notorious con artist. Known across the country and in Europe as the "Duchess of California," she specialized in using her good looks and charm to entice wealthy men into compromising positions then blackmailing them.

◇

asked to go into Aug's Club House where he found and hid a revolver in his sleeve. He then hired a carriage and along with Jackson and the arresting officer went to the Central Police Station on Ninth Street.

Chumley, however, had already gone to the station where he asked a Sergeant Rittweger for string to repair a broken suspender. Five minutes later in walked Snelbaker. Chumley saw him and said, "You godamned son of a bitch!" Snelbaker did not reply but watched Chumley carefully. Chumley continued his threats and moved toward Snelbaker who told him, "Now Chumley, don't come near me." When Chumley continued advancing, Snelbaker pulled the gun and fired several shots, hitting Chumley once in the groin and twice in the stomach. Snelbaker and

After the death of Officer Chumley:

· Jim Chumley, who previously had shot out the eye of his brother-in-law, murdered a co-worker on Christmas Eve, 1882, following a quarrel over a trivial matter. He was convicted of manslaughter and died in prison a few years later.

· Molly Chumley continued to operate her "house of ill repute" on George Street.

· Thomas Snelbaker, following a string of failures in the entertainment business, died in Chicago in 1888.

· Virgie Jackson left Cincinnati and was discovered years later working as a cook in a cheap New York restaurant. She was described as a "large, fleshy woman" nearly unrecognizable from the actress who was "courted and flattered, wined and dined," nearly two decades earlier.

· Ella Chumley met and married a wealthy cigar importer from New York. The Enquirer reported that she was living a "respectable, retired life."

Chapter Three

Jackson were locked up. Chumley was taken to his home. Doctors warned him of the severity of his wounds, but Chumley responded, "I might not have lived the best life, but I am not afraid to die."

Chumley died in his home at 75 Clinton Street on August 10. Snelbaker was convicted of manslaughter on November 23, and then acquitted two years later on grounds of self defense. He died in 1886 and is also buried in Spring Grove. Chumley was known as a religious man. Ironically, his life story as a police officer and father of notoriously troubled children combined so tragically, turning into a great script for modern television and a sad end for a Cincinnati police officer.

MISUNDERSTOOD AND FORGOTTEN

Joseph Earnshaw (1827-1868)

◦ ◇ ◦

ALTHOUGH ADOLPH STRAUCH RECEIVES MOST OF THE ACCLAIM in creating the look of Spring Grove with his landscape lawn design, it is Civil Engineer Joseph Earnshaw who should be equally showered with accolades for laying out the drives, slopes, and lakes with landscape architect Howard Daniels.

Joseph and his three sons (John, Joseph, and Henry) assisted Daniels in producing a completely new design for the cemetery. They located curving avenues through the low-lying areas to provide drainage for the variety of terrain, which in turn reserved elevated land for burials and made the picturesque topography dramatic.

A new method of triangulation was developed by Dr. John Locke of Cincinnati for the United States Coastal Survey to assure precise layout and mapping of the grounds. Earnshaw used this method by staking out equilateral triangles with iron gauges set in the ground at 200-foot intervals. He numbered the triangles consecutively and declared the system as being, "very accurate in a way to establish control over lot boundaries in a seemingly informal, naturalistic landscape with winding avenues, varied topography, and thousands of small private parcels of property." He told the Board that, "if the landmarks of every lot in the cemetery were to be destroyed, they may all be replaced exactly from the record, which would not be the case at any other cemetery in the United States."

Earnshaw was so successful in laying out Spring Grove, he brought his talents to other cemeteries. As noted from the Spring Grove archives, dated September 28, 1854: "Earnshaw (is) granted permission to borrow engineering instruments for a few weeks to lay out some lots in Green Lawn Cemetery in Columbus, Ohio."

Joseph's sons helped their father do much of the surveying in the cemetery

Sketch of a rustic bridge that no longer exists.

until Joseph's death in 1868. The Earnshaw sons continued the work for decades, ensuring the pastoral and beautiful setting we see today.

Edmund Dexter (1801-1862)
Julius Dexter (1840-1898)

◦ ◇ ◦

THE DEXTER FAMILY MONUMENT IS ARGUABLY THE FINEST example of private mausoleum architecture in Spring Grove. It's so impressive, many first time visitors think it belongs to Spring Grove, but the fact is it belongs to the remarkable Dexter family.

Edmund Dexter and his son, Julius, made their fortune in manufacturing whiskey. In his twenties, Edmund established his business and regularly shipped whiskey from Cincinnati to Mobile, Alabama, and New Orleans. Julius was also a senator, the head of the Cincinnati-Hamilton-Dayton Railroad, as well as a prominent supporter of the Cincinnati Art Museum, the symphony, and many other Cincinnati cultural institutions.

Edmund's home on Fourth Street (on the site of the present Western & Southern Life Insurance building) was known for its mahogany and marble. Visitors included the Prince of Wales and Charles Dickens. Interestingly enough, a sculptor by the name of Henry Dexter created a marble bust of Dickens during Dickens 1842 American tour. The bust can be found in the Cincinnati Mercantile Library. The famous home was later occupied by the University Club, before being remodeled for the Western & Southern Life Insurance Company. Eventually it was demolished to build the company's present classic edifice.

This excerpt from the *Commercial Tribune* in 1867, describes the proposal for the Dexter monument in Spring Grove: "The proposed Dexter Mausoleum, James K. Wilson, architect of this city, is now engaged on a mausoleum for the Dexter family. This edifice will cost about $100,000. (About $2 million dollars today!) It will be situated on the northern border of the lake, overlooking the most beautiful part of the cemetery and be built entirely of freestone in the ornamental gothic style. It will consist of a vault containing 12 catacombs, and a chapel 12 feet wide, 31 feet long, and 34 feet high. Around the building and above the vault, will extend a terrace, which will be connected to the main building by flying buttresses. In front will be a portico, on which will be placed a beautiful statue of a female, in the attitude of praying. The interior of the chapel will be of marble and the dome will be supported by marble pillars. The height of the main building will be 48 feet, from the roof to the top pinnacle will be 33 feet, and the grand floor covers, 180 square feet." (Note: The statue of the female was never completed.)

Modeled after the famous Sainte Chapele in Paris, France, the mausoleum/chapel was built by the same architect who designed the historic office building and the small gate house adjacent to the front entrance gates of the cemetery. It has the only known flying buttresses on a private funerary structure in Ohio and possibly the United States.

The exterior of the building was completed but with Prohibition the Dexters' fortune dwindled, so the stained glass windows, for which Sainte Chapele is so well-known, were never installed. In the back right corner of the lower level containing the gothic crypts an elevator to the chapel, operated by a rope and pulley, was to be installed. It never was, but the dark, deep shaft still exists. Left unfinished, the red brick chapel was used by the family for services but without an elevator, the coffins had to be carried up the steps and into the chapel. The interior has been off-limits to visitors for years because of safety concerns. A fourteen foot steeple stood on the roof until it collapsed more than 50 years ago.

Today, the monument is one of the most visited and recognizable locations in Spring Grove. The National Historic

The incredible Dexter mausoleum.

Chapter Four

Joseph J. Mersman had a ten year apprenticeship with Edmund Dexter in the 1800s and reflected on his experience with Dexter in a diary. He mentions Dexter as "taking great delight in bathing," and was inflicted with "a kind of internal pile" (hemorrhoids).

An interesting anecdote, relayed to me by a local Dexter family descendant who remembers a member of the family visiting their distillery in Frankfort, Kentucky, tells of a family legend that Edmund's grandson-in-law, Charles Walker, changed his name to Dexter to gain an inheritance. His father was a Walker and his mother was a Dexter.

Register of Historic Places granted the monument status in the 1980s. The magnificent building was originally planned to be built on Strauch Island. The Spring Grove Board of Directors permitted the Dexters to exchange the island with Strauch, and from what Strauch's great-great-granddaughter has told me, the exchange was not very amicable! No matter the original plan, both the Dexter and Strauch families have two of the most notable sites in the cemetery, across the lake from each other.

Chunkie Singleton (1880-1884)

◦ ◇ ◦

THIS IS A STORY about two requests from the bereaved family of a little girl. One request was granted. The other was not. But the memorial to this young lass remains one of the most beloved figurative statues in the cemetery. In 1884, the four-year-old died from Scarlet Fever in Covington, Kentucky. Her parents, Thomas and Matilda, were no doubt distraught

◦ The years have taken their toll on little Chunkie's statue.

from their beloved daughter's death and the detail carved on their daughter's statue captures their love. The little girl is depicted standing in full Victorian garb from head to toe, including a wide sash, buttons on her high-top boots, and a bow on her frock. She wears a charming hat and carries a parasol which, although folded, seems as though she could open it up at any minute. But the most striking detail of her physical features is the cheeks. They are full and round and make her seem almost real.

You will find the full name of this little lady carved on the marble rock-outcropping base, "Chunkie" Singleton. A most befitting name given that her cheeks are indeed "chunky." It took two years for the family to have the statue erected.

Prior to his death, Chunkie's father, Thomas, applied "for the privilege of erecting a marble statue of a little girl on his lot," which is in Section 16. Board member, George McAlpin, allowed the motion on May 7, 1885. Two years later, Chunkie's statue had still not been erected but in addition to asking for a statue, her father then requested that the statue of his beloved Chunkie be covered with a glass case. This second request was denied; Spring Grove did not permit glass enclosures. I have been surprised at the glass cases I've seen in other Victorian-era cemeteries across the nation that continue to protect statuary from the elements. A few cemeteries in Chicago have great examples of glass-enclosed statues. I will venture to guess that Adolph Strauch feared the enclosures would be damaged too easily and perhaps he felt they would give the burial lots the cluttered look that he so despised.

I like to think that Chunkie didn't need a glass case to protect her. I like to think that she does open the umbrella she holds in her hand whenever it rains or snows on her family cemetery lot.

The Flood of 1937

A TOPIC THAT ALMOST ALWAYS GARNERS COMMENTS from people in the Cincinnati area is the flood of 1937. Considered the worst in Cincinnati's history, it wreaked havoc on the city, and, because of its proximity to the Mill Creek, Spring Grove. It's a sad story in many ways but thanks to the dedication and resourcefulness of cemetery employees, the cemetery recovered from some rather daunting challenges.

The Mill Creek that flows across from the cemetery and Spring Grove Avenue had a history of flooding before adequate flood control began. When it flooded, the Mill Creek backed up and much of the excess water flooded the middle of the cemetery. Imagine monument and markers completely submerged. I found no real reports of caskets floating hither and yon but the photos show that only the tops of otherwise tall, stately obelisks could be seen.

Many visitors today aren't exactly aware of how the 1937 flood affected the cemetery grounds and buildings. It rained continuously for ten days. Now when

Superintendent Salway persuaded the Spring Grove Board in 1884, to build a north gate to allow entry into the cemetery in case of recurring flooding. New suburbs in the north and west areas of the city were springing up, bringing additional visitors to the cemetery, so an additional entrance was needed for them as well.

◇

◇ A person rowing a boat through the flooded streets near Spring Grove.

you enter the main gates of the cemetery, a small bronze plaque can be seen on the west side of the Historic Office building, showing how high the water was during the flood. It was reported that yellow water rose 80 feet above the creek's low mark, inundating "the low-lying land at the front of the cemetery, washing in any debris that floated—lumber from the far side of Winton Road, fences, barrels, oil, and tree trunks, making clean-up a major chore. The poor gathered the masses of dead fish as fertilizer. The silt deposited by the flood eventually proved beneficial." Cliff Radel reported in his 2012 *Cincinnati Enquirer* article that in today's dollars, $7.8 billion worth of property was destroyed from Pittsburgh to Cairo, Illinois. The flood affected everyone.

I am truly amazed at how well the three structures near the cemetery entrance (Historic Office, Gate House, and Norman Chapel) survived the flood. One would have difficulty finding any indication of that flood today, other than the small bronze marker on the Historic Office. But the flood waters did indeed cause much damage to the buildings. The Norman Chapel had to be completely restored following the flood. One of the losses from the chapel was the original organ. James Espy, then president of the cemetery board, ordered a new one after the flood. The Carriage House was almost completely submerged. Luckily the historic records were kept intact. The main offices, where the records and archives were stored, were still downtown at the time. Had they been moved prior to the flood, they more than likely would have been damaged or lost forever—divine intervention perhaps?

Around 2012, the Public Library of Cincinnati and Hamilton County was hoping to get at least 200 photos of the flood for an exhibit but over 700 photos were obtained from the public. And some of those were of Spring Grove. The response from the public was overwhelming but not surprising because the flood was overwhelming to thousands of citizens who to this day talk about it.

The Benton Sphere

◦ ◇ ◦

I WALKED AND DROVE BY THE BENTON MONUMENT FOR YEARS, not knowing the strange story connected to it. Although spherical monuments

The Marion Cemetery in Marion, Ohio (circa 1857) has a spherical monument that is commonly referred to as "The Merchant Ball" and said to mysteriously rotate up to two inches every year. According to the Marion Cemetery website: "In 1929, the monument was featured in 'Ripley's Believe it or Not!'" The dark polished granite sphere on the Benton lot represents several things: the soul, waiting for the resurrection, eternity, or the circle of life.

are not overly common, the dark grey polished orb that stands over the resting place of Anna Benton and her family is impressive. But it's what lies beneath that's most intriguing.

When perusing through the Spring Grove records, I came across the burial stat card for Anna Benton (1869–1931). On the original lot diagram is written an unusual request from a relative or family acquaintance ordering the statue be buried to the right of the monument. I wondered, "What statue?" There is no evidence a statue was ever on the lot, so what happened to the request?

The Benton sphere and the statue before it was buried.

My curiosity got the best of me so I went to Spring Grove grounds manager, Tom Pfeifer, to get to the bottom of the story. "Pfeif," as he is lovingly called by Spring Grove employees, just happened to possess photographs of the monument showing a life-sized granite statue of a woman lying on the ground near the sphere in the late 1980s. Measuring five feet tall, the statue appeared in the photos to be in good shape. When asked what happened to the statue, Pfeif informed me that it had originally been affixed to the top of the sphere, but due to storms and bad weather, it kept getting knocked off. The statue required repair so many times, a relative or family acquaintance ordered the statue be buried in the ground, intact, to the right of the monument. Apparently, they did not want the financial responsibility of having the statue re-attached yet another time. Pfeif also believed no other family members were left to be interred on the lot. After a bad storm in 1989, the family made the final decision for "interment" of the statue.

To my knowledge, the Benton statue in Spring Grove is the only statue to have been buried completely intact. It just goes to show, you never know what mysteries are *literally* buried in cemeteries.

Albert William Bode (1869-1928)

◦ ◇ ◦

ALBERT WILLIAM BODE MAY NOT BE AS FAMOUS as some in Spring Grove, but he has a fascinating story as a circus wagon maker and a politician.

For 28 years, the Bode Wagon Company supplied wagons to all of the major circuses, selling calliopes, animals, and band and general equipment. In 1878, William Bode partnered with Louis Havekotte in the carriage making business. Three years later they made their first parade wagons for the John Robinson circus. Bode sold out his interest in the business in 1885, to establish his own wagon and plow building firm. His son Albert began running the business sometime before 1902. In 1905, he was given the largest order for new wagons in circus history when the Carl Hagenbeck Trained Animal Show ordered 48 wagons at a total cost of $38,000. The company made the transition from horse drawn wagons to building the bodies for motorized vehicles. The last big order of the circus wagons made by Bode's company were for Frank Spellman's *Motorized Circus.* Known as *tableaux wagons,* they were designed to be driven through towns with circus performers in costume on the top. By 1917, the company was moving away from circus wagons to custom truck bodies. The Bode Wagon Company manufacturing plant, located on Central Avenue in Cincinnati, was where many of the motorized wagons were made. The factory caught fire in 1918, but the company survived and eventually became the Bode Finn Company. Today, the company originally founded by Bode has become part of the MH Equipment Company, making equipment such as forklifts and lift trucks.

In his obituary in the *New York Times*, Bode's leadership in the Republican Party and charity work were highlighted, as well as his circus connections. Bode was a delegate to the National Republican Convention in 1920, and served his political

◇ A Bode wagon fit for a clown.

◇

Bode invented and patented, "certain new and useful improvements in picks." His patented toothpick, model no. 438,877, was patented on October 21, 1890, by the United States Patent Office.

apprenticeship in Cincinnati under the infamous George "Boss" Cox, a political boss in Cincinnati during the Progressive Era.

According to Bode's obituary, "It was said that never a man or a woman who lived in the fourteenth ward went to him for aid without receiving more than he asked." Politicians today could learn much from this wagon maker, circus director, and musician!

Myrl E. Bottomley (1893-1956)

◇ ◇ ◇

THE IS A CLOSE CONNECTION BETWEEN THE STORY OF MYRL E. Bottomley, his wife Esther, and hillsides. Hillsides shaped the Bottomley's profes-

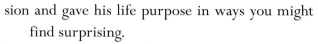

sion and gave his life purpose in ways you might find surprising.

As a professor and writer, Bottomley was a noted contributor in the field of landscape architecture. He helped many professional and non-professional landscapers with the design, maintenance, and planning of American cities especially with how to incorporate hillsides into designs. His contributions to landscape architecture influence design even today.

Bottomley's footstone rests on a hillside that he dearly loved.

Bottomley, born in Charlotte, Michigan, in 1893, served as a lieutenant in WWI on the front lines in France. Bottomley earned his Bachelor of Science degree from Michigan State College in 1916, and in 1922, he earned a Master of Landscape Design from Cornell University. In 1926, he became a professor and the head of the University of Cincinnati's School of Applied Art's landscape architecture program, teaching landscape architecture and city planning classes until 1956.

Bottomley's specialty was in small gardens and the development of suburban and city residential properties. He created an innovative way to identify perennials, known as "the foliage key system," that is used in landscape classes. Bottomley wrote on the art of landscape design to teach homeowners with a "do-it-yourself drive," or to convince those without the drive to simply hire a professional to help them beautify their landscape. His books and lessons contributed to his popularity on the speakers' circuit, and his articulate writing skills led to articles for prestigious home magazines like *Better Homes and Gardens, McCall's,* and *House Beautiful.*

President Herbert Hoover asked Bottomley to serve on a 1931, fact-finding Committee on Landscaping and Planting focusing on American housing and how to solve home ownership problems, like troublesome hillsides. This led to Bottomley's 1944 appointment on the Cincinnati City Planning Commission, whose purpose was to work on the Planning & Design Section of the new *Cincinnati Metropolitan Master Plan.* Bottomley and his cohorts strove to encourage homeowners to take pride in their communities by organizing neighborhoods around schools, civic centers, and business districts. The concept of organized communities was one of Bottomley's most notable contributions to city planning.

A newsletter article from 1953, mentions Bottomley's wife, Esther, who was an economics instructor at Our Lady of Cincinnati College. The article highlighted a style show that was directed by Esther and featured "Round the Clock" fashions from students in her clothing construction course. After Myrl's death, she donated her husband's papers to the University of Cincinnati Archives, which included seven boxes with 119 of his original pencil and ink drawings of landscape designs. Like Myrl, Esther was born in Michigan and died in Cincinnati. It is fitting that Myrl and Esther, lie in eternity beside one another in Spring Grove Cemetery on a beautiful, tranquil hillside.

Adam Edward Burkhardt (1845-1917)

◦ ◇ ◦

A. E. BURKHARDT WAS AN AMAZING MAN. He was a furrier who sold fur garments such as seal skin coats and hats internationally from his shop on Third Street in downtown Cincinnati. Leipzig and London were two of his most important shipping points. Interestingly, he was a founder of the Cincinnati Crematorium. I had the privilege of meeting members of the Burkhardt family when they were photographed for my previous book, *Beauty in the Grove,* and to my delight, the beautiful Burkhardt ladies wore original furs made by their family. The meeting inspired me to learn more of A. E. Burkhardt and his story.

Around 1854, Burkhardt's father died in Bavaria where the family lived. Around the same time, Burkhardt's mother took Burkhardt and his sister to America. But after settling into Cincinnati his mother passed away. Orphaned at age thirteen, he had no choice but to forge ahead, so he began as an errand boy with the famous Mitchell & Rammelsberg furniture factory. At the time, he earned only one dollar a week!

His stint as errand boy was short-lived. After three months, he went to work for Jacob Theis & Co., a business dealing in hats and furs. A penchant for hats and furs spurred Burkhardt to purchase the firm from Theis in 1867. Burkhardt quickly found success. His openings for new inventory were renowned in the Cincinnati area, so much so that he was given the name of "The Father of Openings in Cincinnati." When Burkhardt opened one of his new stores, he did it with panache. He brought in exotic zoo animals, displayed his exposition medals (including one from the Chicago World's Fair), and was known to have the first wax mannequins in Cincinnati. He became president of the Cincinnati Zoo in 1885, and eventually married the daughter of the zoo's founder.

Burkhardt's accomplishments as a craftsman earned him a number of awards, medals, and certificates of merit from expositions, the Centennial celebration, and the Chicago World's Fair. In fact, his display at the Chicago World's Fair was reportedly the finest the world had ever witnessed.

Burkhardt's career was not without misfortune. A terrible fire on July 8, 1891, destroyed Burkhardt's impressive building at the southeast corner of Fourth and

A receipt from 1870, had a logo that listed Burkhardt's company as "Manufacturers of Furs, and Shippers of Raw Skins." Three of the items on the receipt were written for 24 'coons, 4 opossum, and 6 skunk. Add an additional house cat for a total of $12.75!

◇

◇ Burkhardt's monument. The statue of the mourning woman almost looks lifelike.

Elm streets in downtown Cincinnati. The *New York Times* reported, "At eleven o'clock, the splendid structure is a furnace of white flame. The storeroom of this building has been pronounced by the citizens and visitors the finest in America." The loss was estimated at more than one million dollars. The cause of the fire was a faulty switchboard and "dynamo connections" in the plant, which was used for the manufacturing of electricity. Burkhardt used those "dynamo connections" to light the building. The building was considered to be the most palatial mercantile building in the world, and was devoted to the sale of hats and haberdashery. After the building was destroyed, Burkhardt rebuilt his business on Race Street, across from the Shillito's Department Store. His company was then organized into a stock company, consisting of women's furnishings, a cloak factory, and a haberdashery. Two of Burkhardt's sons, Andreas and Carl, ran the Burkhardt Bros. business.

The story behind the man whose company made the beautiful furs so proudly modeled by the Burkhardt girls in *Beauty in the Grove* has brought depth to both the book and the man.

Martin Hale Crane (1821-1886)
William James Breed (1835-1908)

◦ ◇ ◦

WE ALL KNOW OF THAT FATAL DAY IN 1865, when Abraham Lincoln was assassinated, but did you know of his posthumous connection to Spring Grove? Lincoln was interred in a patent metal casket made by Crane, Breed & Company, and both the Crane and Breed families are buried in Spring Grove. First, let's talk about Martin Hale Crane.

Martin Hale Crane was a Massachusetts native. After working as a clerk in a foundry, he along with J.R. Barnes, bought a casket business which came with the license to produce the Fisk burial cast, the first metallic coffin to achieve widespread acceptance and use in the United States. Two months later, Abel D. Breed joined the company and Col. John Mills bought out the interests from Barnes. The company was then reorganized as Crane, Breed & Company. A description from

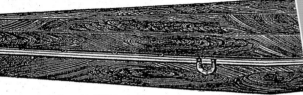

NE, BREED

MANUFACTURERS OF PAT

BURIAL CASES AND CASKE

OFFICE AND MANUFAC

treet, West of Freeman, Cl

STILLMAN

Improvements these Burial Cases are entirely free from those r
d with their name.

IETALLIC BURIAL

f those unpleasant associations which usually accompany the forr
ly its whole length. With the elaborate Silver-plated Mountin,
n elegance any thing of the kind which has ever before been offer
d Caskets are beautifully finished in imitation of the finest rosew
for transportation, and for preservation, are now universally ad
from water, vermin, or other intrusion. Future removal, shoul
nvenience. A delay of days or weeks, awaiting the arrival of a
ion is given in sealing, which may, with care, be accomplished b
and Casket), bodies may be carried to any part of the Globe at an
ver, a sure safeguard against contagious diseases. These advan
in ancient or modern times, has been nvented for the reception

LAYMAN.SC.

he Manufacture of HEARSES, of every
are unequaled by any Establishment ir

The city of Salem, Ohio, was abuzz in 1973, when a strange, mummy-like coffin was unearthed. The strange casket was cast-iron and weighed more than 600 pounds! The discovery drew hundreds of curiosity seekers and speculation of its origin began. Some thought it might have been imported from Europe. The mystery remained, but the patented Crane casket matched that of the Salem casket, leading the citizens to believe they had discovered its maker.

○ A vintage advertisement for the Crane, Breed, & Company.

Cincinnati, the Queen City, 1788-1912 describes the company as, "Everything that pertains to an undertaker's supplies, from the latest appointments in the way of a hearse to the most modern burial casket, and everything in the way of burial-casket hardware is made in this establishment, which is the largest of the kind in the world. A force of workmen, numbering altogether about four hundred, is required to keep up the business of the house. Moreover the company is represented by agents in all parts of the country and the house maintains its position as the leading enterprise of this character in the world."

Martin Crane modified Fisk's casket which resembled an Egyptian mummy allowing it to be mass produced and sell at a lower cost. An advertisement for Crane, Breed & Company caskets in 1864, described the casket as: "The metallic burial casket is entirely devoid of those unpleasant associations which usually accompany the form of a coffin."

The company began a heat and ventilation system in the mid 1860s, headed by Crane. Eventually the division split from the main company becoming the M.H. Crane Estate headed by Martin's son, Harrie, a heating and ventilation engineer. He eventually moved the headquarters to Miami Street in Urbana, Ohio, and then relocated to Chicago, where it became one of the largest heating and ventilating contractors in the city. In 1888, when Cincinnati's City Hall was built, Crane's company supplied the heating and ventilation system.

With the reorganization, Abel's son, William, took over as company president while Abel managed extensive mining interests. The company did so well that Abel was able to move to Cleveland and then to New York. In 1880, the company provided work for "280 men, women, and children (at $1.25 to $2.50 per day)."

The first commercially built gasoline-powered motorized hearse in America was made by the Crane & Breed Company in 1909. It featured a 30 horsepower four-cylinder engine. An ad from the time period proclaimed that it could reach a top speed of 30 miles per hour, which was "fifteen miles per hour faster than any hearse should have to go."

William's son, William D. Breed, eventually took over the company before leaving to pursue a career as an investment banker. The company presidency was then taken over by his brother, Austin Breed in 1909. Fortune didn't always follow the Crane & Breed Company. Austin Breed's death was particularly tragic. In 1924,

Martin Crane has his own stories to tell. He was suspected of having an affair with the beautiful wife of a Covington, Kentucky, liquor distributor named John C. Snell. Crane was almost 60 years old at the time. According to the stories, Snell followed his wife to a rendezvous with Crane and started firing shots, one of which hit his wife in the shoulder. She recovered, but Crane's reputation never did! He became known as a ladies' man who romanced married women!

◇

his maid found him dead in his bachelor apartment with a suicide note. That day he was to appear in court and give testimony in a lawsuit brought against him regarding an unpaid debt of $14,000, incurred by a bookstore he had interest in. They say he was a wealthy man, and this was a minor lawsuit. He really had no need for concern, but the suicide note was addressed to his attorney and apparently referred to the lawsuit.

The Crane & Breed Company made the first automobile hearse, but it was the first glass hearse and patent metal coffin for President Abraham Lincoln's funeral that made them famous. Lincoln could not know, when he visited Spring Grove in 1859, that two future inhabitants of the cemetery, Mr. Crane and Mr. Breed, would be making the hearse for his funeral six years later.

Godfrey Nicolas Frankenstein (1820-1873)

◇

ONCE IN A WHILE, I GET A LITTLE MISCHIEVOUS when giving tours to children or young adults. There always seems to be one youngster in every group who feels the need to cause a bit of commotion, whether it be a smart remark or just impatience. But when I tell them, "The next stop is Frankenstein's grave," they pause. *Frankenstein*, they might wonder, *here*? Many old horror movies begin in an old, spooky cemetery, and Spring Grove is anything but spooky, but there is a story about a *real* Frankenstein in Spring Grove.

This *real* Frankenstein is Godfrey Nicolas Frankenstein, and he was definitely not a monster. He was born in 1820, in the same region as my ancestors, Hessen-

Darmstadt, Germany. After arriving in the United States, the family settled in Cincinnati in 1831, and changed their family name from Tracht to Frankenstein.

The Frankenstein family consisted of gifted artists. Many of Godfrey's siblings and family were painters: John Peter, George, Gustavus, Marie, and Eliza. Of the children, Godfrey was the least reclusive and hypersensitive.

At age thirteen, Godfrey started his own business as a sign painter. Six years later, he became a portrait painter. He gained fame and recognition for his talents when he became the first president of the Cincinnati Academy of Arts. His fame grew in 1844, when he became interested in painting landscapes and completed an iconic painting of Niagara Falls.

Godfrey completed hundreds of individual paintings of the Falls. Two were purchased by the famous singer, Jenny Lind during her first American tour. *Harpers New Monthly Magazine* capitalized on Godfrey's success and reproduced nineteen of his paintings for an issue in August 1953. During the same time, Godfrey was

Of Godfrey Frankenstein's artistic siblings, Eliza, Gustavus, and Marie are also interred in Spring Grove, as well as their parents.

◇ Godfrey Frankenstein's painting of the Mill Creek showcases his love of nature.

Godfrey Frankenstein carved the marble bust of Hon. John McLean, United States Supreme Court Judge, which graces a federal courtroom in Cincinnati.

named "The Painter of Niagara Falls" when he unveiled an enormous panorama of the Falls while in Philadelphia.

The panorama won widespread acclaim because of its combination of beautiful scenery and artistry. The finished panorama was reputed to be a 1,600 foot long by 9 foot wide strip of canvas rolled on wooden spindles. Obviously, there was no sibling rivalry in the family as his sister Eliza and brothers aided in the panorama, arranging the paintings that made up the panorama systematically, incorporating them into a regular series.

Godfrey painted more than just Niagara Falls. His Lagonda Creek painting, which some say represents "the eye of inner man transcending the ego to view God's nature, in the surrounding landscape, and himself, as one" was painted during a storm!

The romantic White Mountains of New Hampshire, became a second home to Godfrey. He frequently painted the dramatic rugged landscape owned by a Dr. Bemis. Godfrey spent so much of his time in the White Mountains, a crag was named in his honor, the "Frankenstein Cliff" located in Crawford Notch.

In Germany, there is a castle named Castle Frankenstein built around 1252. Some claim it was the inspiration for Mary Shelley's novel. While researching the castle, I discovered it was located in Hessen-Darmstadt, the same area where Godfrey Nicolas Frankenstein was born, and where my father's family is from. Who knows? It's possible that Godfrey's adopted surname was also adopted by Mary Shelly for her famous novel, which goes to show you: not all Frankenstein's are monsters.

Joseph R. Mason (1802-1842)

DID YOU KNOW SPRING GROVE HAS A CONNECTION to the famous artist, John James Audubon? I didn't either until a Spring Grove docent, Marsha

Lindner, passed along some fascinating information from fellow Cincinnati history enthusiasts, Bill Hopple, DeVere Burton, and famed wildlife artist, John Ruthven. The story of Joseph R. Mason is one that most certainly deserves to be told!

As many people know, James Audubon traversed the Ohio and Mississippi rivers in the 1820s, creating paintings of American birds he studied along the way. But, he was not alone on those excursions. After showing a rare talent in 1820, at Audubon's drawing academy in Cincinnati, and with skill as a draftsman, a young Joseph R. Mason accompanied Audubon on his river travels. Mason was only 13 years old when he began traveling with Audubon, shooting and retrieving the bird specimens Audubon painted along the way. In addition to shooting and retrieval tasks, Mason's job was to paint floral backgrounds for the now-famous bird paintings. The next time you view an Audubon painting, look for Mason's exquisite work in the background.

Mason's father, a book seller, passed away during the summer of 1822. Mason returned to Cincinnati to help his mother, and began a career as a successful portrait painter in his studio at Fourth and Main streets in downtown Cincinnati.

One of the most interesting aspects of Mason's life was his involvement in a quirky little group called, "The Last Man Society," formed amidst the great cholera epidemic. As the death toll rose during the epidemic, the community struggled to come to grips with the horror around them. On September 30, 1832, seven men got together at Mason's studio and acknowledged their own mortality by symbolically, and figuratively, giving death a toast, so to speak.

On October 6, 1832, the group held a dinner when the epidemic was at its peak and made the following pact: "In a mahogany casket a bottle of wine was placed, and the casket was locked, the lock sealed and the key thrown away. The casket was to be kept by the members of the society, and when six had died, the seventh was, following the death of the sixth, to open it and drink the

A Kentucky Warbler

Joseph R. Mason's grave marker.

wine." It's interesting to note that each of the men survived the epidemic of 1832. Dr. James Mason (possibly related to Joseph) became the first in the group to die five years later. In 1855, when member Fenton Lawson died, fellow member, Henry Tatem, was reported to be delirious and begged that the wine casket be removed from the house, as if it were evil. The last member of the Society was Dr. John L. Vattier and sure enough, as required, he broke open the casket, opened the bottle and drank the wine, in honor of Lawson and Tatem. Mason himself died of pneumonia on October 8, 1842. Apparently, Mason had been so quiet in his personal life, his obituary falsely reported him as being "absent" from the city for seven years. Despite his talent and brilliant work, Mason's mentor, James Audubon, never adequately acknowledged Mason's painted backgrounds for Audubon's *Birds of America*. Audubon signed his own name in pen and Mason's in pencil, leaving Mason's contributions largely unknown to the countless people who have enjoyed his work over the years.

James T. Mathews (1858-1906)

∘ ◇ ∘

SOMETIMES, IF YOU KEEP AN EAR OPEN TO THE STORIES FLOATING around you, you will come across a great and unexpected tale that brings Spring Grove to life. This time, the tale surfaced during a casual conversation with a friend I met over dinner. While discussing the book project, he interjected with, "I have family in Spring Grove." Immediately, I asked him if he had any interesting stories about his deceased family members. Man oh man, did he ever!

My friend's great-great uncle, James T. Mathews, made his fortune as the head of the St. James Medical Company at Fifth and Elm streets, and later as a real estate

The Mathews family monument.

dealer. He left the medical business after deciding not to fight a complaint when the government refused to carry his company's literature. Mathews closed the medical business around 1904, and bought several valuable tracts of land in Bond Hill and the surrounding countryside.

Mathews' story ends sadly. He was shot to death by his brother-in-law on Friday, August 16, in 1906, at his palatial home in Bond Hill. What started as an outing for rest and relaxation near Miamisburg, Ohio, turned into a tragic, unexplainable, and mysterious turn of events.

Mathews appears to have been something of a mystery even to the people who knew him. Some spoke fondly of him. Mathews' niece, Aimee Splain King, described him as "such an attractive, successful person. He was a beautiful sight, riding on his big, handsome horse. I admired him so much that I remember him as a Knight in Shining Armor." His brother-in-law, William, said that when Mathews was sober he was, "as kind and as good a man as ever breathed." Others report Mathews was a surly man, known for his temper. Alcohol was the demon in Mathews' life. When he drank, he reportedly went into an uncontrollable rage. There were reports that Mathews threatened to cut friends and family's hearts out. His problems with alcohol most likely caused his sad, untimely death.

Mathews was married to Mary Elizabeth Hopkins and they had three children. Mary's parents lived with Mathews and Mary after their large home was built. Later, Mathews' brother-in-law, Edwin Hopkins, came to live with them as well. Edwin's father, H.F. Hopkins, was a foreman in Eden Park and his brother, William, was Chief Deputy. Edwin was a railway mail clerk who married a beautiful French woman. They divorced, and Edwin was given custody of his five-year-old son. Hopkins' disposition changed from carefree and jolly to morose after the divorce. Between Edwin's disposition and Mathews' drinking, home life was less than perfect. Mathews and the home had been under surveillance of the police because of fierce arguments. On one occasion, Mathews went to a Walnut Hills saloon and shot at Mr. August Stockman. Mathews escaped charges of shooting with the intent to kill, as Stockman was uninjured.

The day of Mathews' death started with an innocent family trip to the country. The day before, Mathews reportedly made statements about moving out of the house forever, but he joined the family on the trip to Miamisburg, Ohio. When they returned to the house, his mother-in-law went to her room upstairs, and his father-in-law to the stable to look at a new horse Mathews had purchased. Three Hungarian servants were in the rear of the house. What happened next remains a mystery.

Shortly before 8:00 that evening, Mathews reportedly flew into a rage in the hallway on the lower floor. As Hopkins was walking to his room upstairs, Mathews stood angrily at the foot of the stairs. It is reported he suddenly yelled, "If you don't get out of this house, I will cut your heart out." Hopkins thought Mathews was coming to kill him, and knew Mathews had access to either a knife or gun. So he reached for his regulation mail service 38 Smith & Wesson revolver and started down the stairs. *Bam!* Halfway down the stairs, Hopkins opened fire. Four or five shots were fired, the fatal one being one through the left breast, penetrating Mathews' heart.

Hopkins testified in court that Mathews had been, "exceedingly quarrelsome of late." Hopkins claimed he was leaving the house and had actually packed his belongings the day before, in hopes of finding a room in the West End. The day of the shooting was his last in the Mathews house.

Several possible motives for the shooting surfaced from family members since Mathews' death. Some thought there may have been an argument over Mathews' attraction for Hopkins' ex-wife, or perhaps Mathews' treatment of his wife, Mary Elizabeth. Another possible motive could have been Mathews and Hopkins mutual attraction to a girl working on the family farm.

After the shooting, Hopkins fled across the Ohio River and was never prosecuted for the murder. He remarried and moved to California. In 1920, a US Census showed him living in New York City. He died in 1954, in San Diego.

There you have it. Another great story that literally came out of nowhere because of a chance meeting. It reminds me that there are many more interesting and mysterious stories floating around, waiting to be discovered!

The Mermaid in the Grove

◇

HAVE YOU EVER SEEN A MERMAID IN A CEMETERY? It's not the first place I would look for one, but a beautiful mermaid statue sits on the Edwards family lot in Spring Grove. How she got there is a mystery, but her story is remarkable.

When walking along the road near the mermaid statue on a late afternoon or early evening, you can only see the back of the statue. If the sun is setting behind her, she emanates a breathtaking, translucent glow. She is often mistaken for one of the hundreds of female statues in the cemetery. But this one is special—she's a mermaid!

The unsolved mystery is how the Edwards family acquired the mermaid, called "The Origin of the Harp," more than a decade after she was carved. The family was successful and wealthy enough to afford such an impressive piece of artwork.

Walter Edwards, (1839–1888) came to America from England and settled in Cincinnati. After graduating from Woodward High School, he began a sheet metal business on Sycamore Street. The business was a success, and land was purchased at a corner on Eggleston Avenue for the headquarters and main office. The business manufactured ball-bearing buggies and machine handles, and in 1901, began the manufacturing of automobiles.

Business was good and expanded quickly. Edwards built a large factory in Winton Place and hired four hundred skilled mechanics. Branch offices were established in New York and San Francisco, making the company the largest of manufactured sheet metal businesses in the United States. Annual sales amounted to more than one million dollars in the early 1900s.

The mermaid statue was carved in 1887, by a local female sculptress, Louise Lawson, while she was living temporarily in Rome, Italy. She worked in Italy for more than three years before she returned with a distaste for the art scene in Italy. "I should have come home sooner," she remarked. Lawson was annoyed with the 30 percent duty tax that was levied on all works of art brought into America. She still brought back two works of her art, including "The Origin of the Harp" mermaid.

The "Origin of the Harp" is based on a song about a beautiful sea siren that turns into a harp while lamenting her unrequited love for a young man. The lower

The statue was cut from Serrevezza marble, the whitest and purest stone taken from the Carrara quarries in Italy, which were discovered by Michaelangelo during his banishment by Pope Julius II.

◇ The seven-foot-tall statue of the mermaid was originally located in the entrance of Music Hall.

◇

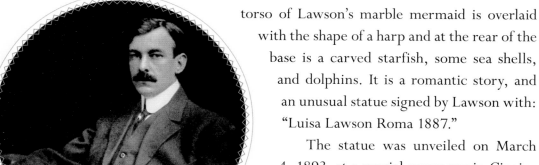

torso of Lawson's marble mermaid is overlaid with the shape of a harp and at the rear of the base is a carved starfish, some sea shells, and dolphins. It is a romantic story, and an unusual statue signed by Lawson with: "Luisa Lawson Roma 1887."

The statue was unveiled on March 4, 1893, at a special ceremony in Cincinnati's Music Hall. Referred to as, "Miss Louise Lawson's Great Work," the audience included many of Cincinnati's high society. Standing at near seven feet in height, the statue stood in a corridor to the right of Music Hall's entrance. But, after the unveiling, the history of the mermaid's journey to Spring Grove remains mysterious. Little is known about her whereabouts until the 1950s, when she was placed on the three-step plinth that leads up to the stylized classical Edwards monument portal.

Walter Edwards

From Songs of 1840, vol. 1

"The Origin of the Harp"- a canzonet (a part-song resembling but less elaborate than a madrigal)

Words by Thos. Moore, adaptations, arrangements, and compositions in vocal music by B. Carr, arranged as solo or duet with accompaniment for harp or piano forte

'Tis believed that this Harp which I now wake for thee

Was a Syren of old, who lived under the sea,

And who often at midnight through the dark billow roved,

To meet on the green shore a youth whom she loved.

[repeat last two lines]

But she lov'd him in vain, for he left her to weep,

And, in tears, all the night, her gold ringlets to steep,

Till Heav'n look'd, with pity, on true love so warm,

And chang'd to this soft Harp the sea maiden's form!
[repeat last two lines]

Still her bosom rose fair, still her cheek smil'd the same,
And her sea beauties gracefully curl'd round the frame,
And her hair shedding dewdrops from all its bright rings,
Fell over her white arm, to make the gold strings!
[repeat last two lines]

Hence it came that this soft harp so long had been known,
To mingle love's language with sorrow's sad tone,
Till thou didst divide them, and teach the fond lay
To be love, when I'm near thee, and grief, when away.
[repeat last two lines]

The whereabouts of the mermaid statue between the late 1800s and 1950s, remains unknown but the artistry of Luisa Lawson and a mermaid in a cemetery both transcend description.

◇

Nathan Flint Baker (1820-1891) and Egeria

◇

THE ITALIAN MARBLE STATUE OF *Egeria* stands elegantly on Strauch Island holding a vessel, as if she were pouring a magic potion into Willow Lake. Her vigil is on a private family lot in the cemetery, but she was never intended as a memorial to the deceased. She represents, instead, a story of one of the oldest families in Cincinnati, and of the success of Nathan Baker, who found international fame as an artist.

Nathan Baker, sculptor of *Egeria*, was the son of John Baker, a successful real estate magnate whose family had deep roots in Cincinnati. His great-grandparents were among Cincinnati's first settlers when they came down the Ohio River in 1790. The Baker family's magnificent Gothic-Revival home, with sweeping views of the Ohio River, is still featured on numerous area home tours, and Nathan's

Egeria was a multitasking water nymph worshipped variously for healing, inspiration, prophecy, wisdom, and an easy childbirth. She also was believed to inhabit springs, fountains, or lakes, as she does today in Spring Grove. Egeria seems to have been the Victorian age poster girl (for those of you who had grandfathers in the war, think "Jane Russell"), and many of her statues were inspired by Lord Byron's poem, Childe Harold's Pilgrimage.

Egeria! sweet creation
of some heart
Which found no mortal
resting-place so fair
As thine ideal breast…

original studio was a charming cottage-like structure near the house.

Nicholas Longworth, one of America's first millionaires, an Ohio Congressman and arts patron, sponsored Nathan's work with Hiram Powers in Florence, Italy, in 1842, helping start Nathan's career as an artist. Powers' studio in Florence, a haven for the arts, was popular with many Cincinnati artists, and a good place for Nathan to learn his craft.

Nathan Baker's Egeria on Strauch Island.

A year later, Nathan went to Rome, where he created his first versions of *Egeria*. The full-figure statue, which figures so prominently in the story of both Nathan Baker and Spring Grove, arrived at Strauch Island after Nathan sent her from Florence for Cincinnati's Western Art Exhibit. The statue was purchased by Walter Gregory as a gift to Adolph Strauch.

Nathan had created his masterpiece, but he wasn't finished yet. Three years after his sculptures were exhibited to acclaim at the Boston Athenaeum, Nathan joined forces with Leavitt Hunt, an old family friend, and in the autumn of 1851, they embarked for the Middle East. They weren't mere tourists, though. They were out to document the Arab world through the new medium of photography and hoped to sell prints upon their return. The daguerreotype itself was barely a decade old, and the enterprising duo of Baker and Hunt wanted to capitalize upon the American fascination with the new process.

Their six-month tour carried them from the pyramids at Giza to Mt. Sinai and the Parthenon. One of their most noted pictures was a photograph of a *ghawdzi* (a woman from a caste of female dancers who performed unveiled in public), which is believed to be the first photograph of a Middle Eastern woman. The entire set— some sixty survive—are considered to be the first photographs from the Middle East, and the pictures are sophisticated in both technique and aesthetics.

It was, however, an idea before its time, and only a few ever appeared on the market. Their idea, though, was correct. The seldom seen photographs are among the rarest of early American paper print photographs.

Near the same time that Nathan Baker created *Egeria*, he also carved an eight-foot marble statue, *Cincinnatus*, the farmer-soldier hero who rescued Rome from the barbarians and became, ultimately, the Queen City namesake. *Cincinnatus*, unlike *Egeria*, met with an ignominious fate. He was placed on a City Hall stair landing but the citizenry complained that he was hindering traffic. Moved outside to the sidewalk, *Cincinnatus* was eventually consigned to the City Hall basement where someone painted his nose bright red. All but homeless, he has subsequently disappeared.

After his adventure, Nathan seemed to have no further interest in photography and returned to Cincinnati where he "pursued the life of an independently wealthy gentleman." He didn't seem to be interested in sculpture, either. The papers reported in 1853 that Baker had "washed his hands of art altogether, having, he declared, almost forgotten how to hold a chisel."

But perhaps having created a sculpture that has been admired by thousands of visitors since the late 1800s was enough. Strauch Island, Willow Lake, and Nathan Baker's *Egeria* have, over time, become intimately linked, symbolizing the beauty and mystery of Spring Grove.

Ren Mulford, Jr. (1859-1932)

ACCORDING TO REN MULFORD, JR., "There's many a cheer between defeat and victory, and every one helps." Mulford's name is another I wasn't familiar with until I started exploring baseball connections in Spring Grove. He has a modest foot stone in section 100 that doesn't tell the story of his accomplishments. His story is one of dichotomies, between his colorful life in sports, legacy of catch phrases we use even today, and his religious devotion.

Mulford's reputation as a clean-cut, respectable Presbyterian was personified when he helped create a writer's department for sports at Cincinnati newspapers. A *Cincinnati Post* journalist referred to its sports department as, "a writer's paradise" and credits Mulford for its formation. As the first president of the Presbyterian

Men of Greater Cincinnati, Ren wanted to keep baseball, and other sports, clean, earning him the nickname "Deacon Mulford" after he wrote an article on religion and sports. Lonnie Wheeler mentioned Mulford's article in his 2007 *Cincinnati Post* article, "Put God at Top of Batting Order."

Mulford was an accomplished sports writer. He was the first reporter to travel with the Cincinnati Reds, and he coined the sport term "hot corner" and popularized the use of the term "fan." Before America used the word "fan," they used words like "crank" or "rooter." Additionally, The Most Valuable Player award was a result of a committee organized by Mulford in 1911.

Often, in Mulford's newspaper sports column, his colorful quotes were listed as "Mulfordisms." In his early days of reporting for the Reds, Mulford once described the team as the "rip-roaring, rushing, rampant, relentless, raging, resourceful Reds." His writing was anything but ordinary or dull. Witness the opening words of his account of a Pittsburgh-Cincinnati rivalry from 1908: "Once in a while, you'll hear some hare-brained ninny, who thinks he has fallen heir to some of the wisdom of Solomon, challenging the squareness of the greatest game on earth. There are a few mortals outside the great Wheel Universities who really think somebody sets up the pins in baseball! I've met them. So has every other lover of the game. The upset of the Reds at home, in the presence of a magnificent outpouring, and the skunking of the Pirates next afternoon at Exhibition Park were incidents that would prove knock-outs for all the Doubting Thomases in Balldom."

Ren Mulford, Jr.

Mulford had a unique talent for words, and many of the phrases we use today have their origins with Mulford's prose. For me, it was hard to believe such a diehard sports "fan" could also be a devoted Presbyterian, but Ren Mulford, Jr. was anything except ordinary!

William Boone Redman (1846-1854)

◦ ◇ ◦

ONE OF THE MOST PENSIVE AND MELANCHOLIC PIECES of sculpture in the cemetery memorializes William B. Redman in Section 46. The lad died from brain congestion at the young age of eight and was interred in the Methodist Burial Grounds in the city. Eight months later, his body was moved to Spring Grove where it has remained.

Turning the corner near section 46, your eye goes directly to the stately Windisch monument, with its depiction of a sacked English abbey. It's impressive, but once you've passed it, an unexpected life-sized sculpture of a dog appears. The marble canine is lying on a pillow-like base, resting its head on its front paws. It's obvious the dog is sad from the mournful look on its face. The unusual sculpture, often mistaken for a Victorian-era sheep which often grace the graves of Victorian children, sits near Redman's grave.

Although I found scarce background history on William and the dog, I was able to find information in the 1906 publication of *Publisher's Weekly,* about William's father, Benjamin T. Redman. In a section called "Obituary Notes," Benjamin is listed as one of the earliest publishers of city directories in America. "The Old Colonial Directory," a combined directory of Philadelphia and New York, reputed to be one of the first of its kind in the country, was issued by William's father.

The Redman dog statue, loyal to the grave.

William is buried next to his parents, Benjamin and Henreitta, and if you look very closely at the dog as it watches over his master, there is another sentimental symbol of melancholia; the dog holds a broken dog chain in its lifeless paw. Little William no longer needs his best friend tethered to a chain. Both he and the dog romp together freely, unchained, in eternal bliss. Man's best friend for life.

The Scottish Travelers

◦ ◇ ◦

FOR SOMEONE WHO STRIVES TO KNOW THE "WHY" OF A STORY, trying to find facts for the Scottish Travelers has been daunting. The Scottish Travelers, people scattered across the country, have been burying their loved ones in Spring Grove for more than one hundred years. I have yet to give a lecture without someone asking me about the mystery surrounding the Scottish Travelers. Some call them "gypsies," but the more respectful term is "the Scottish." Folklore, legends, and rumors surround the Scottish Travelers. Many think it was a gypsy king or queen that started the tradition. But it wasn't.

The Travelers have a proud tradition of placing multiple elaborate floral arrangements on their gravesites. Over the years, I have witnessed fascinating arrangements, all made of flowers, in the shape of: grandfather clocks, baseballs, perfume bottles, and even a box of French fries and catsup bottle! The floral memorials always garnish attention, but the Scottish desire privacy and discreteness, so Spring Grove does not publicize the Scottish burials whatsoever. If you want information from employees, you simply will not receive it. Privacy and respect are foremost.

Recently, I was given a paper written by a member of the local Literary Society who claimed to be related to Scottish Traveler, Bill Gorman. According to a local authority in Scottish Traveler folklore, James Gorman from New Jersey started the Scottish Travelers tradition at Spring Grove in the 1870s, when his teenage son ran in front of a wagon on Spring Grove Avenue and was killed. It was said the family couldn't afford to bury their son, so Spring Grove kindly obliged. The Gormans were so impressed with Spring Grove's generosity, and the beauty of the cemetery, they returned to New Jersey and began spreading the word throughout the Travelers community. The clan in New Jersey told the clan in Florida, who told the clan in California, who told the clan in Michigan, until Spring Grove became nationally known among the Travelers. But as I read on, I came to believe I was reading a story as told by Bill Gorman's great-great grandson. At least that's what I thought.

The story went into great detail of the "gypsy" life. I was shocked at the candidness because, the Scottish Travelers are very private people. I thought this could be my long-sought answers to the origin of the Scottish Travelers in Spring Grove. But some of the reports, and names, started to sound suspect. Gorman talked about the source being from a four-year-old boy who was struck and killed by a horse and carriage on Spring Grove Avenue. I was always under the impression that it was a teenage son and not a young boy. The name of the victim was reported in the story as, "Brian Gorman," which is a very contemporary name for the 1880s. I wanted to believe this source, but something just didn't feel right and it wasn't.

The day after receiving the story, I ran into a friend who has a connection to the Literary Society. With my usual dramatic flair and excitement, I told him about my "discovery" of the Scottish origin in Spring Grove. My friend quietly responded with, "You do know that the paper is fictional, don't you?" I was crushed, almost to tears.

The lead turned out to be a legend, like so many tales surrounding the Scottish Travelers, and I was back to my original assumption that it was the sudden death of John Gorman's teenage son in the 1870s that initiated the Travelers tradition in Spring Grove.

The Travelers continue to bury their loved ones in Spring Grove. Their stunning floral memorials remind us that no matter what the true story is, they honor the deceased with dignity and reverence, color, panache, and mystery. And that's just the way they like it.

Agnes Lake Thatcher (1826-1907)

◦ ◇ ◦

IN SECTION 17, THERE IS A TALL PINK GRANITE OBELISK with the lone name of William Lake Thatcher. No other names. Just William's. That's a shame because his wife has an interesting story with ties to Spring Grove's circus history, and an ongoing mystery regarding the omission of her epitaph and the identity of their "adopted" daughter.

Agnes Mersman was born in Lower Saxony. Her father was a "whiskey drummer" and merchant. She claimed she was born in 1832, although cemetery records list the year as 1826. Agnes eloped with William Lake Thatcher in 1846 and married in New Orleans. The name "Thatcher" was dropped for professional reasons

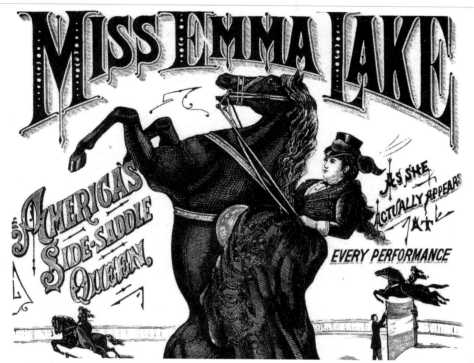

◇ An old advertisement for Agnes's daughter Emma, who followed in her mother's footsteps, becoming a 'side-saddle queen' herself.

and he became William "Bill" Lake. He owned a circus in which Agnes performed as a "world renowned" tight rope walker, equestrian, and lion tamer. William was shot and killed in Granby, Missouri, in 1869, by a man named Killian, who tried to sneak into the circus without paying. Agnes immediately took ownership of the circus, which was touring in 1871, as the *Hippo-Olympiad and Mammoth Circus.* In Abilene, Kansas, she met the town marshal, a man named James Butler, better known as the infamous "Wild Bill Hickok."

Agnes and Wild Bill renewed their acquaintance while he was performing in Buffalo Bill Cody's "Scouts of the Plains" stage show, where it is rumored Hickok couldn't remember his lines and was forced to leave because of poor reviews. Hickok wrote to Agnes, and they reconnected in Cheyenne, Wyoming. At the time, it was rumored Wild Bill was seeing another infamous character, "Calamity Jane" Canary. Jane claimed she had married Wild Bill and he was the father of a daughter they gave up for adoption. But, according to Thatcher historian Carolyn Bowers, "there is no proof that Wild Bill and Calamity Jane met prior to the summer of 1876. Apparently, they met when he was riding into town and she joined the convoy."

Agnes and Hickok married on March 5, 1876, in Cheyenne, Wyoming. Five months after their honeymoon in Cincinnati, Hickok was murdered in Deadwood on August 2, 1876. Agnes was grief-stricken, saying, "It is impossible for a human being to love any better than what I did him. I can see him day and night before me. The longer he is dead the worse I feel." Even on her death bed, she preferred to be called "Mrs. Hickok."

Agnes had two adopted daughters, Emma and Alice. Alice began performing at an early age. Described as graceful and accomplished, she was called the "Fairy Queen of the Arena." Maturing into an accomplished equestrian, she married another rider from Cincinnati, John Wilson. Joining the Robinson Circus, she drowned accidentally in 1867, en route to Mobile, Alabama, and was buried on the Robinson's second lot in section 75.

Agnes's other daughter Emma married into the famed Robinson Circus family. She married Gilbert Napoleon Robinson the author of *Old Wagon Shows Days*. They divorced and she performed as an equestrian with *Buffalo Bill's Wild West Show*. Interestingly enough, Emma was billed as "Emma Hickok" on its European tour, probably to gain the publicity from her famous stepfather's name.

Agnes died in her home in New Jersey on August 21, 1907, and is buried in Spring Grove, on lot 2 in Section 17, with her first husband, William Lake Thatcher.

None of the Thatcher women are memorialized on William Lake Thatcher's obelisk. The truth of their tangled relationships may never be known, creating as much mystery in passing as when they were all living. But let's face it. Don't we all love a good mystery from time to time?

Helen May Butler Young (1866-1957)

◦ ◇ ◦

"STRIKE UP THE BAND!" This story celebrates America's first female band conductor, and reportedly, the world's first female to lead an all-female orchestra. Her expertise and charm brought her fame and success. In fact, one of the world's most famous conductors showered her with praise.

Born in Keene, New Hampshire, in 1866, Helen May Butler Young got an early start in music when she studied violin from the concertmaster of the Boston

The classy leader of the band, Helen May Butler Young.

Symphony Orchestra. Her first violin, of the same vintage as the Stradivarius, was purchased from the concertmaster's private collection.

Young went on to learn other instruments, such as the coronet. In the late 1890s, Helen and friends from the Talma Ladies' Club got together and formed the Talma Ladies' Orchestra.

One of the band's earliest performances was in 1901, at New York City's Orpheum Theater, when Young's band headlined the vaudeville stage. At the time, vaudeville was popular, but often associated with burlesque, otherwise deemed as "tawdry." To de-emphasize the stereotype, and compete with hundreds of men's professional bands, Helen highlighted the military aspect of her troupe.

Helen married her business partner, John Leslie Spahn, around 1901. It was he who changed the name of her band at the Pan-American Exposition in Buffalo from the *Talma Ladies Military Band* to *Helen May Butler and her Ladies' Military Brass Band* to promote his wife's status as the foremost female band leader. John promoted the band as an "Adam-less Garden of Musical Eves." He even went so far as to disguise his gender by signing his name as "J. Leslie Spahn."

In 1906, the tall, blue-eyed Helen advertised in the entertainment weekly, *The New York Clipper*, for, "lady musicians for a band." She ran a tight ship with her girls, who were not permitted, "to flirt or carry on conversation with strangers." Violation resulted in a $5.00 fine. She warned, "kickers and cranks," to stay away and hired only accomplished female musicians from across the country. The saxophone

Helen's band distracted a horrified crowd at the Pan-American Exposition when President McKinley was assassinated in 1901, by playing non-stop for days after the tragic event. One account said that the band may have actually witnessed the assassination. During Teddy Roosevelt's presidential campaign in 1904, Helen wrote a march that was selected as the official song and called it *Cosmopolitan America*. She played a command performance at the White House after the election.

◇

Gem aficionado, Diamond Jim Brady, once danced with Helen. Helen was also friends with Susan B. Anthony.

◇

was not a popular instrument in those days, but Helen was savvy enough to add female sax players to her band and expedite the instrument's popularity. In the winter off-season, Helen taught music lessons and conducted church and theater orchestras.

The group quickly became successful enough to build their own concert hall. Despite the success, Helen fought male chauvinism most of her career. In the finals of a band competition at Madison Square Gardens, Helen captured top honors, winning over a male rival who at one time refused to allow her to play in his band.

Helen's first marriage was ill-fated even after two children were born. Her daughter, Helen May, once referred to herself as a, "trunk baby" because as an infant, she slept behind the stage and to the music of her mother's band. Helen divorced Spahn and married James H. Young. They settled in Cincinnati with her children and opened the Burlington Hotel in 1912 as a boarding house. Eventually, she divorced Young, but continued to operate the hotel until the 1950s. She continued working throughout her life. She formed a band for The Lagoon amusement park in Ludlow, Kentucky, and was recruited by Barnum & Bailey Circus.

So, who was the aforementioned world-famous conductor that Helen impressed so much? None other than John Philip Sousa! In fact, she was often referred to as the "The Female Sousa." Sousa noticed Helen in the audience in his Cincinnati performance and invited her up to direct a number. The next day, he sent her a congratulatory box of chocolates. Helen was the only female that Sousa allowed to direct his band. J.A. Bartlett actually wrote a march and two-step titled "Miss Sousa Jr.," that was dedicated to and played by Helen and her band.

Some of the items from Helen's career are enshrined in the Smithsonian today, such as one of her prized coronets played when "Semper Fidelis" closed concerts, while an American flag was unfurled. One of her large hats she wore at the St. Louis World's Fair is also in the exhibit, as well as her uniforms. A museum spe-

Helen ran unsuccessfully for U. S. Senate in 1936 after a "musical campaign," which included a concert on her $10,000 Stradivarius violin in Covington, Kentucky.

Helen's father was an engineer on the New York, New Haven and Hartford Railroad before investing and designing some of the earliest Pullman cars.

cialist deemed the artifacts important in politics and the emancipation of women. And there is no better homage to that than the crowning piece of the collection—a letter and poem from John Philip Sousa himself.

"Caldonia" Marie Reynolds (1921-1984)

"CALDONIA, CALDONIA WHAT MAKES YOUR BIG HEAD SO HARD?"

Those are the lyrics to a song supposedly written about a lady that I knew only as a tall, lanky character who frequented the streets of downtown, always with a pair of tap shoes draped over her shoulders. At the drop of a hat, she would whip the shoes off her shoulders, put them on, and proceed to tap dance on the sidewalk. I knew there had to be a story behind those impromptu performances that brought so many smiles.

I was curious about what happened to Caldonia when I started my research at Spring Grove. I came across an article from a 1987 *Cincinnati Magazine*, where I learned her given name was Marie Reynolds, though she called herself Caldonia. I had accidentally discovered she was buried in Spring Grove when I unexpectedly passed her headstone and saw the name "Marie Reynolds" on it.

Reynolds' parents, James "Hock" and Mary Jackson, were tap dancers from Lexington, Kentucky, and often took Reynolds to clubs with them. Her father owned a pressing shop and started teaching Reynolds to dance when she was two years old. Her mother worked as a domestic for a prominent Lexington doctor. Reynolds felt she couldn't learn what she wanted in books so she quit school after the fifth grade. Reynolds wanted to entertain more than anything and when she was 21, she went on the road to sing the blues, tap dance, and tell jokes. She was good enough to become a featured performer at the old Cotton Club in Cincinnati at 6th and Mount streets.

○ The elusive Marie 'Caldonia' Reynolds, an early hipster.

She didn't stop there. She went on to New York, with her husband, Larry Reynolds, and became a featured performer at the famous Apollo Club. According to several sources, the blues composer and bandleader, Louis Jordan, was in the audience one evening with the lyrics to a new song he had just written about a woman named Caldonia. His Caldonia was just a melody, but became reality when he saw Reynolds tap dance across the stage. Although he was with his wife, Fleecie, he found Reynolds entertaining and went backstage to tell her that he wanted her to be the Caldonia in his new song. She apparently was so flattered that she got rid of her given name and decided from then on to be known only as Caldonia.

Charles C. Breuer (1845-1908)

○ ◇ ○

MANY PEOPLE ASK ABOUT GHOSTS and the ghost stories of Spring Grove. The fact is there are no substantiated ghost stories, but there are rumors, hearsay, and legends that surround the strange happenings and quirks in the Grove.

One of the most popular stories in Spring Grove involves an impressive bronze portrait bust attached to a large granite pedestal monument on the southeast corner of Section 100. The sculpture, memorializing Charles Breuer, itself isn't extraordinary, it's the eyes.

People who visit the grave often say, "His eyes follow you when you walk past the monument!" Or they wonder if, "His eyes turn red at night!" The eyes are eerie, realistic, and many feel truly unnerving. Because of the stories attached to the Breuer memorial and the eyes, his monument is one of the most popular destinations in the cemetery. Visitors search for the mysterious monument, but don't know the story behind the man with the spooky eyes. In truth, the myths are much more extraordinary than the reality of the man's life.

In 1892, Breuer owned The National Starch Company at 12 West Second Street in Cincinnati. He worked under the auspices of Cincinnati Zoo founder, Andrew Erkenbrecher. Breuer was also listed as a real estate agent at 312 Plum Street, and at one time lived in Clifton at 445 Ludlow Avenue. His second wife was Georgia Gholson, whose father owned the William C. Gholson Fencing Company and held the patent for "block-binding, tension equalizing wire fencing."

There are a few intriguing details to Breuer's story. Saying he wanted to be prepared for his death, he bought two $500 caskets, one for his wife and one for himself. That in itself is not unusual but after a few months, Brewer ordered the caskets delivered to his house and placed under his bed. He defended himself saying, "Why shouldn't I be prepared? I am living well now and want to be assured that I'll be buried right when I am dead. I don't care about all the fuss generally made at funerals. What I want most is to be housed under six feet of dirt and not be put away in a flimsy coffin that returns to dust in a few months time." He goes on to say, "If some of my enemies should dig me up in thirty or forty years after I'm dead, they'll find me just how they found me in life—with the same look of determination on my face. They're trying to rob me of everything I've got but they won't rob me of a decent burial."

Two of his enemies seemed to be Ruth and Helen, his two daughters by his second marriage. Breuer abandoned his two girls after marrying his third wife. Reportedly the girls did not get along with either her or their father. Breuer changed his will giving everything to his third wife and disinheriting the two daughters. In

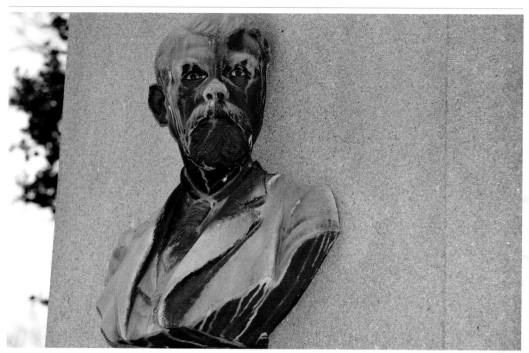

◇ The Breuer monument. Visitors to the monument say, "I always feel like somebody's watching me!" (Which is a line from the song "Somebody's Watching Me," by the musician Rockwell.)

the new will he gave the reasons as, "because of their incorrigibility, abuse, utter disregard for me as their parent, willful association with people I forbade them; for falsehoods, mockery, flinching of the mother's ashes and urn; refusing to live with me or in places I am willing to provide for them, also, for their disrespect in various ways to my wife, who is my sole comfort in my affection." Then one day the girls returned to their Covington, Kentucky, apartment to find nothing but a small bed and two chairs. The next day the stepmother returned but refused to tell the girls where their father had gone. Too young to work, they were supported by neighbors until they learned of their father's whereabouts from the newspaper. Following a series of confrontations where he would strike the daughters and both sides were accused of threatening the other with a gun, he was compelled by the courts to provide $50 a month for their support as the daughters lived in a home for girls.

Breuer's erratic behavior continued. He owned property that he refused to pay taxes on because it was attached in behalf of his daughters and he would rather it be sold to pay the back taxes than allow any of it to go to his girls. Before he could protect the Franklin Building, another of his holdings, lawyers for the girls stopped him, causing most of the building's tenants to leave. When an official for a bank which had been named receiver for the building found a lit fuse in the elevator shaft leading to enough dynamite to take down the building, Breuer was arrested for arson. Although Breuer tried to blame the dynamite on the work of his enemies, he was eventually declared insane and was to be sent to the Longview mental hospital and his property held in trust for his two daughters.

So what about Breuer's mysterious eyes? Some myths say that Breuer was an optometrist who was obsessed with his eyes and when he died, he requested in his will his eyes be removed and incorporated into the bust. Not true. Despite the myths, we know the eyes aren't real. Although the eyes are incredibly realistic, they are actually made of glass.

The eyes aren't the only mystery on the Breuer lot. Look closely and you will notice a large, mysterious slab of concrete near the Breuer monument. It covers the entrance to a series of catacombs containing the deceased bodies of the Breuer family. Adding to the mystery is a purported tunnel beneath the lot supposedly connecting the Breuer catacombs to another set of catacombs on the adjacent lot. It is not known if there is a connection between the two families, other than the rumor of a tunnel.

There you have it—the myth and truth behind the man with the mysterious eyes. Breuer was not an optometrist, the eyes on his memorial are not real, and the tunnel under his cemetery lot may or may not exist. But when all is said and done, Breuer's success in life allowed him to have an eerie likeness, with life-like eyes, which has captured the imagination of countless visitors to Spring Grove!

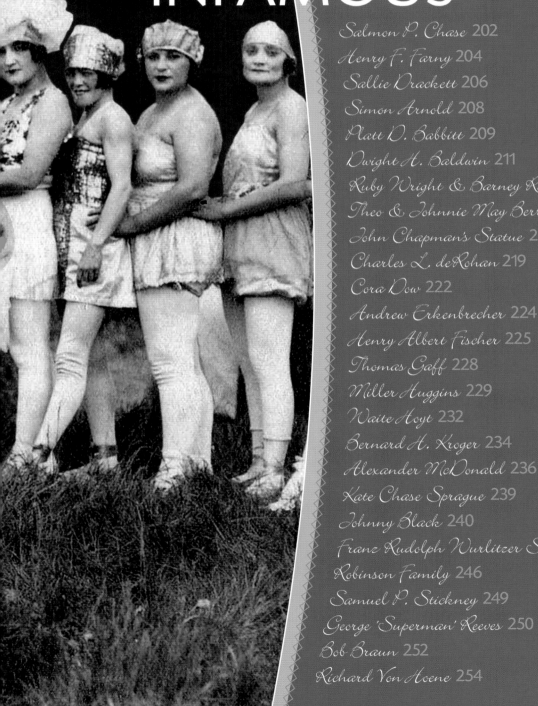

Chapter Five

FAMOUS AND INFAMOUS

Salmon Portland Chase (1808-1873)

◦ ◇ ◦

SALMON PORTLAND CHASE IS AMONG THE MOST RECOGNIZABLE of the notable burials in Spring Grove. The mere mention of his connection to the Internal Revenue Service and the income tax brings an interesting array of comments from our tour participants.

Chase was born in Cornish, New Hampshire, in 1808, and was the ninth of eleven children born to Ithamar and Janet Ralston Chase. When Salmon was nine years old, his father went into bankruptcy and passed away. Chase, to relieve the financial burden on his family, moved to Ohio to live with his uncle, Philander Chase. At that time Philander was the Episcopal Bishop of Ohio and the president of Cincinnati College (now the University of Cincinnati). Chase enrolled as a student at the college but left when his uncle moved east to take another job. Returning home, he enrolled in Dartmouth College. After graduating from Dartmouth, Chase moved to Washington D.C., to practice law before eventually settling back in Cincinnati to set up his own law practice.

In Cincinnati, Chase defended escaped slaves, becoming known as "attorney general for fugitive slaves," as well as those who aided in their escape. He helped politically shape the anti-slavery Liberty Party and later helped form the Free Soil party. This was the beginning of an interesting political career.

With Democratic support, Chase was elected as Senator from Ohio. By 1855, and unable to get Democratic support for his strong abolitionist views, he formed a coalition that included the young Republican Party that was able to get him elected as the Governor of Ohio. Despite his role as a key member in organizing the Republican Party, he failed in his ultimate goal of getting its nomination for president in both 1856 and 1860. However, upon the election of Lincoln, Chase was named to the cabinet post of Treasurer of the United States, becoming a member of what Doris Kearns Goodwin called Lincoln's "team of rivals."

As Secretary of the Treasury, Chase was responsible for the difficult task of financing the Civil War. One of his actions was to recommend the creation of an income tax to be collected by a Commissioner of Internal Revenue. Another was to create a national currency, the first national paper money in the United States, known as demand notes. Before demand notes, private banks issued paper currency. Chase chose the color green for the currency, which led them to be called "greenbacks" because of their distinctive green ink. In what was likely an attempt to enhance his own political standing, he had his face placed on the $1.00 bill. His picture is also depicted on the $10,000 bill, the largest bill to be used in public circulation. Everyone is familiar with the term "In God We Trust," coined by Chase, which he proposed should appear as the motto on the newly designed one and two cent coins. Congress approved and the motto first made its debut in 1864 on the two cent coin. It has appeared on most U.S. coins since then.

Chase's relations with President Lincoln were complicated. Chase's lack of humor supposedly caused friction, and Chase and Lincoln were said to have never understood each other. He supposedly did not like Lincoln's "endless stories," finding them a complete waste of his time, his pride, and his ambition. Several times Chase offered his resignation following a disagreement with Lincoln. Eventually Lincoln accepted it.

Six months later and despite their differences, Lincoln named Chase Chief Justice of the Supreme Court. The Chase Court decided several important cases during the period of reconstruction and in his role as Chief Justice, Chase presided over the impeachment trial of President Andrew Johnson.

Salmon Portland Chase

Chase died in 1873 and was originally interred in Washington. The Spring Grove minutes from June 1, 1882, states: "Surviving daughters of Salmon P. Chase wish to remove his remains from Washington to Spring Grove." Five years later the minutes included this statement on October 7, 1886: "...will receive remains of Chief Justice Salmon P. Chase at the railroad station, take them to the chapel for funeral service." Senator Selden Spencer of Missouri viewed the original modest headstone for Chase while he was in

Stories in the Grove

Cincinnati for an American Bar Association Convention and proposed a "suitable mark of recognition." The result was a dignified granite sarcophagus. Chief Justice William H. Taft spoke at the dedication of the monument in 1923.

And although Salmon's reputed relationship with Abraham Lincoln was strained, Lincoln overlooked Chase's deficiencies and said: "Chase is about one and a half times bigger than any other man that I ever knew."

Henry F. Farny (1847-1916)

◦ ◇ ◦

I LOVE CINCINNATI. One of the reasons is the world-renowned excellence of the art found in our galleries and museums. Undoubtedly, the most recognizable name in the history of Cincinnati art is that of Henry Farny. His oil and watercolor paintings of the Old West and Native Americans, among other subjects, have become internationally known.

Farny was born in Ribeauville, France in 1847, and brought to America five years later by his parents. They settled in Warren, Pennsylvania, in an area frequented by the Seneca Indians. It was there that Farny began his lifelong fascination with Native Americans. Farny and his family later moved to Cincinnati and it was here that his career in art began at a Japan-ware factory ornamenting patent ice water pitchers, then as a chore boy at the Strobridge Lithographing Company. While working at Strobridge, some of his pen-and-ink drawings were published by *Harper's Weekly* which gave him a job in New York on its illustrating staff.

After a year at *Harper's,* Farny, in 1867, desired more advanced training. Working his way to Europe as a deck hand, he traveled to Rome where Buchanan Reed took him on as an apprentice. After a year he went to Vienna, Munich, and then Paris before returning to Cincinnati in 1869. He remained in Cincinnati for two years returning to Strobridge, designing show bills and circus posters as well as submitting illustrations for *Harper's Weekly* and *Century* magazines. Illustrating *McGuffey's Eclectic Readers* was also among his projects. Once again, returning to Europe, he studied briefly in Dusseldorf, then it was back to Cincinnati in 1872, where he began teaching at the Mechanic's Institute. Before the year was up he

◇ One of Farny's paintings of his beloved Native Americans.

returned to Munich. And who painted beside Farny? None other than noted artist, Frank Duveneck.

It wasn't long before Farny returned to Cincinnati where he once again took up teaching at the Mechanic's Institute. When Duveneck followed him back from Munich, Farny turned the class over to him then enrolled as a student in his own class. In 1875, he returned to Europe for a year, this time with Duveneck and John Twachtman.

Farny turned his sights on the West in 1881, where he sketched the Indians of the Standing Rock reservation and brought artifacts back to Cincinnati that he later used in his paintings. On another trip in 1883, the famous Lakota leader, Sitting Bull, was introduced to Farny. Farny had known about Sitting Bull turning himself over to the U.S. military in 1881, and the fascination with Sitting Bull and the Plains Indian life was enhanced. But before coming back to Cincinnati, Farny traveled with dignitaries, like Ulysses S. Grant, on his railroad trip further west. On another trip in 1894, Farny was invited to paint the Apaches at Fort Sill in the Oklahoma Territory. There the famous chief, Geronimo, signed the watercolor sketch that Farny had made of him. *Century* magazine featured Farny's sketches of the Crow Reservation in the Montana Territory.

Eleven of Farny's paintings were considered so outstanding that after he exhibited at the Cosmos Club in Washington, D.C., in 1900, the government bought them for the National Museum. It was during this time that Farny focused more on easel paintings. His subject matter, of course, was the Plains Indians. Probably one of the most noted attributes of Henry Farny's paintings was the fact that the poses of his Native American subjects were candid. No staged poses, just the real thing and a personal tribute to a disappearing world.

Henry Farny's career was among the most prestigious of the Cincinnati area artists and his work adorns the walls of many museums and homes across the world. It's not uncommon to casually stroll through a museum in other parts of the country and come across a Farny painting. My heart swells with pride when I have that experience in other cities and occasionally, countries. Henry Farny is just one of the many reasons to appreciate great art that was created in Cincinnati and the world.

Sallie Bolton Drackett (1858-1934)

◦ ◇ ◦

Sallie and Philip Drackett

NOT A DAY GOES BY THAT WE DON'T either see or use a product made by the Drackett Company, such as Drāno or Windex. Households across the world have been cleaned and shined thanks to the genius of Sallie and Philip Drackett. But Sallie was never given her due until now. Sallie and Philip's great granddaughter, Anne Drackett Thomas, recently said, "Published histories of Cincinnati and the Drackett Company never gave Sallie the credit the family knew she deserved."

Sallie Bolton was born in 1858 in Cleveland as a 6th generation American. Her great-great-great grandfather, Everard Bolton, was a faithful Quaker who purchased land from William Penn's grant. Her great grandfather married the older sister of Betsy Ross, creator of the American Flag. Sallie's family heritage was rich indeed, which may have contributed to her being persuasive, colorful, and energetic; traits that would come in handy later in her life.

In 1880, Sallie was teaching school at age 21 and still living in Cleveland. Three years later, she married Philip William Drackett, a chemist. With Sallie's persuasiveness and energy, it was a match made in heaven and their partnership over the next forty years produced incredible wealth of many kinds for their family. Her Quaker heritage and his entrepreneurial spirit were a perfect combination.

For the next two decades, The Dracketts lived in several cities, with Philip having a number of different employers. By 1890, and with two children, they moved to Chattanooga where Philip and Dr. Marx Block, a Civil War surgeon, formed Block, Drackett & Co., which became a popular and well-known wholesale drug house.

By 1898, the Dracketts appeared for the first time in Cincinnati city directories, Philip being listed as a traveling salesman. In their early 50s, Sallie persuaded her husband to use the contacts he had made over the years and, together, they formed P.W. Drackett & Sons Co. By the 1920s, the company was the largest manufacturer of medicinal quality Epsom Salt in the country.

In the late 1800s, city directories listed primarily men and their businesses but Sallie Bolton listed her own business in the directories as secretary and treasurer of the P.W. Drackett & Sons Co. By 1910, she was a career woman, 10 years before women gained the right to vote! The family venture they built and the products they developed would last through that century and into the next. Sallie was at the center of the company and the center of her family.

The first major consumer breakthrough for the company was in 1923, with the invention of Drāno. It was Sallie who insisted on using the macron over the "a" so consumers would pronounce the name correctly and have no doubt about the purpose of the product. Sadly, Philip and Sallie would not live to see it's lasting success or the success of the next product, Windex, which wasn't introduced until 1935 by their son, Harry, six years after Philip's death and only one year after Sallie died. Both products have become household names.

From now on, when you see a Drackett product or see the name, don't just think of Philip Drackett's story, think of Philip *and* Sallie Drackett's story and their contribution to America's consumer history.

Simon Arnold (1824-1885)

◦ ◇ ◦

QUIRKY ATMOSPHERE, OLD WORLD AMBIENCE, and dinner next to a bathtub are just a few of the experiences you can expect in Cincinnati's oldest bar and restaurant, Arnold's—an ode to the enduring legacy of the founder Simon Arnold, a Cincinnati icon.

Founded in 1861, Simon Arnold's bar, then known as Simon Arnold's Saloon, began as one of Cincinnati's most cherished watering holes. The two buildings that make up the Arnold's establishment were built in the late 1830s. One was a barbershop, the other a feed store, with the courtyard currently at Arnold's once the stable and carriage house. Simon Arnold died in the restaurant from pneumonia on February 7, 1885. His son, Hugo, became owner and purchased the building next door. He opened a café with a separate entrance for female patrons who used the space to escape the cigars and cigarettes from the men next door.

During Prohibition, Simon added food to the menu. The second floor became a dining room and included the bathtub. It's been reported that he once sold gin mixed in the bathtub!

Simon's grandson, Elmer, took over ownership of Arnold's Saloon around 1940 and changed the name to Arnold's Grill. He continued the family tradition of no business on Sundays or holidays. Future owners were respected restaurateurs in their own right, and included brothers Jim Christakos and George Christos (of Christos & Drivorkas restaurant fame). They sold to Alex Chaldekas in 1974 (buried in Section 128) who then sold it to Jim Tarbell, a Cincinnati restaurateur and his wife, Brenda. The Tarbells discovered the open space next door where the stable

It's interesting to note that in the same year that Simon opened Arnold's, Confederate guns bombarded Fort Sumter, Findlay Market was only six years old, and the Roebling Suspension Bridge was five years from completion.

◦ ◇ ◦

Simon Arnold in front of his bar, Arnold's.

and carriage house were, and turned it into a charming courtyard dining area in 1978.

Today, Arnold's continues to thrive as an iconic local gathering spot, serving up "big heaps" of history with their food and drink, keeping many of the traditions first begun by Simon Arnold. When I want to impress out-of-town guests, I request a table upstairs and tell them the story of Arnold's, usually sitting next to the bathtub.

Platt Delascus Babbitt (1823-1879)

◦ ◇ ◦

IT NEVER CEASES TO AMAZE ME HOW HUMAN NATURE serves to shape our lives. Territorialism and a few umbrellas helped shape the life of the talented Platt Babbitt.

Platt D. Babbitt was a famous daguerreotypist and photographer (or "photographist" as he was known in the 1860 census) of Niagara Falls, though he may be better known for his temper and choice of profession than his work. Babbitt made daguerreotypes from 1855 to 1860, and magic lantern stereo views, or slides used in a special viewer, from 1860 to 1870. A daguerreotype is a photograph produced on chemically treated plates of glass or metal. The George Eastman House in New York has daguerreotypes online and they're fascinating.

Babbitt was one of the first photographers to make a career in "tourist" pho-

A photo of Platt's beloved Niagara Falls.

In 1879, another story appeared in the local press, announcing Babbitt's suicide. It described how the man who had worked for decades on the brink of a precipice nearly 180 feet high, had tied a stone around his neck and threw it into a creek no more than three feet deep, where he was later found face down.

Platt isn't the only Babbitt story in Spring Grove. His brother, David, is also there, and his brother-in-law, Charles Rule, was the artist who carved many of the Victorian era stones found in the cemetery.

tography and he set up his business on the American side of Niagara Falls. Very territorial, he acted as if he had a monopoly on photographing tourists at the falls and he and his assistants would wave umbrellas to block the views of other photographers wanting to use "his" spot. Platt was once arrested for fighting with a judge who leased the pavilion space. Some sources say that Platt even stole the Niagara Falls daguerreotypes attributed to legendary Boston daguerreotypists, Southworth and Hawes.

Another photo of Niagara Falls.

One of the most notorious photographs taken by Platt was of Joseph Avery. The photo is considered to be one of the precursors to photojournalism. Avery became stranded in the Niagara River in 1853, and Platt photographed his struggles to survive. Sadly, Joseph was ultimately swept over the falls after becoming fatigued—a dramatic, but unpleasant, way to perish. Babbitt's photograph of Avery was last auctioned at *Sotheby's* for $53,000! You can still see the famous photo on the Library of Congress website. Avery's plight was also memorialized in a poem written by William Dean Howells.

On my last visit to Niagara Falls, I couldn't help but imagine an angry Platt Babbitt shooing away other photographers with an umbrella. From the number of amateur photographers at the falls, he would have been busy!

Dwight Hamilton Baldwin (1821-1899)

◦ ◇ ◦

I'VE FOUND THE NAMES BALDWIN AND WURLITZER synonymous with keyboards ever since I learned to play the organ and piano in my youth. Imagine my surprise at learning the patriarchs of both families are interred in Spring Grove. I knew the Baldwin Piano manufacturing and corporate headquarters were on Gilbert Avenue in Cincinnati, but was surprised to learn of the Baldwin family connection to Spring Grove.

Dwight Hamilton Baldwin was born in Erie County, Pennsylvania, on September 15, 1821. Coming from a family of devout Presbyterians, Baldwin had originally aspired to be a minister. He attended Oberlin College in 1840 and enrolled in the Preparatory Department where he learned not only ministry, but music as well.

After leaving Oberlin, he travelled to Maysville, Kentucky, where he taught music and Sunday school in country churches. In 1850, he reportedly taught singing at the Ebenezer Church in Cabin Creek, Kentucky. He and his family then travelled to Ohio, where he taught music in Brown and Adams counties. After that, he moved to Cincinnati and taught music in the Cincinnati Common Schools for a salary of $100 a month. His students, who became more and more interested in pianos and reed organs, regarded Baldwin as an expert keyboardist and teacher.

In 1862, Baldwin left teaching and began selling reed organs and pianos. His background in music must have been an advantage in sales. In the *Biographical Encyclopedia of Ohio* from 1876, Baldwin was listed as a ruling elder in the Third Presbyterian Church in Cincinnati, where he reportedly increased attendance in Sunday school to an all-time high in 1875.

Baldwin first advertised in the *Cincinnati Daily Gazette* in 1865 as a dealer in pianos and organs. The ad for his business at 92 W. Fourth Street stated, "Chickering

◇ The Baldwin piano manufacturing company and corporate headquarters on Gilbert Avenue.

Chapter Five

It was not until after Baldwin lost their Steinway franchise in 1887 that the colleagues decided to begin designing and building their own keyboard instruments.

Pianos are undoubtedly the cheapest in the market. For superior tone, durability, and elegance of finish, there are no pianos that will compare with Chickering's." The ad in the 1865–66 *Directory* lists Baldwin as a "Dealer in Pianos, Melodeons, and Boudoir organs." At one time, Baldwin also sold Steinway pianos as a franchise.

Baldwin's business moved many times in Cincinnati, however, the famous Pike Street Opera House at 65 W. Fourth Street brought Baldwin tragedy. On March 22, 1866, the Pike Street building burned to the ground. A local newspaper account reported: "In the second story of this building was the piano room of D.H. Baldwin. The stock on hand consisted of twenty-two pianos, only one of which was saved. Mr. Baldwin can at present give no idea of his loss."

The Baldwin Company eventually recovered and went on to become one of the most successful piano companies in America after Baldwin partnered with his bookkeeper, Lucien Wulsin, in 1873. With the help of Wulsin, the Baldwin Company flourished. Baldwin pianos have been played by notable musicians, both amateur and professional, including Liberace, Aaron Copeland, and President Harry Truman. Today Baldwin is owned by another iconic musical business, the Gibson Guitar Company.

Ruby Wright (1914-2004)
Barney Rapp (1900-1970)

SARAH VAUGHN'S SIGNATURE SONG, "POOR BUTTERFLY," was one of the most popular songs performed by vocalist and Indiana native Ruby Wright. Wright sang "Poor Butterfly" on Ruth Lyons' 50-50 Club television show in the 1950s and '60s to the delight of the audience, but Wright's story is much more interesting than a single song.

Ruby Wright was comfortable in and out of the spotlight.

Ruby's singing career began in 1930 with a simple phone call from two friends who attended Indiana University. They asked Ruby to join them in starting a female singing trio. For the modest fee of $10 a week, the friends, who named themselves the Call Sisters, sang at a northern Indiana resort known for its big-band dance music.

Wright left the Call Sisters to perform with The Charlie Davis' Orchestra in Milwaukee. She later joined bands in Chicago and New York. While performing in New York, she met the love of her life, Barney Rapp, the leader of Barney Rapp and His New Englanders. Rapp was amazed by Wright's talent, and she became the "chirp," or female singer, in his orchestra. Their love grew, and they married in 1936 before touring the country together.

Rapp's orchestra was successful in venues across the Cincinnati region, including the Beverly Hills Supper Club, the Lookout House in Fort Wright, Kentucky, and Coney Island's Moonlight Gardens. They eventually opened their own successful nightclub, The Sign of the Drum on Reading Road in the Bond Hill section of Cincinnati. When Wright became pregnant, Rapp needed a replacement singer for the club.

Rapp discovered a young kid from the west side of Cincinnati with a great set of pipes. Her name was Doris Kappelhoff. She auditioned and was hired, but Rapp thought she needed a shorter, more entertainment-friendly name. He convinced her to change her name to Doris Day. Not only did her career blossom with the name change, it eventually became a household name and she a beloved figure in the music and entertainment business.

Wright could have become jealous or resentful of Doris Day's success but she harbored no ill feelings against her replacement. She was supportive of Day and her success in Hollywood. Wright was a lady of great character, and too busy and happy for resentment. Wright stayed home for several years, raising four daughters, but she never stopped performing. In the morning, Wright lovingly awoke her girls by singing "God Bless America."

In the 1950s, Wright eventually resumed her career locally with a successful 20 year run on WLW television with the beloved Ruth Lyon's 50-50 Club as well as popular recordings at King Records. She closed the Lyon's holiday show each season with her signature "Let's Light the Christmas Tree." Her recording of the song sold 250,000 copies in 1958, an astounding number for the time.

Had Ruby not been such a kind and sweet lady and supported Doris Day's success, "Poor Butterfly" may have been a bittersweet commentary on resentment instead of the beautiful song it is today. The lamenting butterfly in the song proclaims she will die if her love doesn't return. In Ruby Wright's case, she never lamented a career lacking international stardom. She didn't need it. The love of her hometown and the love of her children and husband were more than sufficient.

The Barney Rapp Band was a popular attraction at the Cincinnati Reds' Crosley Field, and often performed during games.

◇

◇ Doris Day and Barney Rapp

Theodore M. Berry (1905-2000)
Johnnie May Berry (1910-2002)

◦ ◇ ◦

WHEN I WORKED AS A SPEECH AND LANGUAGE PATHOLOGIST, I had the privilege of working with a wonderful pre-school teacher by the name of Johnnie May. She was soft-spoken, quiet, and dignified. I worked with her students and always looked forward to my time in her class. Many years later, I discovered how her story connected with the story of my home, Cincinnati.

Johnnie May was the wife of Cincinnati's first African-American mayor, Theodore M. Berry. He was born in 1905 in Maysville, Kentucky, to an unwed and deaf mother, Cora Parker. They lived in poverty while she worked as a laundress. Berry was young when he moved to Cincinnati with his mother and family. In Cincinnati, he was placed in Jennie Porter's Stowe School in the West End. His education not only instilled in him the yearning for excellence, it provided him with a penchant for grace and dignity that became the hallmark of his career. His grace and dignity however, were put to the test in 1924, his senior year in high school, when an essay he wrote on Abraham Lincoln was initially rejected by an all-white panel of judges. Determined and confident, Berry persevered by re-entering his essay under the pseudonym *Thomas Playfair*. This time, his essay won and he became the first African-American valedictorian at Woodward High School.

Berry worked at a steel mill in Newport, Kentucky while he attended the University of Cincinnati College of Law. After graduating, he began a legal career that led him to the civil rights movement. In 1945, he was instrumental in defending three Tuskegee Airmen who attempted to integrate an all-white officers club, and he served as legal counsel for the NAACP. Berry litigated for fair housing in Cincinnati and worked for the Community Action Program.

President Lyndon Johnson appointed Berry to the head of the Office of Economic Opportunity's Community Action Programs. Berry spearheaded such programs as Head Start, Legal Services, and the Job Corps. In 1972, he was elected Cincinnati's first black mayor and served for four years. The *Cincinnati Enquirer* reported that the inaugural audience was likely the largest to crowd into the City Council Chamber.

Today, Berry is not only remembered as Cincinnati's first black mayor, but a man who fought social injustice and inequality for citizens of every race, creed, and color. Former Cincinnati mayor, Charlie Luken, referred to Berry as "one of the greatest Cincinnatians of all time. A kind man, an intelligent man, a true statesman in every respect, he led our city to a better place in the area of civil rights." Both the International Freedom Park and the former Produce Drive on the Cincinnati riverfront were named in his honor—lasting legacies of a great man and leader of the community.

Theodore Berry

Theodore M. Berry's story ended when he passed away in 2000. One of my favorite quotes by Berry, mentioned in his obituary, was from Proverb 31:9, "Open thy mouth, judge righteously, and plead the cause of the poor and needy." He certainly embodied that proverb for a community of friends, family, colleagues, and the citizens of the Cincinnati area and beyond.

The statue of John Chapman, aka "Johnny Appleseed" (1774-1847)

◦ ◇ ◦

TO BE CLEAR, JOHNNY APPLESEED IS NOT BURIED IN SPRING GROVE. But a special statue located at the top of Section 134 has led to rumors, myths and legends worthy of the legacy of Johnny Appleseed.

The story of Johnny Appleseed has a special place in American folklore. We imagine him as a vagabond character wandering the frontier with a walking stick and sack full of apple seeds. Most of us grew up imagining Johnny Appleseed as a whimsical, imaginary character. The truth is, only the name, Johnny Appleseed, was fictional.

The true story centers on a Swedenborgian missionary from Massachusetts by the name of John Chapman.

Records of Chapman's birth from the First Congregational Church in Leominster, Massachusetts, indicate he was born on September 26, 1774. His father, Nathaniel, was a farmer and carpenter, and served as a Minuteman at Concord under General George Washington in the Revolutionary War fighting in "Capt. Pollard's Company of Carpenters."

Chapman worked on the family farm before eventually taking off on his own to explore the wilderness. The first recorded evidence of Chapman planting apple trees is from 1804, written by his sister in a promissory note. John deemed himself "called" to a mission in the West. As he made his way to western Pennsylvania, he navigated a large boat of apple seeds down the Ohio River. After landing, he planted apples over miles of Ohio countryside and thus became known as Johnny Appleseed.

Chapman was quite a character in his own right, and lived up to the name, Johnny Appleseed. It is reported he was a loner but could be

◇ Johnny Appleseed statue.

Chapter Five

quite social in the right situation. He was known to give girls pieces of ribbon and amuse children by doing such things as walking on hot coals and sticking pins in his feet. People welcomed him because of his wit and charm. Some considered Chapman rather quirky, which has been attributed to a kick in the head he received from a horse. Even his clothing was considered strange.

Chapman died around 1847 from pneumonia and was buried in Ft. Wayne, Indiana. His exact burial place in Ft. Wayne has been disputed for many years, however a beautiful bronze statue of Johnny Appleseed was commissioned by Spring Grove in 1968. Robert C. Koepnick, the head of the Dayton Art Institute at that time, created the sculpture which is at the top of Section 134 as a memorial to the horticultural and missionary work of John Chapman. In Koepnick's sculpture, Chapman is immortalized raising an apple tree seedling in one hand and holding a book in the other. The inscription plaque on the sculpture reads: "Saintly in his daily life, he loved life in all its forms and had a joyous will to help the earth yield its fruits. Bible in hand and sack of seeds swinging from his shoulder, he planted many apple orchards that live today in this region. May he be remembered in fact as well in legend for his godliness and goodness."

In Chapman's obituary from the *Fort Wayne Sentinel,* it is written: "He lived to an extreme old age, probably being not less than 80 years old at the time of his death-though no person would have judged from his appearance that he was 60." Johnny Appleseed was a true American icon, and his memorial in Spring Grove has become very popular with visitors and tour participants.

In a last, little twist of irony, Chapman's grandfather, Edward (five generations removed), willed to his second wife "ten good bearing fruit trees near the end of the house" upon his death in 1678. Little did grandfather Edward know that five generations later, his descendant would forever be associated with one of the most popular "bearing fruit trees" in America, the apple tree.

Charles L. deRohan (1924-2005)

◇

FOR DECADES, PEOPLE HAVE WRITTEN STORIES WITH PENCILS. We used pencils in grade school. We wrote with them. We sharpened them. And some of us even chewed on them! Remember when you were young and looked forward to buying those colorful yellow pencils in preparation for the new school year? I have the distinct memory of putting my yellow pencils in the pencil tray underneath the lid of those old wooden school desks. This is a story about an unlikely connection between those yellow pencils and Spring Grove.

The story begins with Charles deRohan, who was an aristocrat and son of Prince Charles Victor deRohan of France. The title "Princes of Royal Blood" was bestowed upon the deRohans from their cousins, who were kings of France. The family, originally from Brittany, was once one of the most powerful aristocratic families in France, however, during the French Revolution they fled to Austria.

His father married a British national Maria Anna von Hardmuth in 1923, and Charles deRohan was born a year later. Maria was an heiress to the Josef Hardmuth pencil empire. More than 200 years ago, her Austrian family pioneered a ceramic-based graphite pencil. Later the company introduced a new bright yellow pencil called the Koh-i-Noor creating a tradition of associating the color yellow with high quality pencils that remains today.

Living in Czechoslovakia at the outbreak of World War II, the Prince and one of his brothers were imprisoned in a Nazi concentration camp in Lauffen, Germany. Fortunately, in April of 1945, deRohan was liberated by the American Army and he joined the British Liberation forces. Following the war, the Russians seized the family's home and properties leaving them a small pencil factory in Somerset, England and one in Bloomsbury, New Jersey. DeRohan moved to New Jersey in 1948 to run the pencil factory before it was eventually sold and he moved to Cincinnati, the home of his wife, Virginia Durrell. Later on, he worked for First America Corporation and then as Vice-President of Leasing Company, Inc., taking charge of finance and equipment leasing.

I find it highly ironic that the yellow pencils that I lovingly used in grade school had a connection to Spring Grove and since that revelation, it's hard for me to use a yellow pencil without thinking of the deRohan family and Spring Grove!

It is interesting to note that Josef Hardmuth was originally an architect, builder, and inventor who bequeathed monuments in Vienna. It's likely that I have seen some of his monuments on my visits to Zentralfriedhof cemetery in Vienna.

Chapter Five

The Plain Dealer December 3, 1836, page 11: "Mammoth Potato-The Prince Charles deRohan, who introduced the potato deRohan into France, otherwise called the monster potato, lately sent one to Paris, which would afford a plentiful meal to more than twenty persons. In the computation of the size of this potato from the data furnished, it would be all important to know of what nation to call the twenty persons. It would take a thumping large potato to satisfy the appetite of twenty sharp children of the Emerald Isle."

◇ Princess Maria Anna deRohan

Cora Dow (1868-1915)

◦ ◇ ◦

FOR ME, WHAT USED TO BE A ROUTINE TRIP to the drug store now evokes the story of Cora Dow. The woman challenged and rose above male chauvinism in the 1800s to become a dynamic presence in the business world. President William Howard Taft described Dow as "a woman who was a master of her own fate, who from early life lay down and adopted, as a means of achieving usefulness for herself and her kind, a plan of life of action which she maintained until her death with extraordinary consistency and strength of character."

Cincinnati was the home to one of the first and largest drug store chains in America, Dow Drug Store. It was founded by Edwin B. Dow in the West End of Cincinnati during the late 1800s. Before opening his drug store Edwin peddled porous plasters from a wagon. While traveling throughout Ohio, he was often accompanied by his daughter, Cora, preparing her for a career in the drug store business. When her father became ill in 1885, Cora, putting aside her dreams of a career in music, began managing much of the business.

A quote from Dow states how her need for survival overtook her yearning to become an opera star: "Frankly, we did not yearn a lot for pharmacy. We did want grand opera, and had an ambition to stand behind the footlights and pour forth volumes of melodies to delighted audiences. But there was the matter of bread-winning, and so I studied pharmacy and powders and pills, and then, as now, I enjoy harmony with the crowd and not from the stage. It is all right, but after twenty-five years we still confess to an ambition to star in Wagnerian roles."

Cora Dow went on to revolutionize drug store products. Feeling women were important customers, it wasn't uncommon to find fresh flowers scattered throughout her establishments. She added other little touches to make her stores cheerful as she recognized the difficulty of having to purchase items for ill relatives and friends.

At age 20, she started chain-store pharmacies when she opened her second store on Race Street. Eventually she made Dow Drug Stores one of the largest chains in the United States. Much of her success was from slashing prices as Dow adhered to the principal of rapid turnover at a small profit per unit of sale. This raised the ire

8902
Interior of Dows Drug Store, 7th & Race Sts., Cincinnati.

◇ Famous actor, Tyrone Power, worked at Dow Drugs in College Hill.

of male druggists and she was "sued, blacklisted, hounded and threatened." She was reportedly followed by detectives and put in jail at one point. She fought back, and her quest for success made her even more determined and vigilant. She ate and slept in the back of the store, even doing janitorial work. I love Dow's view on the failure of retail businesses: "There are three (reasons.) These are: ignorance of the principle of rapid turnover and large volume at small profits, lack of capital, and dry rot." When she died in 1915, Dow owned 11 stores.

The exterior of Dow Drug Store.

Our story on Dow ends with her most interesting quote about females becoming pharmacists: "So, I contend that beautiful women can be pharmacists without spoiling their beauty, either of person, disposition, or character." I think she succeeded with all three and in a way, her success did indeed become of Wagnerian proportions.

Stories in the Grove

Dow's love of music continued after her death by bequeathing much of her estate (equaling millions today) to the Cincinnati Symphony. Her other outside interest was animals. She campaigned across the nation for horses to receive two-week vacations every year!

Andrew Erkenbrecher (1821-1895)

I LOVE TELLING VISITORS THE STORY OF HOW I LOVED to order dinner at a Mt. Adams restaurant that was in the old Rookwood Pottery building just so I could order the "Erkenbrecher Burger." Say that fast ten times! I had no idea who Andrew Erkenbrecher was or what he did for Cincinnati's history but his story quickly unfolded when I first began searching for stories a decade ago.

Andrew's family came from the Bavarian village of Heilegersdorf. In 1835, they brought Andrew with them to America, living in New York before coming to Cincinnati. Andrew eventually found employment working on the Colonel Gano farm in the suburb of Carthage. It didn't take long before he became a clerk in several stores and eventually purchased a mill which he later combined with a starch factory. It was there that he made his fortune after developing new methods of "efficiently manufacturing corn starch that would not immediately spoil." He later added a factory away from the city in Morrow, Ohio.

It wasn't until after the Civil War that Andrew used his wealth for philanthropic purposes. The most notable of those was his leadership in the formation of the Cincinnati Zoo, one of the first in the nation. During a plague of caterpillars in the area around 1872, Erkenbrecher and some friends decided to import around one thousand birds from Europe

Andrew Erkenbrecher

that would devour the destructive insects. Perhaps we can blame our overpopulation of starlings in the area on Erkenbrecher? He built a garret in an old "Colonial-roofed residence" in Burnet Woods, near the campus of the University of Cincinnati, to house the birds. When the birds became accustomed to the environment, he would release them so that they could eat the caterpillars. Upon the successful release of the birds, Erkenbrecher and others formed the *Society for the Acclimatization of Birds* in 1873 to acquire the birds so that they could start chomping away on the caterpillars. Later that year, the Society changed its name to The Zoological Society of Cincinnati. Erkenbrecher's prized collection of birds was the main exhibit when the zoo opened in 1875.

Mr. Erkenbrecher was the first president of the Cincinnati Telephone Company and the director of Spring Grove from 1872 to 1885. He died on the Fourth of July in 1895 at age 50. Isn't it funny though that I can't eat a hamburger now without envisioning a flock of birds flying over my plate? May the Erkenbrecher burger rest in peace.

Henry Albert Fischer (1828-1918)

◦ ◇ ◦

AFTER HIS EDUCATION IN GERMANY and a challenging voyage to America, Henry Albert Fischer found his way to Cincinnati and made a name for himself. Fischer's story is one of perseverance and fortitude that others with similar obstacles may have found too challenging to overcome. And although his lasting legacy was as a founder and savior of the Cincinnati Zoo, it was his work ethic that I found most impressive.

Fischer was born in 1828 in Hanover, Germany, into a family of four sons and a daughter. At age fifteen, he studied to become a salesman in Hildesheim, Germany. His first job was short-lived when his boss, known to be a "strong" drinker, was found dead in his office from a stroke. The boss's wife took over the business but Fischer hated her. So when her husband died and Fischer's contract became void, off he went to find a job elsewhere. After apprenting for two years in Peine, Germany, Fischer was "the happiest man in the world" when his father managed to scrape up enough money to send him to America around 1845.

○ Fischer family photograph

Fischer's voyage to America was challenging. He was on a boat with 286 passengers and conditions were brutal. Most of the time, they were sailing in stormy weather. Their meals consisted of salted beef, herring, prunes, and Zweiback. After 108 days, the ship finally arrived in New Orleans. Fischer's arrival was met with melancholy. His best friend, with whom he had traveled from Germany, died of yellow fever. Fischer was now alone in a new land but dealt with his situation by helping other immigrants from Europe transition into a world foreign to them.

Fischer found that the language difference didn't fare well in his quest to become an American merchant. Jobless, the ship's captain took Fischer under his wing and procured a position for him in the laboratory of an apothecary. It was another short-lived job when Fischer was told to cook a large kettle of sarsaparilla (pronounced "sasparilla"). He was sidetracked when the boss made him go to a saloon, thus neglecting the boiling sarsaparilla. Upon return to the apothecary, they were met with a room full of scalding sarsaparilla. Goodbye, apothecary job!

The visit to the saloon was not Fischer's last. His next job was working in a saloon with a "mean man" as his boss. Fischer was most likely used to dealing with less-than-congenial supervisors so he remained in the saloon position until he enlisted as a soldier with the third dragoons in the Mexican War. He was described as "a wiry, slender man, angular and stern in appearance but underneath was very kind and most level-headed." You would have to be somewhat level-headed to deal with the odds Fischer was exposed to. After two years in the military, he received an honorable discharge. Soon after he returned to New Orleans, he was in an accident that left him in critical condition, spending months in a hospital. That didn't slow Fischer down though. He regained his strength and decided to come to Cincinnati and start anew.

It was 1849, and a cholera epidemic was sweeping Cincinnati—a depressing and desperate time. Fischer searched for nine months to find a job and once again, found work in a saloon, but this time, the saloon was connected to a German theater on the canal between Main and Sycamore Streets. He worked hard and in 1851 was able to open his own cork shop. The same year, he met and married Babette Ackerman and they had seven children. According to the city directories and his great-grandson, they lived in two or more locations before settling on Woodburn.

Fischer had many other accomplishments in his life, such as being a member of the Turners Club in 1855, and founding the first tin can factory in this part of the country in 1861. The Albert Fischer Manufacturing Company made cans and canned vegetables. Around 1877, the factory moved to Hamilton, Ohio, and the name was changed to the American Can Works. When hand-made cans were no longer feasible, Fischer began using the latest machinery. As a result, the company was able to sell cans to other canning factories all over the country. Fischer then added lard pails and buckets to his manufactured items. A Cincinnati City Directory listed Fischer as a "preserved fruit pickler" in 1864, and then as proprietor of "the Star Preserve Works, canned meats, fruits and vegetables" in 1880. Wait. There's more. In 1884, Fischer's company was listed as "sole packers of 'Star' boneless pig feet!" His "catsup works" was noted as operating only in summer months. But Fischer's most well-known credit was as one of six original founders of the Cincinnati Zoo, and more importantly, saving the zoo from foreclosure.

The *New York Times* reported in 1898 that George Hafer and Fischer were appointed as receivers of the zoo "upon application of the stockholders," who reported a debt of $70,000. Mayor Gustav Tafel preceded Hafer as a receiver. They said that litigation loomed "which would bring permanent injury to the property." Fischer was authorized to borrow $12,000 but held down the amount to $6,200. He challenged the citizens to patronize the zoo and increase attendance. Citizens were forever in Fischer's debt for his accomplishment.

"Mean" bosses, stormy voyages, almost catastrophic injuries, overflowing sarsaparilla, none of which kept Henry Albert Fischer from his accomplishments. He was a true role model for overcoming adversity and hardship. The next time I have a nice, cold sarsaparilla, I shall make a toast to Mr. Fischer and his success!

Thomas Gaff (1808-1884)

◦ ◇ ◦

I LOVE TO "EXPLORE MY ENVIRONMENT" by taking day trips in the car from time to time. One of my favorite area historical spots is the Hillforest Mansion in Aurora, Indiana. I had walked past the Gaff family monument for years in Spring Grove and later learned that Hillforest was the Gaff family home in the 1800s.

Thomas Gaff was an industrialist and financier in Indiana but he learned the process of paper making from his father and the distilling business from his uncle Charles in Brooklyn, New York. Eventually, he and his brothers, James and John, formed a partnership and opened a distillery in Philadelphia that rapidly became a success. But because of the Panic of 1837, the brothers had to find other opportunities. They decided to move their business to Aurora when they were offered tax incentives and land. Thomas arrived in 1843 and established the T. & J. Gaff & Co. Distillery on the banks of Hogan Creek, one block north of downtown Aurora. Their distillery made bourbon, rye, and Thistle Dew scotch whiskey. Aurora beer was featured from the Crescent Brewing Company that they also owned. The beer was exported to Germany because of its high quality. Thomas partnered with the Fleischmann family at one time.

There were other interests in the Gaff family: farming, turnpike and canal construction, a foundry and machine works, silver mines in Nevada, a jewelry store, two Louisiana Plantations and their mill in Columbus, Indiana, which produced the "first ready-made cereal in the world," *Cerealine*. I'm exhausted just thinking about their involvement in so many businesses!

The Gaff brothers also owned a fleet of steamboats that were used to transport their brewing and distillery products. On a spring afternoon in 1853, their steamboat, the *Forest Queen*, which would become the headquarters for General William Tecumseh Sherman during the Siege of Vicksburg, "glided to a stop at a dock in Aurora." Noted architect, Isaiah Rogers, was one of the passengers and was there to meet with Thomas Gaff to see the proposed site for Hillforest. The design by Rogers was a modified version of Italian renaissance style but with a steamboat appearance made by the wide, rounded porch that was likely ordered by Gaff. The suspended staircase in the front hall resembles a grand salon of large luxury riverboats of that era. Thomas loved the Ohio River and he often watched it from a telescope in a circular room that was called the third-floor belvedere, above the ladies' sitting room. That was because ladies were not permitted in his retreat! Huurrumph!

Thomas Gaff and his brothers were also involved in civic affairs that included backing Aurora's first utility company, the Aurora Gas and Coke Company. He even served as president. James was the first of the Gaff brothers to build a home in the city, known as Linden Terrace, named for Linden trees that he imported from Germany for landscaping.

A beautiful, large, polished pink, granite column graces the Gaff lot in Section 20. Atop the column is a bronze allegorical female statue.

It's virtually impossible to re-visit or take out-of-town guests to Hillforest without thinking of the Thomas Gaff family and their contribution to so many American products. It's no longer just about a house, it's about a family and their history.

Miller Huggins (1878-1929)

◦ ◇ ◦

I ADMIT IT. I DID NOT KNOW WHO MILLER HUGGINS WAS until I started researching Spring Grove notable burials. I wish I had known his story sooner. Huggins' story stems from the strict guidance of his English immigrant father, who deemed education more important than baseball, not unlike my own father.

Huggins grew up in Cincinnati, to a *very* strict father whom he feared would discover his desire to play baseball. His solution was to use an assumed name, re-

Roller skating became another interest of Miller during the off-seasons when he worked in area skating rinks. The fascination with the sport continued for the rest of his life.

◇ Miller Huggins, the only man who could keep Babe Ruth in line.

portedly William Proctor or Cummings. After graduating from Walnut Hills High School he got a law degree at the University of Cincinnati before he abandoned law for baseball. William Howard Taft, then a professor at U.C., reportedly suggested Huggins follow his dreams in the world of baseball.

Baseball brought Huggins together with another notable family of Spring Grove residents—the Fleischmann's of Fleischmann's yeast and margarine products. It was Max and Julius Fleischmann who, in 1900, signed Huggins to play baseball, when he was still using the name of Proctor, for their semi-professional team, the Mountain Athletic Club. The team played in Fleischmann, New York named after the family, largely for the amusement of wealthy visitors. The Fleischmann's were known to pay the players well and provide a first rate experience. A few years later, Max and Julius, partnering with the infamous Garry Herrmann and "Boss" Cox, bought the Cincinnati Reds. On April 15, 1904, Miller Huggins made his professional debut with the Cincinnati Reds as a second baseman after being traded from the St. Paul team of the Western League.

Huggins suffered from chronic lack of sleep, headaches, and lack of appetite, symptoms which later were compounded by a skin disease known as erysipelas. Despite his health problems, he was amazingly accomplished on the baseball field. He was traded from the Reds in 1910, and in 1913, became the St. Louis Cardinals' manager. Six years later, the hapless, losing New York Yankees hired Huggins as their manager and he turned the franchise around. The Yankees went on to win six pennants and three World Series under Huggins. In fact, they were the first World Series wins in the history of the team. Among his players were Waite Hoyt, Babe Ruth, and Lou Gehrig. By 1927, the Yankees were considered the best team in the history of baseball, accomplished under the guidance of their manager, Miller Huggins.

But Huggins was not easy to work with. He often fought with Babe Ruth, to the point where Ruth called 5'6" Huggins,

Miller Huggins

Stories in the Grove

"a little twerp." In 1925, when Ruth was absent for three consecutive games, Huggins fined him $25,000, ten times the amount other players would have been fined. Another time, Huggins threatened to throw a drunken Babe Ruth off a train.

Despite having at first to hide his connection to baseball, when Miller died, all American League baseball games were cancelled to observe his funeral. It was estimated that more than 10,000 people lined the streets of New York. Among the pallbearers were "The Babe" and Lou Gehrig. The same day, his body was brought back to Cincinnati on a train and another public viewing and service were held. Three years later, the first memorial in Yankee Stadium was for Huggins. He was inducted into the Baseball Hall of Fame in 1964. In fact, Babe Ruth is quoted as saying of Huggins, "He was the only man who knew how to keep me in line."

Waite Hoyt (1899-1984)

◦ ◇ ◦

FOR CINCINNATIANS WHO FOLLOWED BASEBALL in the 1940s, '50s, and '60s, Waite Hoyt was the voice of the Cincinnati Reds. But before that he was also a New York Yankee pitcher, artist, and mortician. Mortician? Yes, Waite's story is not just about baseball. He was full of surprises and it was his beautiful widow, Betty, who enlightened me on his colorful background that involves a story about a stint in the mortuary field.

Hoyt's baseball career began with the New York Yankees in 1918. He played with legends such as Babe Ruth and Lou Gehrig. His baseball career ended in 1938, and in 1942, he began a 24 year career in broadcasting with the Cincinnati Reds.

When he wasn't playing baseball or broadcasting, Hoyt was also an artist and stage performer. In the 1920s, he performed vaudeville in the off-season with J. Fred Coots, the man who later wrote, "Santa Claus is coming to Town." On the vaudeville circuit, Waite sang while Coots played the piano. Through his Vaudeville connections, Waite met Mae West and became golf partners with Bob Hope.

Hoyt was a self-taught painter, and his painting of Reds' great, Ted Kluszewski, can be seen in the Cincinnati Reds Hall of Fame. However, Hoyt's most surprising job experience was not with the living.

For years, I had heard rumors that Hoyt once worked for Spring Grove. I wanted to know the truth, so I visited his second wife, Betty Hoyt. As friends of my family, the Hoyts were part of my father's career with the Cincinnati Reds. Hoyt was my father's mentor before he started his career in the Reds radio booth. In fact, while my dad was the youngest player to ever pitch in the major leagues at age fifteen, Hoyt was also fifteen when he signed with the New York Giants and began pitching batting practice.

I went to Betty to learn more about Hoyt's stint during the off season and his connection to cemeteries. Her tale not only shed light on the connection, but proved highly entertaining.

Betty explained the story in a letter she wrote in 2003:

"Waite was never an undertaker at Spring Grove or anywhere else in Cincinnati. His only work in that profession took place in New York during his playing days with the Yankees. During the early 1920s, he married the daughter of the owner/operator of the largest and most successful funeral home in Brooklyn. Since Waite was fond of Mr. Pyle (his father-in-law), he often helped out at the home when they were busy or in the offseason. Those tasks could have been picking up and transporting remains from homes or hospitals to the funeral home, reception during lay outs/funerals, or driving a hearse or limousine in funeral processions. Although he was often present at the preparation of a body, he never participated because he had no formal training in that field or a license. He did have thoughts that it was a profession he'd pursue deeper after his baseball career ended. During those years, Waite lived in Brooklyn for a while and then moved to Westchester County. For some personal reason, Waite had a falling out with Mr. Pyle and decided he'd open his own funeral home in Long Island. That he did and hired Mr. Pyle's chief embalmer/mortician. All went well until the mortician suddenly died. He was unable to hire another qualified mortician and the business failed. Later, his marriage failed, along with hopes of a future in that profession."

Coincidentally, Hoyt was nicknamed "The Merry Mortician." According to Betty, Miller Huggins was Hoyt's hero. Hoyt suggested to Betty that he be buried near Huggins' grave site. And so he was; on a beautiful ridge in section 103. Waite Hoyt, New York Yankee pitcher, radio announcer, artist, and mortician, shows there often *is* more to the story if you're willing to dig a little deeper.

◇ Waite Hoyt was a true Renaissance man–baseball player, radio announcer, and mortician.

◇

Hoyt was a pallbearer at Babe Ruth's funeral and, in 1969, he was inducted into the National Baseball Hall of Fame.

Bernard Henry Kroger (1860-1938)

◇ ◇ ◇

IF YOU'RE FROM THE CINCINNATI AREA, you're probably familiar with the Kroger grocery store chain, founded by Bernard "Barney" Kroger. But his legacy didn't start with grocery stores, it started with tea.

Born in 1860 in Cincinnati, Kroger was fatherless by age 13. He left school and became a farm worker but the work never appealed to him. In 1875, on a cold night in December, he quit farming and walked thirty-five miles back to Cincinnati.

Back in the city, he started his career in groceries selling tea and coffee door to door. He was soon manager of the Imperial Tea Company. A year later when the owners refused to make him a partner he quit and joined B. A. Brannigan to open the Great Western Tea Company. At first, unfortunately, the business was an "unmitigated disaster." The Ohio River flooded, submerging their business. In addition, their wagon wrecked and the horse was killed by a train. As I said, it was a disaster.

Bernard Henry Kroger

Kroger and Brannigan borrowed money, a lot of money, to reopen their business. When in 1884 the two men couldn't agree on opening a second store, Brannigan sold his half of the interest in the prospective Kroger Foods company for a mere fifteen hundred dollars. It was a 400% profit for Brannigan, and at the time, he might have thought it was a good deal. But the Kroger company was about to take off.

I was surprised to read Kroger was considered a "crank," and was proud of the label. He sat at his office desk and faced his staff to make sure they were working. He hummed and used "extremely colorful" language. But Kroger knew groceries. When he managed the Imperial Tea Company, he insisted on testing the products before they were sold. If a product didn't meet his approval, Kroger simply refused to sell it.

Kroger kept long hours, often from dawn to midnight. His mother and brothers were the first managers. In fact, "Mother Kroger's" home-made pickles and sauerkraut were Kroger's first name brand items. Competitors made fun of the grocery's blue and white color scheme but Kroger kept innovating. His business was the first to operate its own bakery, the first to combine meat and grocery stores under one roof, and one of the first to hire female cashiers. Success allowed Kroger to expand

Barney had a particular affection for the blind beggars he noticed on street corners. He and fellow philanthropist Frances Pollak helped found the Cincinnati Association for the Blind.

○ Kroger expected everyone to work just as hard as he did.

beyond Cincinnati. In 1902, he changed the name from Great Western Tea Company to Kroger Grocery and Baking Company. At that time, he owned forty stores!

A grocer has a hectic and stressful life, so Barney cut back his work and began golfing and charity work. His contributions included a roof on his golf caddy's church and a swimming pool for Condon School.

When Barney decided to sell Kroger in 1928 to Lehman Brothers, he owned more than 5,000 stores nationwide. He retired to Cape Cod, where, I imagine, he could sit on the beach, be as cranky as he liked, and drink a nice cup of tea.

Alexander McDonald (1836-1910)

○ ◇ ○

I OFTEN GET WEARY OF VISITORS WHO FIND IT AMUSING to make jokes about the Alexander McDonald family mausoleum when we approach the monument on guided tours. We often hear "Is this Ronald's family?" Ha ha. But the jokes fade to awe when they learn of Alexander's story.

I first learned of Alexander McDonald through his great-niece, Nancy, after she had taken one of my very first tours. I didn't know much of his legacy, but Nancy enlightened me on some of the lesser-known facts.

Alexander's father was a landscape gardener who settled in Chillicothe after he emigrated from Scotland around 1851. The family home on the Scottish island of Iona was called "Dalvay," as was their iconic and stately mansion in Clifton which he built at a cost of more than $600,000. A country home on Prince Edward Island in Canada was also reportedly worth a small fortune. But his career actually began by working in his uncle's starch factory in Chillicothe, Ohio.

Being one of his uncle's best workers, Alexander was able to create starch companies throughout the nation. He and his brother opened a store in the Camp Washington area of Cincinnati and called it Alexander McDonald & Brother Starch Company. Then they opened a store that sold coal oil by wholesale and commission at 57 Walnut Street.

In 1863, Alexander started his first company to sell oil, which led him eventually to become the president of Standard Oil Company of Kentucky. The headquarters was in Louisville, Kentucky and later moved to Cincinnati. Alexander was successful, and was said to have conducted the largest merchandising business in the United States. If that wasn't enough, he also was the director of the Big Four Railroad, Vice-President of the Cincinnati Art Museum, director of the College Conservatory of Music and May Festival Association, and a banker.

◇ Old Alexander McDonald did not have a farm. He had oil.

Alexander became partners with his son-in-law, Edmund K. Stallo, in the building of the Mobile, Jackson & Kansas City railroad line. 410 miles were actually built and bonded for $30,000 a mile but unfortunately, Alexander died before its completion. It was reported that debts from his liquid assets reduced his worth but other reports indicate that he died a very wealthy gentleman.

The princesses Laura and Helene.

The McDonald family consists of some royalty. Alexander's granddaughter's, Laura, married Prince Francesco Rospigliosi of Italy and Helene married Prince Michel Murat of France. Helene however had an interesting relationship before her marriage to Prince Murat. The *New York Times* reported that her father broke off her engagement to the grandson of Admiral Count Bonde of Sweden's royal family because he feared that "she and Mr. Florman would be uncongenial." I suspect he wasn't happy to learn that her betrothed was also the son of a masseur! Alexander's daughter, another Laura, married a relative of Johann Bernard Stallo, the physicist who wrote *The Concepts and Theories of Modern Physics* in 1882.

Laura and Helene were groomed in the finest of fashion and wealth. Estimates of their inheritance ran as high as fifty million dollars and as low as fifteen million dollars. Either way, not a bad inheritance! Around 1900, Alexander's worth was said to be less than five million, leading to speculation that it "may easily have been a matter of unhappy uncertainty in his mind as to whether or not he was even solvent." But the girls were far from destitute, with a hefty inheritance from their grandmother.

But even with the royal family connections, McDonald's legacy was not without controversy. In 1911, a *New York Times* article reflected on the fact that McDonald's fortune was much less than previously thought. People assumed that Alexander had simply mismanaged his wealth but it was a case of the reported wealth not being there in the first place. The amount from the McDonald estate was estimated at $300,000.

When visitors make jokes about the McDonald name in reference to the hamburger chain, it's Alexander McDonald who has the last laugh. He didn't need golden arches to memorialize a story like his!

Kate Chase Sprague (1840-1899)

◦ ◇ ◦

KATE CHASE SPRAGUE WAS THE ONLY SURVIVING CHILD of Salmon Portland Chase and his second wife, Eliza Ann Smith. Her father confessed in his diary that "The babe is pronounced pretty. I think quite otherwise. It is however well formed and I am thankful." Kate was named after Salmon's first wife, and his first daughter, whom were both named Catherine.

Kate's relationship with her father began at birth. He loved her, but "with reservations." His life was filled with personal tragedies, including the death of his first wife and two daughters, and his wife's family had been ravaged by tuberculosis. Kate found herself trying to cope with the mix of "loving concern and emotional distance" from her father during most of her life. This in turn led her to create quite a legacy of her own when she married a wealthy politician, William Sprague, in 1863. He became the governor of Rhode Island and supported Kate's father in his political aspirations. Sprague had been widowed for almost twenty years prior to marrying Kate in Washington, D.C.

Kate became "The Belle of Washington Society" and was described as being "young, remarkably beautiful, regal, and captivating." Abraham Lincoln referred to her as "young and handsome." But not everyone thought so highly of her, including Lincoln's wife, Mary Todd, who had as she said "battles royal with her." Mary even forbade her husband to dance or talk to Kate. Kate's beauty may have been a factor in Mrs. Lincoln's seemingly jealous remarks but Kate added to the tension by coming to the receptions at the White House as a guest and upstaging the first lady by holding court on her own account. Many of Kate's actions were for the purpose of enhancing her father's political career including a nomination for the presidency in 1864. All in all, Kate's advice was so highly sought that some have labeled her as the "only woman in the history of the United States who had such political influence."

Although Kate was the talk of the nation with her penchant for purchasing extravagances at one time, she actually died in poverty. There were very few mourners and no famous people at her funeral. But President McKinley was kind enough to make sure that her body was sent back to Cincinnati in a "special car." Her three daughters accompanied her body back to Cincinnati.

Kate and William's daughter, Ethel, was the last in the family to be interred on the Chase lot in 1938. It's interesting to note that Ethel married a surgeon by the name of Frank Donaldson, who was with Roosevelt's Rough Riders.

Johnny Black
(1891-1936)

◦ ◇ ◦

I'VE ALWAYS felt a connection, a tenuous connection perhaps, to Johnny Black. I have family roots in Hamilton, Ohio, and Black, the man who wrote the song "Paper Doll" made famous by the Mills Brothers, lived most of his life in Hamilton, even though he was born

◦ Salmon Portland Chase thought his daughter, Kate (pictured here) to be ugly when she was born.

Chapter Five

in St. Louis. His father, John L. Black, lived on Sycamore Street in Hamilton. John was a musician and operated a music store in the city. He was a traveling one-man band who played the violin, coronet, drums, and piano, and performed magic tricks.

At 17, Black left Hamilton and traveled to Chicago to perform with Joe E. Lewis. There he became a favorite of Al Capone, and then decided to continue on the vaudeville circuit sharing billings with Jimmy Durante, Joe E. Lewis, Jack Benny, Eddie Cantor, Ira Gershwin, and Hoagy Carmichael. Impressive company! Locally he appeared in a vaudeville show in Chester Park, an amusement park next to Spring Grove Cemetery.

After time, his career going nowhere, Black went to New York to seek a show business break. In New York, he met and fell in love with an "oriental dancer" appearing at the Winter Garden on Broadway. She asked Black to write a new "oriental" number. That night he wrote his first hit, "Dardanella" in just an hour while working in his kitchenette. The song appeared in the movie *Two Girls and a Sailor* and in the 1949 movie, *Oh You Beautiful Doll*. A *New York Times* story from 1936 mentions the origin of "Dardanella." "Fred Fisher of 308 W. 104th Street, who holds the copyright on 'Dardanella,' said yesterday that Johnny Black had come to him seventeen years ago with several unfinished songs, the best of which later developed into the hit. Fisher said Black only had the tune in simplest form and that the music, the lyric and the choice of a title were completed later." The article goes on to say, "Black was said to have cleared about $12,000 on the song, selling his interest early. Fisher estimated that 6,000,000 phonograph records and 1,750,000 sheets of the song were sold."

One of Black's hit records, "Paper Doll."

While Black worked as a piano player and songwriter, several stories have surfaced over the years as to what Johnny did to supplement his income. Most stories cover the origin of his most famous song, "Paper

Hamilton was once called "Little Chicago" because of its gangster history, especially during Prohibition.

◇

Doll." Some say he became a boxer, and the woman he fell in love with left him because she loved a songwriter, not a boxer. Another version placed the origin in Chicago with a song named "My Doll" about a young showgirl who became "Paper Doll." "Paper Doll" was introduced in the movie musical, *Hi, Good Lookin'* by the Delta Rhythm Brothers in 1942. Lena Horne sang "Paper Doll" in the 1944 movie *Two Girls and a Sailor.* The rest was history. The song was a hit and a share of the royalties was awarded to his first wife.

Black's unfortunate death was tragic, and worthy of his legendary music. In the early 1930s, he played the piano and sang in Butler County, Ohio, nightclubs. He eventually bought a nightclub in the city of Hamilton and called it The Dardanella Club after his hit song. One night in 1936, Black argued with 20-year-old customer, Edward C. Moorman, over a $.25 tip left on the bar. Afterward, some say Black walked out of the club, others say that he was pulled out by the two young men. He was then either hit, pushed, or fell, hitting his head on a cement step. Edward was arrested and his companion, Julius Murray, held as a material witness. Black died afterward and was placed in an unmarked grave in Spring Grove. He was quoted as saying "Fame is climbing a greased pole for ten bucks and ruining a suit worth fifteen."

In 1972, the *Hamilton Journal News* publicized Black's story and learned of his unmarked grave. Soon thereafter, a memorial was donated to his memory.

The epitaph on his simple granite footstone now reads: "Composer of 'Dardanella' and 'Paper Doll'/The Happiness His Music Brought/Will Live Forever." The marker, created by the Greater Cincinnati Monument Dealers, has an etching of a musical lyre in honor of his accomplishments.

That tenuous connection grew stronger when I discovered, not long ago, that as a boy, I often dined with my parents and attended a banquet at a popular dinner club named Eaton Manor, which was formerly Johnny Black's Dardanella Club!

Franz Rudolph Wurlitzer, Sr. (1831-1914)

◦ ◇ ◦

AS A YOUNG BOY, I CLEARLY REMEMBER SEEING THE WORDS, "The Mighty Wurlitzer" in reference to one of the most famous organ makers. At the time though, I knew nothing of the story beyond "The Mighty Wurlitzer" organ.

If you've visited famous Radio City Music Hall in New York, then you've most likely seen the largest of the Wurlitzer organs. The Chicago Theater supposedly has the oldest Wurlitzer organ but perhaps the most famous Wurlitzer organ is in Blackpool, England, in the Blackpool Tower Ballroom.

The Wurlitzer empire of musical entrepreneurship began in the late 1600s with flute maker Nicholas Wurlitzer, from Markneukirchen, Saxony. Little did Nicholas realize that a descendent, Franz Rudolph Wurlitzer, would become one of the world's most famous makers of musical instruments.

Franz Rudolph Wurlitzer came to Hoboken, New Jersey, in 1854. He had no money and barely spoke English. He founded his music business part-time in 1856 when he was working for foreign bankers at the Heidelback, Seasongood & Co. in Cincinnati. He invested $700 for musical instruments supplied by his family in Germany and opened a one-room office as the Rudolph Wurlitzer Company. By 1860, Wurlitzer's wholesale operations were nationwide and a retail store, offices and stockrooms were operated at 123 Main Street in downtown Cincinnati. Within ten years of its founding, Wurlitzer had become the largest outlet for band instruments in the U.S. The military was his biggest customer.

Wurlitzer created a handwritten catalogue listing all of the instruments and accessories he carried in 1879. In 1882, the first Wurlitzer piano was made. One of Wurlitzer's first inventions came in 1899 with the first coin-operated

Rudolph Wurlitzer tuning up with a fellow violinist.

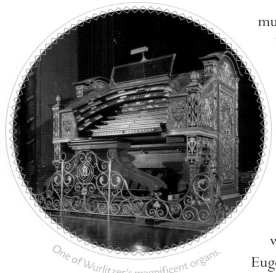
One of Wurlitzer's magnificent organs.

musical instrument by Wurlitzer, called the Wurlitzer Tonophone. It was termed "a granddaddy of the juke box." In 1906, Rudolph Sr. retired and his son, Farny, ran with the company.

Some found it odd that Wurlitzer would choose the quiet town of Tonawanda, New York, for its phonographic division headquarters and plant site. Tonawanda was a haven for skilled wood craftsmen. Wurlitzer negotiated with Eugene DeKleist's already established Barrel Organ Works to produce Wurlitzer's Tonophone. In 1908, Wurlitzer bought out DeKleist and the North Tonawanda Plant became Wurlitzer's manufacturing center, not only for the continuation of the DeKleist line of instruments, but for "The Mighty Wurlitzer" pipe organs.

"The Mighty Wurlitzer" organ was introduced by Farny Wurlitzer and Robert Hope Jones, and was in wide use before the "talkies" were introduced to the movie world.

A 1910 Wurlitzer catalogue listed more than 50 coin-operated musical instruments. A major item in the catalogue was the Concert Piano-Orchestra—a giant instrument which featured instrumentation of 30 oboes, 56 violins, 30 violas, 30 piccolos, 30 flute—an entire orchestra!

The small company founded by Franz Rudolph came to dominate the instrument industry across the world. The company not only made musical instruments, home stereos, electronic organs, and keyboard instruments but also radios and refrigerators. Before 1940, an estimated 3,000 Wurlitzer pipe organs were built and the slogan "Gee, Dad, It's a Wurlitzer" became a trademark. *The Billboard* reported in 1956 that "those who could not play, pushed a button, turned a crank, lit a lamp or put a nickel in." The Wurlitzer Company was bought by Baldwin in the late 1980s and today, you might see the name Wurlitzer on some models sold by Baldwin, the enduring legacy of Franz Rudolph.

The Music *that gives* Realism *to the* Pictures

THE WURLITZER NE MAN ORCHESTRA

The Wurlitzer family made a connection to local Cincinnati artists when Rudolph married Leonie Farny, daughter of famed artist Henry Farny, in 1868. They named their son Farny Wurlitzer, who eventually worked for his father.

A visit to Grandma's house was much more fun if she owned a Wurlitzer and let you play it.

Robinson Family

◦ ◇ ◦

LIGHTS! CAMERA! ACTION! One of the most colorful and fascinating stories in Spring Grove is centered on one of the most interesting and exotic monuments in the cemetery, the Robinson Family mausoleum. As the owners and founder of the John Robinson Family Circus, The Robinson family included circus workers, an actress, equestrian riders, tightrope walkers, and yes, even a clown!

The biographies of most circus performers in the 1800s are notoriously unreliable. John "Uncle John" Robinson claimed to be the son of a Scottish soldier in the American Revolution, who got his first glimpse of circus life in 1817, when he ran away from home to join the Buckley & Wicke circus in Newport, Rhode Island. He became a bareback rider. John worked with a number of travelling shows and circuses, and during his career, John performed as a "stilt dancer" and was known as a "Herculean Horseman." Eventually he found his own circus around 1824, although it was more of a show than a circus initially. Much of this may not be true. The first mention of him in any way connected to a circus was in 1832. While he may have been connected to a circus earlier, it was probably as a worker. He only appears to have become an owner of a circus in 1842.

Robinson's early form of advertising for the John Robinson Show consisted of an old mule with a pair of saddle bags, which held a six week supply of posters and six paper boxes of tacks. An agent for the circus would tack the posters on trees, barns, and anywhere else tack hammers were allowed along the show route. And the band? Well, it consisted of Robinson himself, playing a fiddle while sitting with his back against the center pole.

The "big show" evolved into "the big family circus" known for its elaborate costumes and staging around 1863 when Gilbert Robinson became treasurer of The John Robinson Family Circus. Gil married Emma Lake, who was an expert equestrian rider. Gilbert, Eldred, and John Robinson traveled for 23 years as partners. At one point, there were "four circuses, three 'menageries' with two stages, a herd of performing elephants, and 1,000 rare and costly animals." The most famous of those animals was Tillie the Elephant. Tillie's death in 1932 created a public stir.

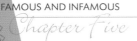

◇ You, too, can wear a unitard if you run away and join the circus!

Area schools were dismissed and a "three cannon salute" was performed by three of Tillie's fellow elephants in front of the entire village of Terrace Park, a community near Cincinnati where the Robinsons resided.

Tillie's death isn't the end of her story. Amazingly, part of Tillie the Elephant actually ended up in the home of a Robinson descendant. Intrigued? This story begins many years ago, when one of my co-workers gave me a photograph of herself with Ellanora Robinson, a descendant of John Robinson, on a visit to Ellanora's Hollywood home. Ellanora became a friend and shared many stories of her family's colorful

Another great clown connected to the Robinson Circus is one of the most famous clowns in history, Emmett Kelly, Sr., who met his wife at the Robinson Family Circus. His wife was performing a trapeze act with her sister in 1923 when they met. Kelly's clown/mime character was called "Weary Willie." I had a wonderful encounter with "Weary Willie" when I was four years old, backstage after a performance at the Cincinnati Gardens. At that time, I didn't know the legend of "Weary Willie," but will never forget his magical sad face. (Kelly is interred in Rest Haven Memorial Park in Lafayette, Indiana.)

history, including the story of Tillie's death. Apparently the elephant was too big to bury intact, so umbrella stands were made from Tillie's legs! I occasionally have to squelch the rumor that Tillie is buried in Spring Grove. It's reported that Tillie's eternal resting place is in Terrace Park, Ohio.

Ellanora Robinson has her own colorful story worthy of the Robinson family name. Ellanora worked in Hollywood as an actress, using the stage name Ellanora Needles. While filming a movie in 1940, she met actor George Reeves (see Reeves story), who played Superman on TV. In 1944, she and George appeared in the movie *Winged Victory* and fell in love. They were married for nine years before divorcing.

Even the Robinson Family mausoleum has an interesting story. Over the years, the mausoleum filled up with both family and circus members, creating a need for another private lot. The family purchased a separate lot in Section 75 that includes the resting place of an adopted daughter, Cora, an equestrian rider, and a clown.

But it wasn't enough just to have more space, the Robinsons needed a resting place worthy of their legacy. An interesting entry from the original Spring Grove Board Minutes, dated April 2, 1874: "John Robinson applied to keep remains of his daughter and grandchildren in the public vault until chapel he's about to build on Lot 2, Sec. 19 is finished, he having the bodies hermetically sealed up-allowed by

Eventually, Robinson's posters were made by the *Cincinnati Enquirer* job department until the building burned. No problem. John F. Robinson, Jr. built his own plant with the help of three Civil War vets (A.O. Russell, Robert J. Morgan, and James M. Armstrong) and began the nation's greatest printing companies, eventually becoming the U.S. Playing Card Company. Near the turn of the century, the famous Strowbridge Lithography Company made Robinsons' posters, which are now prized possessions.

Board." The family members were finally interred in their final resting place once the marble and limestone mausoleum was completed, looking a bit like the famous elephant house at the Cincinnati Zoo.

So after many circuses and a few movies, today "Old John" and most of the Robinsons rest peacefully in the family mausoleum, next to many circus performers. They continue to entertain the world in death as they did in life, surrounded by one of the most exotic and entertaining private resting places in Spring Grove.

Samuel Peckhill Stickney (1808-1877)

◦ ◇ ◦

FOR YEARS I PASSED A VERY STOIC-LOOKING marble portrait bust on a monument in an off-the-beaten path in the cemetery. It's an impressive sculpture of a gentleman who appears to be a distinguished states-man or politician. The patriarch of the family is the subject of the portrait bust and the story of him and his family is truly "monumental."

As I came to discover, the man depicted in the portrait bust, was an equestrian, ringmaster, instructor, and circus owner. Samuel P. Stickney, known as "Old Sam" by those in the circus world, was from Boston and joined the circus profession as a "fill up" when he replaced performers from time to time. His career started by training and riding horses with the Price & Simpson Circus in 1823.

The portrait bust on Stickney's monument.

In 1828, Stickney Sr. performed with the Washington Circus in Philadelphia, causing quite a stir by carrying Charles J. Rogers on his shoulders during his performances. He ended the act by leaping through a large balloon, with Rogers still on his shoulders! Then around 1852, Stickney Sr. trained and performed with a horse named Cincinnatus. That was impressive but not as much as his act "The Courier of St. Petersburg," which he performed on six to eight horses! Stickney Sr. obviously had a sense of humor. From 1853 to 1855, he portrayed a drunken soldier equestrian in his act called "Monticello."

Stickney Sr.'s family included a variety of circus performers. His son married Kate Robinson, daughter of famed circus owner John Robinson. His daughter Rosaline was the first accomplished female equestrian in America. Another daughter, Sallie Louise, married a circus performer who "astonished the public, in his unparalleled disguise as a woman, under the celebrated alias of 'Zoyara.'" I found his eldest son, Samuel Stickney, Jr. to be one of the most interesting circus members in the family.

Stickney, Jr. started as a hurdle rider, when he trained and rode horses with the Joe Cowell Circus. The following year, he appeared in winter engagements with Quick & Mead Circus, but his equestrian career ended early when he injured his ankle. Off to Philadelphia he went to study. Upon his return, he became successful in the ring as a Shakespearean clown! John A. Dingess said, "As a jester he was witty, original, and chaste. His voice was full and strong and his every word could be heard in the most remote recesses of the tent." Stickney Jr. started a one-ring wagon circus that eventually joined the John Robinson Circus.

In 1864, Stickney Jr. married a member of the Sherwood Circus family, Ida Sherwood. Their son, Robert, became a non-professional and their daughter, Cora, was in a vaudeville juggling act with her husband, W. R. Johnson. Stickney Jr. died in 1921 at his home in Chicago.

I find it ironic that Stickney Sr. died in Cincinnati while visiting a friend when he slipped on an icy sidewalk as he was leaving Wood's Theater. His friend just happened to be John Robinson.

The moral of this story: a stoic-looking marble portrait bust isn't necessarily a memorial to a politician or statesman. He could have been the father of a clown!

George "Superman" Reeves (1914-1959)

◦ ◇ ◦

HE WAS FASTER THAN A SPEEDING BULLET, more powerful than a locomotive, and able to leap tall buildings in a single bound, but he couldn't find a resting place in Spring Grove. George Reeves portrayed the iconic Superman on the 1950s television show, and although Reeves ashes rest in Altadena, California, he did have a brief "stint" in Spring Grove's White Pine Chapel. The story of his stay in Spring Grove is quite a saga.

Reeves was born to Don and Helen Brewer in Woodstock, Iowa, in 1914. Shortly after his birth, Helen divorced her husband and moved to Pasadena, California, where she met and married Frank Bessolo.

The White Pine Chapel where Reeves' body was held.

In California, George became an actor. In fact, he changed his last name to Reeves at the urging of Warner Brothers Studios when he signed a contract after his appearance as Stuart Tarleton in the classic *Gone with the Wind*.

Spring Grove enters the story with Reeves' maternal grandparents, George and Eliza Jane Lescher, who are indeed interred in Spring Grove. One of Reeves' relatives on his mother's side lived in Cincinnati, and was buried on a family lot in Spring Grove in 1857. Up until 1945, the family had been buried in the family lot.

Reeves' death remains a mystery. It has never been proven whether he was murdered, or if he committed suicide in his Hollywood home in 1959. His mother, Helen Bessolo, had difficulty at first deciding where she wanted her son to be laid to rest. At first, she wanted a private mausoleum built for him on her grandparents' lot in Spring Grove. She sent a telegram to Spring Grove on August 18, 1959, requesting permission to have a private mausoleum built "for my son, Superman."

While Helen Bessolo waited for a response from Spring Grove, she ordered Reeves'

Reeves allegedly had a hard time fighting his own demons.

body sent to Cincinnati, where it was temporarily stored in the White Pine Chapel. Spring Grove sent a letter of regret, explaining there was not sufficient space to erect a mausoleum on the family lot. Bessolo then ordered her son's remains be cremated, which was performed at the Hillside Chapel in Cincinnati on February 10, 1960.

Bessolo had Reeves' ashes sent to her in Hollywood, where she kept them in an urn on her baby grand piano until they were eventually placed in a niche in Mountain View Cemetery's Pasadena Mausoleum in Altadena, California. Today, Reeves' niche is lovingly marked with an inscription that includes "My beloved son, Superman."

Robert "Bob" Braun (1929-2002)

∘ ◇ ∘

AS TEENAGERS, WE ALL WANTED TO BE COOL. We wanted to be part of the "in" crowd. Impressionable as we were, some of us wanted to stand out from the others. The story of my "coolness" was almost decimated as a teen appearing on the local television show, *Bob Braun's Bandstand*. No doubt, Braun went to his grave in Spring Grove without knowing the affect that fateful evening in the WLW television studio had upon me.

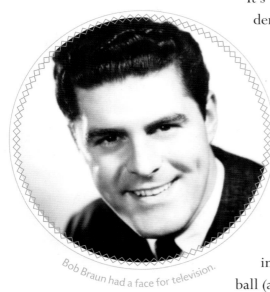

Bob Braun had a face for television.

It's rare to talk to any Cincinnati area resident over the age of 50 who doesn't remember WLW radio and television singer Bob Braun. As a sidekick to the cherished Ruth Lyons on her *50-50 Club* television show, Braun was kind of like Ruth's Ed McMahon (sidekick of late night talk show host, Johnny Carson). But Bob Braun was a cool guy, suave and debonair in most people's eyes. At least I thought so.

Braun was born in Ludlow, Kentucky, in 1929 and his career actually began in baseball (a likely reason that he and my dad were good friends). Braun hosted a summer weekend radio show for knothole baseball on WSAI-AM radio when he was at the young age of 13. Then six months before commercial television began in 1947 in Cincinnati, Braun sang on an experimental station, W8XCT, on Harris Rosedale's variety show. Around 1949, Braun was hired by WLWT and WLW-AM as the result of winning first prize on the *Arthur Godfrey Talent Scouts* show. Many females remember Braun as the handsome lifeguard during summers at Coney Island's "largest flat-surface pool in North America."

As a child, I remember watching Braun pantomime popular songs locally on *The Dottie Mack Show,* which was broadcast nationally on the DuMont Network. In 1957, he started substituting for the popular television pioneer, Ruth Lyons, on her live *50-50 Club* show. Ruth Lyons retired in 1967 and Braun was the logical replacement. He later starred on his own show, *The Bob Braun Show,* until it was canceled in 1984. A new career began for him in Los Angeles after that by hosting talk shows, parades, and doing commercials. It was Dick Clark who consulted with Braun's son, local television news personality Rob Braun, to go into broadcasting.

Braun became good friends with *American Bandstand*'s Dick Clark and hosted a similar show on WLWT that brought me to the studio when I was fourteen years old. Going downtown to a taping of *Bob Braun's Bandstand* as a teenager was a goal of many teenagers. I was ready to tear up the dance floor on *Bob Braun's Bandstand.* It was time to be cool and strut my stuff on local television!

Lights, camera, action. It was "Beach Party Night" on the show and my friends and I were dressed in our grooviest beachwear. The song "Barefootin" was popular at the time and when Braun played it, everyone took their shoes off and proceeded to do the limbo on-camera. At one point during the show, I took a break to drink a bottled soda. After all, I was thirsty from all of the 'barefootin.' Not wanting to miss clapping to the beat of the music, I leaned over next to a cameraman and put my bottle of soda on the floor. The next thing I knew, I had knocked it over. Dark, bubbly liquid spewed out of the bottle but not after making enough noise to get Braun's attention. I felt Braun's eyes leering at me upon hearing the sound of the bottle crashing to the floor but he was a professional. He carried on as if nothing had happened. But there I was, being totally "uncool" on the most popular dance show in town. But it made no matter to Braun. He was a professional. He knew how to handle such things. But then after all, he was the coolest of the cool.

Richard A. "The Cool Ghoul"
Von Hoene (1941-2004)

◦ ◇ ◦

I'M CONSTANTLY AMAZED at how many visitors assume notable or famous people have elaborate gravesites with expensive markers or monuments. Famed architect Samuel Hannaford has no marker or monument whatsoever. Artist Henry Farny has a modest head stone. One of the most colorful Cincinnati area television personalities has a simple marker which tells the visitor nothing of his contributions except on Halloween.

Richard A. Von Hoene received a Master of Arts degree in theater from the University of Cincinnati and started his career as a staff announcer and copywriter for WCPO radio. In the early 1960s, he was a broadcaster on "Bob Smith's Monster Mash" program. When Von Hoene moved from radio to television, *The Cool Ghoul* was born on Von Hoene's popular Saturday night horror film show, *Scream In*. As host, Von Hoene entertained his viewers by dressing in ghoulish attire, complete with a bright red fright wig and his signature plaid hat. Even the Cincinnati Reds admired *The Cool Ghoul,* bestowing him with a Reds jersey and the number "0." Von Hoene became royalty when he was named the Goetta King at a local goetta fest.

Scream In, went off the air at the end of the 1970s, but Von Hoene continued his public persona by reprising his *Cool Ghoul* character occasionally on television and for charitable events. He rarely, if ever, charged for his appearances.

A local affairs television program, "Insight Cable," employed Von Hoene as a news anchor, reporter, and talk show host for *Northern Kentucky Magazine*. Guests on his show included Chubby Checker, Cloris Leachman, Dean Jones, and Judy Collins. He worked until his untimely death in 2004 of an apparent heart attack. So beloved was *The Cool Ghoul* that a 30-minute tribute to his life and work was broadcast on local television.

Von Hoene now rests peacefully on a public lot in Spring Grove. No one would ever know that *The Cool Ghoul* is buried there. There are no carved ghouls on his marker, no mention of his work on television, and no mention of his induction into Ripley's Believe it or Not Horror Host Hall of Fame in 2011. But every Halloween, a lone pumpkin is mysteriously placed on his gravesite, memorializing not only a man who was a cool ghoul, but also a true humanitarian.

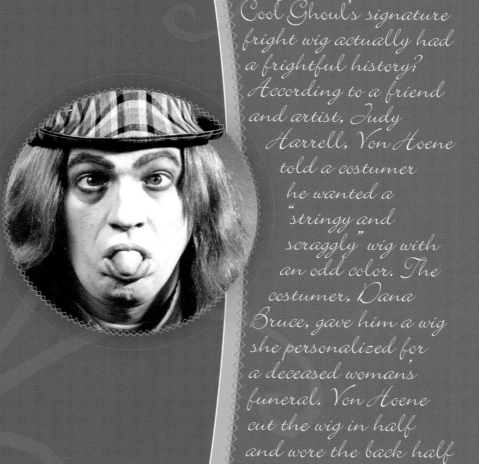

Did you know that The Cool Ghoul's signature fright wig actually had a frightful history? According to a friend and artist, Judy Harrell, Von Hoene told a costumer he wanted a "stringy and scraggly" wig with an odd color. The costumer, Dana Bruce, gave him a wig she personalized for a deceased woman's funeral. Von Hoene cut the wig in half and wore the back half during his entire career as The Cool Ghoul.

◇ The Cool Ghoul aka Dick Von Hoene.

LAST WORDS

Strauch, Adolph (1822-1883)

◦ ◇ ◦

IT'S IRONIC, AND APROPOS, that the final story I write for *Stories in the Grove* involves Spring Grove's master landscaper, Adolph Strauch. There wouldn't be a book if there hadn't been the genius and ambition of Adolph Strauch, and I wouldn't be the person I am today without the Strauch family.

This story begins with an unexpected phone call in the summer of 2006 from Cassie Eckhardt, a descendant of Strauch living in St. Louis. She introduced herself as the great-great granddaughter of Adolph Strauch. A Strauch family funeral was taking place the following week on the family's island in Spring Grove.

It's true, Strauch Island is owned by the family. It's located in one of fifteen lakes in the cemetery. It's no wonder the family owns the island. Adolph Strauch changed the cemetery landscape, making it the landmark it is today. He was a genius. I couldn't believe I was talking to a living descendant of Adolph Strauch. "You're Spring Grove royalty!" I exclaimed.

In the late 1850's, Adolph Strauch transformed Spring Grove into the first landscaped lawn-designed cemetery in America. His vision revolutionized the design of cemeteries across the world. Strauch "de-cluttered" Victorian-era cemeteries- no more lot fencing, multiple upright markers on private lots, and no more benches. Before coming to America, he was master gardener for both the Hapsburg Imperial gardens in Vienna and the Royal Gardens in London. Strauch established an impressive reputation before "accidentally" coming to Cincinnati.

In the mid-1850s, Strauch visited America. He started in Texas, then traveled to Niagara Falls. During a stopover in Cincinnati, Strauch missed his connection. He had a calling card given by Robert Bowler of Cincinnati after Bowler requested an impromptu tour of London's royal gardens. As luck would have it, Strauch remembered Bowler's card. Bowler was the president of the Kentucky Central Railroad and owned a dry goods business. He lived on an estate called Mt. Storm; one of many baronial estates in the Clifton suburb of Cincinnati. Bowler yearned for more manicured, refined grounds at Mt. Storm, and convinced Strauch to remain in Cincinnati to landscape his property. Bowler's neighbors witnessed Mt. Storm's transformation, and hired Strauch to give their homes European-style landscapes. Strauch quickly became a success in Cincinnati!

Strauch landscaped Cincinnati's beautiful Eden Park, Burnet Woods, the northern Cincinnati suburb of Glendale, and other locations in the area. Spring Grove hired Strauch to be the master landscaper in 1854, and on October 16, 1860, he became the Superintendent of Spring Grove. Although recognized nationally, Strauch immediately noticed the clutter that plagued the cemetery, so he designed a new plan of design. He imagined open vistas and fantastic views by clearing the lot fencing and other extraneous objects, including cast iron animals, wire settees, and trellises.

The master himself, Adolph Strauch.

His revolutionary design removed expensive lot fencing and other clutter. He convinced lot owners to remove the clutter through a combination of "consolation" plot markers and persuasion. Within 7 years, Strauch managed to rid the cemetery of all fencing. Considering a significant number of family lots were fenced in, Strauch's achievement is remarkable. Strauch became the most famous and influential cemetery landscaper in America. Other cemeteries sought his advice and service, including nearby Greenwood Cemetery in Hamilton, Ohio, to Forest Lawn Cemetery in Buffalo, New York.

Against his own landscaped lawn plan, Strauch quietly planned for an Egyptian pyramid on his burial site, modeled after the grandiose pyramid on the burial site of his mentor, Hermann von Pueckler, in Germany's Muskau Park. The only evidence of the pyramid-plan is a hand-drawn illustration on an archival map of Spring Grove Cemetery.

As significant and remarkable as Adolph Strauch's story is, it's my chance meeting with his great-great granddaughter in the cemetery that has inspired me most. When Cassie made the first phone call to me in 2006, I knew I was meeting a very special person; not only was I meeting "Strauch royalty," I was fascinated by the spiritual energy surrounding her and the family.

◇

Cassie initially asked if I would give the family a tram tour following the funeral service. Reluctantly, I said yes, thinking it odd to give a tour after a funeral. A few days after the first phone call, Cassie called again; this time, she asked if the former lead horticulturist, Whitney Huang, and I would actually attend the service with the family. Now I was nervous- I was going to be surrounded by Spring Grove royalty!

The day of the funeral was surreal with perfect weather. The family was solemn, but they were proud of what their ancestor accomplished. It was a small gathering that walked slowly over the stone bridge onto the island. Then it happened, as if the cemetery were honoring the Strauchs. Two swans appeared on the lake, and birds gathering to witness the service. The turtles emerged from the water. It was like a scene from a movie: magical, surreal, and spiritual.

Strauch died in 1883 in his home from pneumonia, on the property of his beloved Spring Grove Cemetery, but even today you can see his hand guiding the fortunes of Spring Grove. Noted writer Henry Howe aptly said Strauch's landscapes were "lovely as a dream." Adolph Strauch was indeed Spring Grove's *dream maker*.

Sources:

Crouch, Tom D. "Up, Up and-Sometimes-Away." The Cincinnati Historical Society Bulletin. Vol 28 Summer 1970 No.2. Print.

Eckhardt, Cassie. Personal interviews and correspondence. 2006-2013.

Howe, Henry. *Historical Collections of Ohio.* Norwalk, Ohio: The Laning Printing Co., 1896. Print.

Linden, Blanch M. G. *Spring Grove: Celebrating 150 Years.* Cincinnati: Cincinnati Historical Society, 1995. Print.

Rattermann, H. A. Don Heinrich Tolzmann, ed. *Spring Grove and its Creator: H. A. Rattermann's Biography of Adolph Strauch.* Cincinnati: The Ohio Book Store, 1988. Print.

Strauch, Adolphus. *Spring Grove Cemetery: Its History and Improvements, with observations on Ancient and Modern Places of Sepulture.* Cincinnati: Robert Clarke & Co., 1869. Print.

In September of 1855, another noted aeronaut from France, Eugene Godard, made a "grand and novel Balloon Voyage" over Spring Grove with Madame Godard.

"While scanning the city from this point, it presented in shape the appearance of a huge frog, with its hind legs distended. The Cemetery grounds had the appearance of a ribbon, shaped something like the "true-lovers knot," and the country round teemed with villages and avenues as adjuncts to the great Queen City." John Wise, aeronaut, while flying over Spring Grove Cemetery on October 9, 1851.

Immortal and Perpetual Words

◦ ◇ ◦

WHEN I'M NOT RESEARCHING NEW MONUMENTS or sleuthing new stories, I study epitaphs—the final commemorative words inscribed on the memorials of Spring Grove residents. Some are funny, and others are melancholic. Whether happy or sad, the words give us glimpses into the stories of Spring Grove residents.

In Adolph Strauch's biography, by H. A. Ratterman, Strauch states a proper epitaph, "should be plain and simple. This will be best given in the beautiful language of Wordsworth: 'An epitaph is not a proud writing shut up for the studious; it is exposed to all—to the wise and the most ignorant; it is condescending, and lovingly solicits regard; its story and admonitions are brief, that the thoughtless, the busy, and the indolent may not be deterred. Not the impatient tired. The stooping old man cons the engraven [sic] record like a second horn-book [a primer for study]; the child is proud that he can read it, and the stranger is introduced by its meditation to the company of a friend—it is concerning all, and for all.'"

"An inscription for the dead," says another eminent writer, "should be simple in style, sparing words, modest in eulogy. The long and labored epitaph is seldom read. Glowing encomiums are received with distrust. Excessive praise, fulsome always, seems especially so when heaped on the dead. These are principles generally acknowledged—though, in practice, so often disregarded. Resignation and calmness are to be expected in a Christian epitaph, but coldness and studied effect are inconsistent with sepulchral mention."

I've collected a few of the parting words that have made me laugh, weep, and remember the souls they were intended to honor.

War-related Epitaphs

◦ ◇ ◦

- "Daughter of a Revolutionary Soldier." (Lucinda Woods, 1898)
- The Ohio 5th Voluntary Infantry monument, erected in 1895 by the regiment's survivors, commemorates the soldiers who fought for the 5th Ohio Volunteer Infantry Regiment during the Civil War serving the Union Army from 1861 to 1865. The epitaphs read: "In memory of the dead of the 5th Regt. Ohio Vol. Infantry. Total enrollment 1,871 men mustered for 3 mos. April 20, 1861. Remustered for 3 Yrs. June 19, 1861. Veteranized Jan. 23, 1864, mustered out of U.S. service, July 26, 1865 with 213 men. Erected by surviving comrades, A.D. 1895. A bronze owl plaque on the monument reads: "Boys keep the Colors up."
- "Served in War of 1812. Died. Universally regretted for his many virtues." (Major William Stanley, 1814)
- "Fell at Stone River Dec. 31, 1862." (Albert G. Williams died in 1862 from wounds received in battle in Tennessee).
- "Born Nov. 28, 1831, died at Great Mountain Pass, July 19, 1861, of wounds received while scouting." (William D. Gault, 1861)
- "Marched out of Camp Benson, August, 1862. Drum corps playing, 'The Girls I left Behind Me.' " (Isaac Stokes, 1852)
- "If he was as good as he was a soldier, you must be proud of such a boy. Captain N. E. Symmes, 110th O.V.I. wounded at Battle of Cedar Mountain, 1862." (John T. Coverdale, 1862)
- "Jonathan Mullen, Jr., Co. H. 23 KY. Infantry USA. Fell at the Battle of Chickamauga on his 25th birthday, Sept. 19, 1863."
- "In memory of Cornelius R. Sedam who died May 9, 1823 in the 64th year of his age. He emigrated to the West in the year 1791 and was the first to clear and settle upon the land on which his remains now rest. He was a Col. in the United States Army and served with Washington, Harmer, St. Claire, and Wayne. He was also a member of the Hon. Cincinnati Society. As a man he was a warm and fast friend, a zealous Christian, and honest man.

His sons erect this monument to his memory. This monument and remains removed from the family burying ground at Sedams-ville, by the great-great grandchildren, January 1916."

Isn't That Sweet?

◦ ◇ ◦

Even auto buffs are memorialized in stone.

- Belle Zopff's modest footstone simply exemplifies love as her name is spelled in tiny carved hearts in granite. Belle was born in Manchester, Ohio, in 1884 and died in 1927 at age 43 from leukemia in Des Moines, Iowa.
- "Born in London England, Jan 18, 1801. Fell asleep, September 23, 1872."
- "Only God knows how we miss her." (Chunkie Singleton, 1872)
- "I Am Not Alone." (Edward C. Roll, 1896)
- "Heaven may never be the same." (Dossie Upson, 1993)
- "The force be with you...always." (Douglas E. Mize, 1995)
- "If I...can help one fainting robin onto his nest again I shall not live in vain." (Doris Bars Hall)
- "She went home." (Alzina Green)
- "Beneath a sleeping infant lies, to earth its body is lent, more glorious shall hereafter rise, tho not more innocent. When the arch angels trump shall blow, and souls to bodies join, millions will wish their lives below had been as short as thine." (William Baker, 1829)

GRANDMA
SHE HATH DONE
WHAT SHE COULD

As only grandmother's can.

- "Too soon in youth, death drew me to a cool grave. How harsh to be parted from you, my parents! Rash work undid me. But weep not. Now I see a better light." (Christian Berne, Jr., 1861)
- "She hath done what she could." (Dorothea Woehrman, 1898)
- "A child wife and mother of whom the world was not worthy." (Mary Ann Boyd, 1845)
- "He was a man, take him for all. I shall not look upon his like again." (Actor James E. Murdock, 1893)
- "He being dead yet speaketh. Meet me Papa, Mama, and Frank. Meet me in Heaven." (Miller Huggins, 1929)
- "I miss thee from our home, Fannie. I miss thy winning face, I miss thy kind and willing hands, I miss thee every place." (Fannie H. Wise)
- "Love-ya!" (Mary Ann McCullough, 1996)
- "Meta Louise Siegrist, there is always sunshine here. 1905-1933."
- "A little bud of love to bloom with God above." (Dorothy M. Short, 1923)
- "Forever and ever, do not stand at her grave and weep. She is not there, she does not sleep. She is a thousand winds that blow. She is the diamond glints on the snow. She is the sun-ripened grain, she is the gentle autumn rain. When you awaken in the morning's hush, she is the swift, uplifting rush of quiet birds in circled flight. She is the soft stars that shine at night.
  Do not stand at her grave and cry, she is not there. For with the Lord, she is every-where." (Stuart Chantilas, 1998)
- "Living in greener pastures." (Leona M. Workman, 1987)
- "She's an eagle when she flies safely home." (Connie S. Honchell Strobel, 1993)
- "Teach me to live that I may dread, the grave as little as a bed." (Landon Rivers, 1868)
- "I am happy." (William Solomon, 1888)

Catrice clearly loved bingo.

- "I love you." (Frank D. Brockell, 1990)
- "I love you too." (Hilda Mae Brockell, 1976)
- "Death only makes a ripple when the bubble of life bursts." (R. Bissel, 1885)
- "If we could sit across the porch from God, we would thank Him for lending us to you." (Jason Faris, 1986)
- "In memory of our dear children. Their star went down in beaut and it shineth sweetly now in the bright and glorious diadem that decks the saviour's brow." (William Box, 1896)
- "Only sleeping." (Anna D. Pannell, 1945)
- "She was lovely." (Marcella Pochat, 1954)
- "Let it be said of me, 'She tried.' Let it be said of her children, 'She did.'" (John Wright McCracken)
- "When she had passed, it seemed like the ceasing of exquisite music." (Mabel Grace Opplinger, 1953)
- "Just away." (Charleen L. Reed, 1933)
- "Preaching by the roadside." (Della Spencer, 1982)
- "Thanks for stopping by. Live, Laugh, Love." (Sherwood "Woody" B. Faison Jr., 1985)
- "You weren't my mother, but I was your little girl." (Mattie Webb, 1986)
- "I burned my candle at both ends; it did not last the night. But ah, my foes, and oh, my friends, it gave a lovely light!" (Lawrence C. Coates, 1931)

Tragedy and Sorrow

- "Afflictions some four months he bore, physicians were in vain. 'Till God was pleased by death to last and ease him of his pain.'" (John S. Shillito)
- "Sacred to the memory of Wm. K. Merrill who was drowned in the Ohio River at Cincinnati, June 16, 1848, aged 17 years and 4 months. A kind and dutiful son and affectionate brother. His exemplary conduct was equaled by few and excelled by none. He cometh forth like a flower and is cut down.

He fleeth also as a shadow and continueth not."

- "Gone in the morning and there is no night there."
- "Died at the burning of the Pacific Hotel, St. Louis Mo., Feb. 20, 1858." (Ammi Lord, 1858)
- "Thomas Mason, a native of Montpelier, Maryland, who died amoung strangers in Cincinnati, July 23, 1855. Aged 32 yrs, 8 days. A generous heart, a cultivated mind, a friend sincere, and a brother true. Sleep beneath this silent grave." (Thomas Mason, 1855)
- "Sons of E. & J. Norton lost from off the steamer, *Memphis* on the Mississippi River, June 9, 1849." (Edmund and James L. Bepler, 1849)
- "William Worsham, died on board the steamer *Memphis* on August 11, 1858, aged 36 years."
- "Killed on the U.S. steamer, *Champion* on the Red River, April 27, 1864, aged 51 years." (David V. Stewart, 1864)
- "Died on the flag ship, *Tempest* at mound city Illinois, on June 15, 1865." (Benjamin F. Baker, 1865)
- "Abraham B. Hart died from effects of a railroad accident in Philadelphia on February 5, 1856."
- "Here lie the remains of John Broadfoot Smyth who was delivered from a polluted and polluting world." (1837)
- "Died by collision of steamers, *Danube* & *McFarland* in 1839." (John W. Keely, 1839)
- "J.W. Meal born February 6, 1822. Killed on his plantation in Arkansas while writing at his desk by an unknown assassin, March 23, 1868."
- "Lost at sea, Henry Powell, 1821-1888."
- "Our Helen and Harry, Au Revoir." (1906)

A simple tribute of love.

- "In memory of Robert H., son of James and Hannah B. Cross. Drowned in the Ohio River of Cincinnati on August 4, 1849. 13 years, 5 months, and 16 days."

The Last Laugh

◇

- One shocking epitaph was a mystery when it was first seen on a newly placed headstone. Irreverent? Perhaps. But the truth of the matter is, it was done in jest. A family member reported that the wife was born on Halloween so of course, witches are iconic with the holiday. Her epitaph reads: "Ding dong, the witch is dead," and beneath is a depiction of a witch riding a broom. That pretty much explains the witch reference. On the opposite side of the marker is an even more shocking symbol and epitaph; a hand gesture depicting a peace sign and the words, "Read between the lines." But I'm happy to report that the gesture was not meant as an insult to the husband. Turns out he received much joy from sitting on his front porch, giving passerby's the "gesture."

- "The nurseryman stood at the golden gate. His head was bent and low. He merely asked the man of fate which way he ought to go. 'What have you done?' St. Peter said, 'To seek admittance here.' 'I ran a nursery down on earth for many and many a year.' St. Peter opened wide the gate and gently pressed the bell. 'Come in,' he said, 'and choose your harp. You've had your share of hell.'" by Euonymus. (Edwin "Bud" Tepe, 1985)

A shocking yet humorous headstone.

◇ Richard Renneker was a doctor with a good sense of humor.

- "I rest my case." (Walter S. Houston II, 1979)
- "Gone fishing." (Charles Phelps Taft, 1983)
- "Pilot" (Thomas Noonan, 1993)
- "Co-Pilot" (Dorothea H. Noonan, 1969)
- "Come and see me in my new home." (Earlene Knell)
- "Promoted July 29, 1916." (Mrs. Major Sprak, 1916)
- "Takin' care of business." (Charleen L. Reed, 1933
- "That's all." (Ray J. Niesen, 1987)
- My all-time favorite epitaph is for Dr. Richard E. Renneker, who died in 1995. At the top-center of his simple footstone is his name, birth, and death date. There is a small asterisk by his middle initial. In the lower left corner is the matching asterisk which reads: "See other side."

Sources Cited

◇

"Acquitted of Murder." *Times Recorder.* Zanesville, Ohio. October 11, 1927.

Acts of the Legislature of West Virginia, at its Eighteenth Session. Wheeling: James B. Tanney, Public Printer, 1885.

"AGS Field Guide No. 8: Symbolism in the Carving on Gravestones." The Association for Gravestone Studies. Greenfield, MA: The Association of Graveyard Studies, 2003.

"Albert William Body". *New York Times.* October 18, 1928.

"Alleged Violators of Dry Laws before Court." *Indianapolis Star.* November 25, 1920.

Allen, Lee. "The Saga of Cincinnati's Charlie Grant." *Cincinnati Times*-Star. November 2, 1957.

"Alexander McDonald." *New York Times.* March 20, 1910.

Amnéus, Cynthia. *A Separate Sphere: Dressmakers in Cincinnati's Golden Age, 1877-1922.* Lubock: Texas Tech University Press. 2003.

"An American Sculptor-Louise Lawson." *The Daily Graphic, New York.* March 15. 1889.

Andrew, Karen. "Edwin McClure, 87, WWII veteran: Helped develop the U.S. ZIP code.". *Cincinnati Enquirer.* April 5, 2004.

_____. "Ruby W. Rapp, 90, radio, TV personality." *Cincinnati Enquirer.* March 22, 2004.

Arboretum. Cincinnati: Cincinnati Historical Society, 1995.

Archambeault, Mary. "Debunking Cincinnati-The Stories behind the Stories." http://archinbolt.wordpress.com

Architectural Foundation of Cincinnati. "Pedretti Family." http://www.architecturecincy.org

Arnold's Bar and Grill. Androski,

Ronda & Brett. "History". www.arnoldsbarandgrill.com.

"Art and Artists Abroad: The Return of Miss Louise Lawson." *New York Times.* October 18, 1887.

The Art of Restoration. "Case History-John Robinson's Circus-Congo." http://theartofrestoration.com

"Auto Hearses Will Soon Be Seen Here as Automobiles are Now Permitted in Spring Grove Cemetery." *Cincinnati Enquirer* April 28, 1911.

Backes, Karen. "Tony Sarge." *TC Puppet Monitor.* Spring, 1998. http://www.tcpuppet.org

Bahra, Peter J. "Refreshing Enjoyment, Healthful Excitement: Early Bicycling in Cincinnati." *Queen City Heritage.* Spring, 1996.

Ballard, Sarah. "Fabric of the Game: The Baseball Uniform Has a History as Colorful as the Players who have worn it." *Sports Illustrated.* April 5, 1989.

Bannon, Anthony. "Photography Changes What Tourists Want to See." http://click.si.edu.

Baptist Heritage. "Ohio Baptist Sites." http://www.baptistheritage.com

Bartlett, John Russell. *Dictionary of Americanisms-A Glossary of Words and Phrases Usually Regarded as Peculiar to the United States.* Second ed. Boston: Little, Brown and Company, 1859.

Baseball Reference. "Miller Huggins." http://www.baseball-reference.com.

Billman, Rebecca. Lenore Wingard obituary. *Cincinnati Enquirer.* February 12, 2000.

Bills, Sheryl. "After a Lifetime of Lonely Shadows, Teacher Basks in Death's Warm Sunlight." *Cincinnati Enquirer.* 1969.

The Biographical Encyclopedia of Ohio of the Nineteenth Century. Cincinnati: Galaxy Publishing Co., 1876.

The Biography Channel. "George Reeves. http://www.biography.com.

Birnbaum, Charles. "1810-1865 John Notman." The Cultural Landscape Foundation. http://tclf.org.

Bliss, D. W. "The Story of President Garfield's Illness." *Century* Magazine. 1881.

Blount, Jim. "Butler County Biographies." Hamilton, Ohio: Past/Present/Press, 2001.

_____. *Little Chicago: A History of the Prohibition Era in Hamilton and Butler County, Ohio.* Past/Present/Press 1997.

Bogler, Doreen, and others. *In Pursuit of Beauty: Americans and the Aesthetic Movement.* New York: Metropolitan Museum of Art, 1986.

Bonanos, Christopher. "Zooming Twenties: Tony Sarg's Busy, Busy New York." New York Magazine. http//nymag.com

Bottomley, M.E. *The Art of Home Landscape.* New York: A.T. DeLaMare Company, Inc., 1935.

Brian McKenna. "Miller Huggins, Outside the Majors." Baseball Fever. http://www.baseball-fever.com.

Brown, Ellen. "Monumental Tales." *Cincinnati Magazine.* September, 1976.

Brown, Thomas Allston. *A History of the New York Stage from the First Performance in 1732 to 1901.* New York: Dodd, Mead and Company, 1903.

Burnham, Patricia and others. *Montana's State Capitol: The People's House.* Montana Historical Society Press, 2002.

Burrage, Henry S. *Baptist Hymn Writers and Their Hymns.* Portland, Maine: Brown Thurston & Co. 1888.

"Business Vs. Politics." *New York Times.* November 13, 1898.

Calos, Katherine. "Sword found its way back." *Richmond Times-Dispatch.* July 17, 2011.

Campbell, Polly. "Arnold's a landmark for 150 years." *Cincinnati Enquirer.* March 2, 2011.

Causeway Costal Route . "How the Giant's Causeway was Formed.". 2008. http://www.causewaycoastalroute.com.

"Cemetery Notice." *The Gazette.* June 18, 1878.

"A Change of Mistresses." *The National Police Gazette: New York.* August 21, 1880.

Chilton, John. *Let the Good Times Roll: The Story of Louis Jordan and His Music.* University of Michigan Press, 1997.

Christ Church Cincinnati. "History & Traditions- In the Beginning." http://christchurchcincinnati.org.

Cincinnati Art Museum. "Discovering the Story: A City and Its Culture." http://www.discoveringthestory.com.

Cincinnati Caledonian Pipes and Drums Band. "Cincinnati Caledonian Pipes and Drums Band history" http://www.cincypipesanddrums.org.

Cincinnati Historical Society Library and Archives "Theodore M. Berry." http://library.cincymuseum.org.

"Cincinnati Letter." *The St. Louis Lumberman.* July 1, 1909.

"Cincinnati's Charlie Grant." *Cincinnati Enquirer.* March 11, 1901.

"Cincinnati's Rich Men." *New York Times.* December 10, 1880.

Cincinnati: The Queen City, 1788-1912. Chicago-Cincinnati: Clarke, S.J. Publishing Company, 1912.

Cincinnati 1781-1943, WPA Guide. Cincinnati: Cincinnati Historical Society, 1987.

"Cincinnati Woman Leaves $42,000 to Former Employee." *Cincinnati Times-Star.* April 25, 1949.

Clipson, Addison J. "The Caledonian Society of Cincinnati: A History from 1827 to 1977." Caledonian Society. http://www.caledoniansociety.org.

Civil War Trust "Joseph Hooker Major General November 13, 1814-October

31, 1879." http://www.civilwar.org.

Coachbilt. "C. Ahreds & Co. 1868-1891-American Fire Engine Co." http://www.coachbuilt.com.

Coffin, Levi. *Reminiscences of Levi Coffin, the Reputed President of the Underground Railroad.* Second ed. Cincinnati: Robert Clarke & Co., 1880.

Comley, W.J. and W. D'eggville, M.D. *Ohio, the Future Great State: Her Manufacturers, and a History of Her Commercial Cities.* Cincinnati and Cleveland: Comley Brothers Manufacturing and Publishing Company, 1875.

Coney Island Park. "Sunlight Pool." *Coney Island Cincinnati-Sunlight Pool.* http://www.coneyislandpark.com/sunlight_pool.php.

Connecticut Women's Hall of Fame. "Evelyn Longman Batchelder." http://cwhf.org.

Cook, William A. *King of the Bootleggers: A Biography of George Remus."* McFarland Publishing, 2008.

"Coroner Blames Coroner." *Cincinnati Enquirer."* June 7, 1943.

Cunningham, Mia. *Anna Hubbard: Out of the Shadows.* Lexington, Kentucky: The University Press of Kentucky, 2001.

"Curious Effects of a Brain-Injury." *Popular Science.* September, 1872.

"Daguerreotype View of Cincinnati." http://www.codex99.com.

"Dardanella Writer is Killed by Blow." *New York Times.* June 10, 1936.

Day, Michele. "Carving a history." *Cincinnati Enquirer.* May 17, 2003.

Derdak, Thomas and Lisa Mirabile. *International Directory of Company Histories,* Vol. 2. St. James Press, 1990.

Doane, Kathleen. "Chester Park was once city's top entertainment destination." *Cincinnati Enquirer.* September 2, 2012.

_____. "Family Matters." *Cincinnati Art Museum Member Magazine-* Spring/Summer 2012. Cincinnati Art Museum.

_____. "Spring Grove's park-like design met original vision." *Cincinnati Enquirer.* http://cincinnati.com.

Dodge, Andrew R. and Betty K. Koed. *Biographical Dictionary of the United States Congress, 1774-2005.* Government Printing Office, 2005.

Don't Fence Me In. Music by Cole Porter. Lyrics by Robert Fletcher and Cole Porter. 1934.

"Dr. Leland Clark, Brilliant Researcher." *Cincinnati Post.* September 27, 2005.

The Dragonfly. Cincinnati Art Club (newsletter). Spring Grove archives.

Drew, Chris. "The Cincinnati Red Stockings: The Team That Shaped Modern Baseball." Society for Cincinnati Sports Research.

Durrell, Lucile. *Memories of E. Lucy Braun.* Ohio Biological Survey: Biological Notes No. 15. Cincinnati: Stucky & Reese, 1981.

Dyer, Mike. "Legend is loud and clear." *Cincinnati Enquirer.* May 13, 2012.

"Egyptian Pyramid Covering Cemetery Lot Asked in Will." *Cincinnati Times Star.* February 2, 1949.

Eliason, Norman Ellsworth. *Tarheel Talk; and Historical Study of the English Language in North Carolina to 1860.* Chapel Hill: University of North Carolina Press, 1956.

Ellard, Harry. *Base Ball in Cincinnati: a History by Harry Ellard.* Cincinnati: Press of Johnson & Hardin, 1907.

"Emerson Kemsies," *Ohio Journal of Science,* July, 1971. http://hdl.handle.net.

Erwin, Paul F. "Scottish Gypsies and their Burial Customs: Facts and Folklore." *Urban Resources- Vol. 4, No.3, Spring 1987.* Cincinnati: Metropolitan Services, 1987.

"Experts shed light on clans." *Cincinnati Post.* February 26, 2002.

"Factory to Use Checks to Frustrate Bandits." *The Lima News.* August 2, 1928.

"Fair Norwood Archer National Champion." *The Cincinnati Enquirer.* September 23, 1904.

Farmer, Russell. "The Lunkenheimer Co., Part. 2." http://gasengine.farmcollector.com.

"Farny paintings to be exhibited in restored Indian Hill school." *Hamilton Journal News.* June 19, 1975.

Fein, Zachery. "Geology of the Cincinnati Area-Compiled Reports, Spring, 2008." Zachery Fein. http://zfein.com.

"50 Years Ago in Cincinnati: March 5, 1893." *Cincinnati Enquirer.* March 5, 1943.

"The Fighting McCook's." *Carrollcountyohio.com.* Carroll County Ohio History. http://www.carrollcountyohio.com.

Fischer, Henry Albert. "Henry (Albert) Fischer's Partial Autobiography." ca 1908.

Fisher, Linda A. and Carrie Bowers. *Agnes Lake Hickok: Queen of the Circus, Wife of a Legend.* Norman, OK: University of Oklahoma Press, 2009.

Fleischman, John. "This is Cincinnati in 1848. Fascinated Yet?" *Cincinnati Magazine.* May, 2011.

Ford, Henry A. and Kate B. Ford. *History of Cincinnati, Ohio with illustrations and biographical sketches."* L.A. Williams & Co., 1881.

Fowler, Elizabeth J. "Kitaro Shirayamadani and the Creation of Japanese Rookwood." *American Ceramic Journal Rookwood.* Brooklyn, NY: The American Ceramic Circle, 2006.

_____. "Kitaro Shirayamadani, Japanism, Art Nouveau, and the American Pottery Movement, 1885-1912." Ph.D. dissertation. University of Minnesota, 2005.

"The Fritz J. and Dolores H. Russ Prize." *Ohio University Magazine.* March 28, 2013, http://www.ohio.edu

Fuentes, Dave. "Horror Host Hall of Fame: The Cool Ghoul!" http://terrordaves.com.

Funding Universe. "History of Drackett Professional Products." http://www.fundinguniverse.com.

Gagel, Diane VanSkiver. *Ohio Photographers 1839-1900.* Nevada City, CA: Carl Mautz Publishing, 1998.

Gallico, Paul. *Olympic Pool.* July 28, 1934.

"Gang Suspect Killed by Cop." *Newark Advocate.* June 11, 1929.

"Garden Sanctuary Lawn Crypt sculptures." Spring Grove brochure. Cincinnati: Spring Grove Cemetery & Arboretum, 1976.

Garraty, John Arthur and Jerome L. Sternstein, ed. *National Cyclopedia of American Biography.* New York: Harper & Row, 1974

"German Red Cross is to Benefit From Luedeking $515,000 Estate." *Cincinnati Times-Star.* May, 11 1939.

Giffin, William Wayne. *African Americans and the Color Line in Ohio, 1915-1930.* Ohio State University Press, 2005.

Girdwood, Charles. "Blackpool Tower Ballroom Wurlitzer." http://www.girdwood.co.uk.

Glenn, Alex E. *The Ark, and the Odd Fellows' Magazine.* January, 1848.

Golden, James T. Jr. "Monument Marks Grave, But Actress's Body's Small Card Reveals Real Burial Place." *Cincinnati Enquirer.*

"Golden Wedding Anniversary." *Cincinnati Enquirer.* June 2, 1901.

Goodman, Rebecca. "Cleon Wingard helped neediest". *Cincinnati Enquirer.* April 15, 2005.

_____. "Charles L. de Rohan, 80, aristocrat, doted on kids." *Cincinnati Enquirer.* March 5, 2005.

_____. "Leland Clark created devices that save lives." *Cincinnati Enquirer.* September 27. 2005

Goshorn, Alfred Traber. *Literary Symposium on Cincinnati.* Cincinnati: Robert Clark & Company, 1888.

Goss, Charles Frederic. *Cincinnati, the Queen City, 1788-1912.* Cincinnati: S. J. Clarke Publishing Company, 1912.

Gowan, Phillip and Homer Thiel. Ed. Hind, Philip. "RMS Titanic facts and history." *Encyclopedia Titanica.* http://www.encyclopedia-titanica.org.

Grace, Kevin. *Legendary Locals of Cincinnati.* Charleston, South Carolina: Arcadia Publishing, 2012.

Grant, Tina. *International Directory of Company Histories.* Volume 65. St. James, MO: St. James Press, 2004.

Greater Cincinnati Police History Society "Special Police Officer Armstrong Chumley." http://www.gcphs.com.

Grebe, James. "The Wurlitzer Piano Company-Grebe Piano." Yesterday Once More Publications. http://www.grebepiano.com.

Greve, Charles Theodore. *Centennial History of Cincinnati and Representative Citizens.* Vol. 1. Chicago: Biographical Publishing Company, 1904.

Grob, Dave. "Rare Uniforms on the Auction Block." Mears Memorabilia. http://www.mearsonline.com.

Gulley, Frank. "Odd Fellow Memorial." *I.O.O.F. Newsletter.* 1993.

Guschov, Stephen D. *The Red Stockings of Cincinnati: Base Ball's First All-Professional Team and its Historic 1869 and 1870 Seasons.* Jefferson, North Carolina: McFarland & Company, 1998.

Hall, Jacob Henry. "Dr. W.H. Doane: Composer of Hymns." *Biography of Gospel Song and Hymn Writers."* New York: Fleming H. Revell. 1914.

Hamilton County Ohio Exploration Society. "Hamilton County Hauntings and Legends.". http://www.ohioexploration.com.

Hannavy, John, ed *Encyclopedia of American Photography.* Routledge-Taylor & Francis Group: New York, 2007.

_____. "Porter, William Southgate (1822-1889)." *The Encyclopedia of Nineteenth Century Photography, vol. II.* New York: Routledge Reference. 2008.

Hart, Albert Bushnell. *American Statesman:*

Salmon Portland Chase. Boston: The Riverside Press, 1899.

Hass, Ed. "Schacht Cars and Trucks: Made in Cincinnati, Oh 1904-1940." http//www.oocities.org.

Haverstock, Mary and others. *Artists in Ohio-1787-1900. A Biographical Dictionary.* Kent State University Press, 2000.

Heer, Fred. J. *Ohio archeological and historical publications: Ohio History,* Ohio Historical Society, 1908.

Hehman, Maureen. "The Last Will and Testament of Ruth Hooke." *Cincinnati Enquirer Magazine.* March 10, 1974.

"Helen May Young Dies at 90; Led First All-Woman Brass Band.". *Cincinnati Post.* June 17, 1957.

Henderson, Metta Lou and Dennis B. Worthen. "Cora Dow (1868-1915)-Pharmacist, Entrepreneur, Philanthropist." Cincinnati: Lloyd Library and Museum. *Lloyd Library.org.* http://www.lloydlibrary.org.

Herbert, Walter H. "Joseph Hooker Biography." http://www.civilwarhome.com.

Herrick, Cindy. "Rich in History." *Clifton Chronicle.*

Herz, Walter. "Sarah Otis Ernst." *Dictionary of Unitarian & Universalist Biography.* Unitarian Universalist Association. http://www25.uua.org.

_____. "Influence Transcending Mere Numbers: The Unitarians In Nineteenth Century Cincinnati." *Queen City Heritage,* Winter, 1993.

"Highlights of the May Calendar- (Garden Club of America)." *New York Times.* May 1, 1966.

Hillforest Historic House Museum. "Hillforest History." http://hillforest.org.

Hillman, Charles. "The Genealogy of the Brisbane Family in South Carolina." http://www.hillmanc.fsnet.co.uk

Historical Society of Pennsylvania.

"Complimentary dinner to Alfred T. Goshorn, Cincinnati, April 4, 1877." http://discover.hsp.org

"History." Koh-i-noor Hardtmuth A.S. http://www.koh-i-noor.cz

Holden, Craig. *The Jazz Bird*. New York: Simon & Schuster, Inc., 2001.

"Holds 7 worlds Records." *Life* (magazine ad). July 19, 1937.

Honey Bee Home. "Herman Suhre Monuments." http://67.55.50.201/honeybeehome

Horstman, Barry M. *100 Who Made a Difference: Greater Cincinnatians Who Made a Mark on the 20th Century*. Cincinnati: *Cincinnati Post*. 1999.

Hosea, Lewis M. *Cincinnati Superior Court Decisions*. Cincinnati: The W.H. Anderson Co., Law Publishers, 1907.

Hover, John Calvin, et al. *Memoirs of the Miami Valley. Vol. III*. Chicago: Robert O. Law Co., 1920.

"How a Woman Built Up a Million Dollar Business." *The Progressive Grocer. volume 1*. January, 1922.

Howe, Henry. *Historical Collections of Ohio an encyclopedia of the State: History Both General and Local*. State of Ohio, 1908.

Huffman, Barbara. "John Beatty Rebuilt Mike Fink." *Cincinnati Enquirer*. May 30, 2010. http://news.cincinnati.com

Hughes, Jon C. "The Short Life and Death of 'YE GIGLAMPZ'." *The Cincinnati Historical Society Bulletin*. Summer 1982.

Hunt, Tamara Robin. *Balloons Over Broadway-the true story of the puppeteer of Macy's Parade*. New York: Houghton Mifflen Harcourt Publishing Co., 2011.

"Hunted Slayer Found Shot to Death on Road." *Lima News*. May 17, 1928.

"Indian ball player secured by McGraw for Baltimore club." *Chicago Tribune*. March 24, 1901.

Indiana Memory Digital Collections. "A.E. Burkhardt & Co. Furs and Raw Skins Receipt c1870: Clark County Collections." http//cdm16066.contentdm.oclc.org

Ingham, John N. *Biographical Dictionary of American Business Leaders, vol. 2*. Westport, Connecticut: Greenwood Press, 1983.

"The inventive tradition." *Cincinnati Post*. December 17, 2003.

"It Has Served the Public 79 Years." *Cincinnati Times-Star*. April 25, 1940.

J.Paul Getty Museum "Platt D. Babbitt." http://www.getty.edu

Japan America Society of Greater Cincinnati. "Kitaro was Cincinnati's first and perhaps most famous Japanese resident." http://jasgc.org

"Japanese Marks-Shirayama Kitaro." http://www.waiapo.com

Jarvits, Janet. "Joy of Cooking: a listing of the American editions." http://www.cookbookjj.com

John Chapman obituary. *Fort Wayne Sentinel*. March 22, 1845.

"Johnny Appleseed: A Pioneer Hero." *Harper's New Monthly Magazine*. November, 1871.

Johnson, Maria Miro. "The 'Female Sousa' could really strike up her brass band." *Providence Sunday Journal*. May 30, 1993.

Jones, James O. Co. *Southern Ohio and Its Builders*. The Southern Ohio Biographical Association, 1927.

Jones, Robert Ralston. *Papers read before the Literary Club Historian's evening, 1921 and 1922*. Cincinnati, December 25, 1922.

Joy of Cooking. "All About Joy." http://www.thejoykitchen.com.

Kashner, Sam and Nancy Schoenberger. *Hollywood Kryptonite: The Bulldog, the Lady, and the Death of Superman*. St. Martin's Press, 1996.

Keating, Michael. *Cincinnati Enquirer Tristate Magazine*. August. 17, 1986.

Keister, Douglas. *Stories in Stone: A Field Guide to Cemetery Symbolism and Iconography*.

Layton, Utah: Gibbs Smith, 2004.

Kiesewetter, John. "Bob Braun Braun's Life at 70." *Cincinnati Enquirer*. April 20, 1999.

Kirwin, Liza. *Lists: To-dos, Illustrated Inventories, Collected Thoughts, and Other Artists.* Princeton Architectural Press, 2010.

Knippenberg, Jim. "TV era passes with Von Hoene." *Cincinnati Enquirer.* February 8, 2004.

Kraft, Joy. "From Orphaned Immigrant to Furrier Magnate." *Cincinnati Enquirer.* May 12, 2013.

Kranz, Cindy. "Rare vase goes for 36 grand." *Cincinnati Enquirer.* December 5, 2010.

Lamphier, Peg A. *Kate Chase & William Sprague: Politics and Gender in a Civil War Marriage.* Nebraska: University of Nebraska Press, 2003.

Langsam, Walter E. *Biographical Dictionary of Cincinnati Architects, 1788-1940.* Cincinnati: Architectural Foundation of Cincinnati, 2008.

Langsam, Walter E. and Alice Weston. *Great Houses of the Queen City.* Cincinnati Historical Society 1997.

Leading Manufacturers and Merchants of Cincinnati and Environs. New York, Boston, Cincinnati, & Chicago: International Publishing Co., 1886.

Leavitt, Michael Bennett. *Fifty Years in Theatrical Management.* New York: Broadway Publishing Company, 1912.

"Leon Van Loo." *Cincinnati Commercial Tribune.* January 15, 1907.

"Letter List." *The Billboard.* July 24, 1943.

Linden, Blanche M. G. *Spring Grove: Celebrating 150 Years.* Cincinnati: Spring Grove Cemetery & Arboretum, 1995.

Lindenmeyer, Kriste. "Views from the Life of Paul Briol: Cincinnati's Unconventional Photographer." *Queen City Heritage-The Journal of the Cincinnati Historical Society.* Vol. 47. No. 3. 1989.

Litscape. "The Origin of the Harp." http://www.litscape.com.

Lloyd, James B. *Lives of Mississippi Authors, 1817-1967.* University Press of Mississippi, 2009.

Loveland, Erma Jean and Robert S. Harding. "Helen May Butler Collection, 1898-1937." http://amhistory.si.edu/archives/d5261.htm.

Ludwig, Charles. *Levi Coffin and the Underground Railroad.* Wipf & Stock Publishers, 2004.

Lumber World. July 1, 1909. Chicago: Lumber World Publishing Co., 1909.

Mallon, Bill. "The 1904 Olympic Games: Results for All Competitors in All Events with Commentary." La84 Foundation. http://la84foundation.org.

"Man Implicated in Hiatt Murder Held for another Killing." *Times Recorder.* Zanesville, Ohio. August 13, 1927.

Martin, Douglas. Obituary for Robert A. Moon. *New York Times.* April 14, 2001.

_____. "Theodore Berry, Civil Rights Pioneer, Dies". *New York Times.* October 17, 2000.

Martin, Johnes. Abstract. "Archery, Romance and Elite Culture in England and Wales c. 1780-1840." Oxford, UK: Blackwell Publishing Ltd., 2004.

Maschmeier, Edward. "I Remember When." Spring Grove Bulletin. November, 1960.

McCay, Bob. "Going Out in Style." *Cincinnati Magazine.* April, 1978.

McClung, D. W. ed. "Albert Fischer Manufacturing Co., Canners and Can Makers." *The Centennial Anniversary of the City of Hamilton, Ohio.* 1892.

McGill. "The Ingall's Building." http://www.arch.mcgill.ca.

McLean, Jan Briol Chinnock. "What a Father!" *Queen City Heritage- The Journal of the Cincinnati Historical Society.* Vol. 47. No. 3. 1989.

Means, Howard. *Johnny Appleseed: The Man, the Myth, the American Story.* New York: Simon & Schuster, 2011.

"Melody and Oratory Unite." *Cincinnati*

Enquirer. January 16, 1916.

Merrill, Peter C. *German Immigrant Artists in America: A Biographical Dictionary.* Lanham, Maryland & London: The Scarecrow Press, Inc. 1997.

Mersman, Joseph J., ed. Linda A. Fisher. *The Whiskey Merchant's Diary: An Urban Life in the Emerging Midwest.* Athens, Ohio: Ohio University Press, 2007.

Meyer, Richard E. *Ethnicity and the American Cemetery.* University of Wisconsin: Popular Press, 1993.

"Miller Huggins Dies; Many Pay Tribute" *New York Times.* September 26, 1929.

Missouri Botanical Garden "Buxus Sempervirons Joy.". http://www. missouribotanicalgarden.org.

Moffit, Sally. "Italians as an Ethnic Group in Cincinnati." University of Cincinnati. Libraries. http://www. libraries.uc.edu

Moore, Thomas. *The Poetical Works of Thomas Moore.* London: Frederick Warne and Co., 1881.

Mooseheart Child City and School. "Moosehaven: City of Contentment." http://www.moosehaven.org

Morgan, Robert. *Lions of the West: Heroes and Villains of the Westward Expansion.* Chapel Hill, North Carolina: Algonquin Books of Chapel Hill, 2011.

Mulford, Ren, Jr. "Red Philosophy- National Game Faces Greatest Prosperity." *Sporting Life.* July 4, 1908.

_____. *Sporting Life.* "Red Bomb Shell. Jack Barry's Rebellion Stirs Cincinnati." July 7, 1906.

Murphy, James L. *The Salem Mummy from Echoes.* Columbus OH: Ohio State University, October, 1978.

National Park Service. "National Historic Landmark Nomination." http:// pdfhost.focus.nps.gov

Nell, William Cooper. *The Colored Patriots of the American Revolution.* Boston: R. F. Wallcut, 1855.

Nelson, S.B. and Runk, J.M. *History of Cincinnati and Hamilton County; their past and present."* Cincinnati: S.B. Nelson & Co., 1894.

"New Gift Angle." *The University of Michigan Today."* Summer, 1976.

Newman, Larry. "Florence Groff's Dream of Final Splendor." *Milwaukee Sentinel.* April 3, 1949.

Niven, John. *Salmon P. Chase: A Biography.* New York: Oxford University Press, 1995.

NNDB: Tracking the Entire World. "Barney Kroger." http://www.nndb. com.

"No Millions Left to Stallo Girls." *New York Times.* November 18, 1911.

Norberg, John. *Wings of their Dreams- Purdue in Flight."* Purdue University, 2003.

Northern Kentucky Views. "History of Crittenden Community." http://www. nkyviews.com

Nuxhall, Phillip J. *Beauty in the Grove.* Wilmington, OH: Orange Frazer Press, Inc., 2010.

"Obituary Notes." *Publisher's Weekly, Volume 70.* New Providence, NJ: R.R. Bowker Company, 1906.

"Odd Fellows, The." *Cincinnati Daily Gazette.* September 21, 1881.

"Odd Fellows' Monument, The." *Cincinnati Daily Gazette.* 23 August 23, 1881.

Ohio History Central. "National Road." http:// www.ohiohistorycentral.org.

_____. Ohio History Central. "Alfred T. Goshorn" http://www. ohiohistorycentral.org

_____. "Salmon P. Chase." http://www. ohiohistorycentral.org

Ohio Law Bulletin,Vol. 52. Jan. 7, 1907. Norwalk, Ohio: The Laning Company, 1907.

Ohio's Progressive Sons. Cincinnati: Queen City Publishing, 1905.

"$1,200,000 Paid for The Hamilton Plant of American Can Co." *Hamilton Evening Journal.* October 14, 1914.

"Only Surviving Founder of Cincinnati

Zoo." *Cincinnati Times-Star*. January 10, 1917.

O'Neill, Tom. "Ted Berry Local hero." *The Cincinnati Enquirer*. October 16, 2000.

"Opinion of Court is Sought on Otto Luedeking Bequest to Red Cross In Germany." *Cincinnati Enquirer*. November 20, 1951.

"The Origin of the Harp: Miss Louise Lawson's Great Work Unveiled at Music Hall." *The Commercial Gazette*. March 5, 1893.

Ossad, Steven L. "The Fighting McCooks." *Military History*. October, 2005.

"Our Boys Did Nobly." *Sports Illustrated*. April 30, 1956.

Owen, Lorrie K. *Ohio Historic Place Dictionary, Volume 2*. Somerset Publishers, 2008.

Palanci, Jennifer. "Career Biography of Photographer James F. Brown." 2009.

Patton, Mark and Mark Abramson. "Frankenstein: A frightfully nice place for Halloween celebration." www.stripes.com.

Peat, Wilbur David. *Indiana Houses of the Nineteenth Century*. Indianapolis: Indiana Historical Society, 1962.

"Pet Dog Buried in Spring Grove. "*Cincinnati Post*. 08 December 8. 1905.

Petroski, Henry. *The Pencil: A History of Design and Circumstance*. New York: Alfred A. Knopf, Inc., 1989.

Pfeifer, Thomas (Spring Grove Cemetery & Arboretum grounds manager). Personal accounts and interviews. 2011-2013.

Phelon, Wm. A. "The Team That Never Was Licked." *Baseball Magazine*. January, 1917.

Pih, Richard W. *Ohio History: The Scholarly Journal of the Ohio Historical Society, Negro Self-Improvement: Efforts in Ante-Bellum, Cincinnati, 1836-1850* .Volume 78, Summer 1969. Columbus: Ohio Historical Society, 1969.

Placzek, Adolph K., ed. *Macmillan Encyclopedia of Architects- Vol. 3*. New York: Collier-Macmillan, 1982.

Plattner, Steven W. "Paul Briol- An Appreciation." *Queen City Heritage-The Journal of the Cincinnati Historical Society*. Vol. 47. No. 3. Cincinnati Historical Society, 1989.

Povich, Shirley, and others. *All Those Mornings…at the Post. Washington Post*. Ed. Maury Lynn, David Povich and George Solomon. New York: Public Affairs, 2005.

Powers, James. "Miss Groff's Dream Pyramid Stands on Six-Foot Base (No $40,000 Vision)." *Cincinnati Enquirer*. April 10, 1957.

"Probably a Million Lost." *New York Times*. July 19, 1891.

"Protest Filed by Auto Club Against Rule." *The Times Star*. July 18, 1919.

The Public Library of Cincinnati and Hamilton County. "The Cincinnati Panorama of 1848" http//1948.cincinnatilibrary.org

Purdue University. Cooper, Ralph. "Chirp, Early Birds of Aviation." http://home. earthlink.net

Radel, Cliff. "1937 Flood has Powerful Hold on Cincinnati." *Cincinnati Enquirer*. January 21, 2012.

_____. "Our Titanic Connections- Women Returned, Men Didn't." *Cincinnati Enquirer*. April 13, 2012.

_____. "Ruby Wright will live on in the echoes of her music." *Cincinnati Enquirer*. March 14, 2004.

Ravo, Nick. Lenore Wingard, 88, Swimmer Who Won Two Olympic Medals." *New York Times*. February 15, 2000.

Reidel, Jennifer. "Caldonia, Caldonia." *Cincinnati Magazine*. June, 1985.

Raney, Jack. "Pyramid Really Shrinks." *Cincinnati Enquirer*. June 21, 1953.

Rattermann, H. A. *Spring Grove and its Creator: H. A. Rattermann's Biography of Adolph Strauch*. Cincinnati: The Ohio Book Store, 1988.

"Receiver for the Cincinnati "Zoo." *New York Times*. January 22, 1898.

Reifel, August J. *History of Franklin County, Indiana: her people, industries and* institutions." Indianapolis: B.F. Bowen & Co. Inc., 1915.

Renfro Funeral Services, Inc. "Renfro Funeral Services History." www.renfrofuneralservice.com

Rhodes, Greg and John Erardi. *The First Boys of Summer.* Cincinnati: Road West Publishing Company.

Right Worthy Grand Lodge of the United States and the Sovereign Grand Lodge of the Independent Order of Odd Fellows. Vol.10. Baltimore: The Sovereign Grand Lodge of the Independent Order of Odd Fellows, 1882.

Riley, James A. *The Biographical Encyclopedia of the Negro Baseball Leagues.* New York: Carroll & Graf Publishers, Inc., 1994.

Rodriguez, Junius P. *The Historical Encyclopedia of World Slavery: A-K, Vol. II, L-Z.* ABC-CLIO, 1997.

_____. *Slavery in the United States: A Social, Political, and Historical Encyclopedia, Volume 2.* 2007. http://books.google.com

Rogers, Millard F. *Randolph Rogers; American Sculptor in Rome.* University of Massachusetts Press, 1971.

_____. *Rich in Good Works: Mary Emery of Cincinnati.* Akron OH: University of Akron Press, 2001.

Rosa, Joseph G. *The West of Wild Bill Hickok.* Norman, OK: University of Oklahoma Press, 1994.

Rosen, Steve, "A Moment in Time Preserved 163 Years, Newly Accessible." *New York Times.* May 21, 2011.

Rutledge, Mike. "Dead in the Water." *Cincinnati Enquirer.* January 13, 2012.

Rynor, Vivien. "Art; Photography's Early Images Keep the Nation's Past Alive." *New York Times.* August 19, 1990.

"Sale of East Walnut Hills home for $100,000." *Cincinnati Times-Star.* January 8, 1949

Sanderson, Kirk. Excerpts from speech given by PGM Kirk Sanderson at Spring Grove. June 6, 1993. Spring Grove archives.

Sarg, Tony. *Up & Down New York.* New York: Universe Publishing, 1926.

Schulz, Janice. "A Look into the World of Landscape Architecture. University of Cincinnati Libraries. http://www.libraries.uc.edu.

Schulze, Mildred. "Woman archer set for Hall of Fame." *Norwood Enterprise.* March 27, 1975.

The Sea Breeze, Volumes 20-30. "Doings at Vineyard Haven Bethel." Boston: Boston Seaman's Friends Society, October 1907.

Seidman, Sandra R. "Early Steam Manufacturing-The Lane and Bodley Company, 1850-1920." Cincinnati Triple Steam. http://cincinnatitriplesteam.org

Seidner, Rosemary. "Le Château." *Upstairs, Downstairs Home Tour* supplement to *Cincinnati Magazine.* May 2002.

Severance, G. A. "Samuel P. Stickney." *Circus Scrapbook.* No. 13. Cincinnati. March 20, 1820.

Severson, Kim. "Does the World Need Another 'Joy'? Do You?" *New York Times.* November 1, 2006.

"Shall it be a Race Course?" *The Gazette* February 20,1887.

Shelby County Historical Society. Wallace, Rich. "Shelby County Woman is First Female Architect in Ohio." June 1997. www.shelbycountyhistory.org.

Sheraton, Mimi. Marion Rombauer Becker, 73 Dies; Co-author of 'The Joy of Cooking.'. *New York Times.* December 30, 1976.

"Shirayamadani at the Cincinnati Art Museum." *The Grains of Rice* newsletter. Cincinnati Chapter Japanese American Citizens League, July, 2012.

Shirk, Ida M. "Descendants of Richard & Elizabeth (Ewan) Talbot." *American Weekly.* Day Printing Company, 1927.

Sicherman, Barbara and Carol Hurd Green. *Notable American Women: The Modern Period: A Biographical Dictionary.* Cambridge, MA: Belknap Press of Harvard University Press, 1980.

Sifakis, Stewart. *Who Was Who In The Civil War.* New York: Facts on File, Inc., 1988.

"Signal Bell Disturbs Mourners, so Whistle is Substituted." *Cincinnati Enquirer.* October 8, 1912.

"Sixty Years of Cincinnati Zoo Financing." *Cincinnati Enquirer.* Ca 1931.

Slout, William L. *Olympians of the Sawdust Circle: A Biographical Dictionary of the Nineteenth Century American Circus.* Rockville, MD.: Wildside Press LLC, 1998.

Smith, D.E. Huger. "Dr. William and Anna Brisbane." *The South Carolina Historical and Genealogical Magazine.* Volume 14. South Carolina Historical Society, 1913.

Society for American Baseball. McKenna, Brian. "Charlie Grant." www.sabr.org

Spengler, Teo. "What is the meaning of the thistle?" Ehow http://www.ehow.co.uk

Stern, Joseph S. Jr. "Cincinnati's Butch Cassidy and the Sundance Kid." *Queen City Heritage.* Summer 1992.

Stevens, E. B. M.D. and others. *The Cincinnati Lancet & Observer, Volume 13 & Volume 31.* E.B. Stevens, Publisher, 1870.

Stickney, Samuel P. "Thirty Years with The Horse." New York: Murray Publishing 1855.

Strauch, Adolph. *Spring Grove Cemetery-Its History and Improvements* Cincinnati: Robert Clarke & Co., 1869.

Steves, Rick. "Père Lachaise Cemetery Tour." Rick Steve's Europe Through the Back Door. http://www.ricksteves.com.

Stickney, Samuel P. "Thirty Years With The Horse." New York: Murray Publishing 1855.

Stinson, Tamia. "Cincinnati Shopping History." *A-Line* magazine. July 12, 2011.

Strauch, Adolphus. *Spring Grove Cemetery: Its History and Improvements, with Observations on Ancient and Modern Places of Sepulture."* Cincinnati: Robert Clarke & Co., 1869.

"Style Show Features 'Round The Clock' Fashions; 12 To Model Own Creations." *The Edgecliff.* April 14, 1953.

"Superman" Dedicated to the Young." *Cincinnati Business Courier.* January 18, 2013. http://www.bizjournals.com.

Taos and Santa Fe Painters. "Henry Farny." http://www.henryfarny.com.

Thacker, John Adams. *The Cincinnati Medical Repertory, Volume 4.* Cincinnati: The Medical Journal Association, 1871.

Thayer, Stuart and William L. Slout. "John Robinson's Early Days." *American Circus Anthology, Essays of the Early Years.* ed. William L. Slout. Circus Historical Society. http://www.circushistory.org.

Theobald, Mark. *Memoirs of the lower Ohio Valley: personal and genealogical.* Vol 1. Federal Publishing Company. 2004. http://www.ebooksread.com/authors-eng/federal-publishing-company.shtml.

Thomson, Peter G. *Cincinnati Society Blue Book and family directory.* Cincinnati: Peter G. Thomson, 1879.

"Tiny Flower-Covered Casket." *Cincinnati Enquirer.* December 8, 1905.

Titus, Richard O. "What's In a Name? An Inquiry into the Identity Theft of Platt Delascus Babbitt." *The Daguerreian Society Newsletter.* May-July 2008. http.www.luminous-lint.com

Tolles, Thayer. "American Women Sculptors". *Heilbrunn Timeline of Art History.* The Metropolitan Museum of Art. http://www.metmuseum.org

Tony Sarg's Sea Monster. 1937-NHA Research Library Film Collection. Nantucket History. http://www.youtube.com

Torrens, Roberta J. "Jim Brown: A Story in Pictures." *Ohio Valley Chapter/American Society of Media Photographers*. Decmber1, 1996.

Tracy, Stephen C. *Going to Cincinnati: A History of the Blues in the Queen City.* University of Illinois Press,

Trapp, Kenneth. "Rookwood and the Japanese Mania in Cincinnati." *The Cincinnati Historical Society Bulletin* 1981.

Tremain, Henry Edwin. *In Memoriam, General Major-General Joseph Hooker.* Cincinnati: Robert Clarke & Co., 1881.

Turner Classic Movies. "The Court-Martial of Billy Mitchell (1955)." http://www.tcm.com

"Underworld Figure Killed in Duel with Detective." *The Coshocton Tribune.* Coshocton, Ohio. June 11, 1929.

University of Cincinnati "History of CCM." College Conservatory of Music University of Cincinnati. http://ccm.uc.edu

Venable, William Henry. *A Centennial History of Christ Church 1817-1917.* Cincinnati: Stewart & Kidd Company, 1918.

Warminski, Margo. "Upstairs Downstairs" *Cincinnati Magazine.* May, 2008.

Wayne, Tiffany K. *American Women of Science Since 1900.* ABC-CLIO. 2010.

"Wealthy Patent Medicine Man is Shot to Death." *Commercial Tribune.* August 17, 1906.

Weather Review, Vol.12. Washington: U.S. Government Printing Office, 1884. http://books.google.com

Webb, Nedd. "Lenore Wingard-Remembering the Berlin Olympics." *Cincinnati Enquirer Magazine.* August 17, 1986.

Whalen, Charles and Barbara. *The Fighting McCooks-America's Favorite Fighting Family.* Westmoreland Press, 2006.

Wheeler, Lonnie. "Post Sports Department a Writer's Paradise." *Cincinnati Post.* Dec. 31, 2007.

"Why Did Wurlitzer Pick N. Tonawanda?" *The Billboard.* August 25, 1956.

"Widowed by Her Brother." *Cincinnati Post.* August 17, 1906.

"Will Asks Pyramid-Tomb But Cemetery Says No." *Cincinnati Post.* February 2, 1949.

"Will Provides $20,000 Fund For Flowers on Burial Plot." *Cincinnati Times Star.* October 19,1944.

"William James Breed." *New York Times.* December 25, 1889.

Willis, James A. and others. *Weird Ohio.* New York: Sterling Publishing, 2006.

Worthen, Dennis B. "Dow Drugs an early discounter." *Kentucky Enquirer.* May 24, 2010. http://nky.cincinnati.com

Wulsin, Lucien. "Dwight Hamilton Baldwin (1821-1899) and the Baldwin Piano Company". The Newcomen Society in North America, Vol. 5. Issue 25.1953.

"A Wurlitzer at Helm 100 Years." *The Billboard.* New York: New York. August 25, 1956.

"Wurlitzer World of Music Built on Century of Growth." *The Billboard.* August 25, 1956.

Personal interviews, correspondence, and papers

Barrett, Peter. 2007.

Bowers, Carolyn "Carrie" 2007.

Burt, DeVere. personal April, 2013.

Deborah Spencer Rose. April 9, 2004.

Dewitt, Jackie. June 13, 2007.

Dracket, Anne. April 8, 2013.

Eckhardt, Cassie. 2006 - 2013.

Ellanora Robinson Rose. December 8,1997.

Gordon, Andrew. April 18, 2013.

Greensfelder, Jim. June 13, 2007.

Hopple, William. personal April, 2013.

Hoyt, Betty. Personal September 30, 2003 and 2003-2007.

Huenefeld, Thomas E. 2007-2012.

Johnson, Eric. 2005.

McClure, Judy and Jewell McClure. 2008-12.

Naberhaus, Annie, 2011.

Palanci, Jennifer. February, 2013.

Rhodes, Greg. 2012-2013.

Ruthven, John. A. April-May, 2013.

Hennessy, Rose 2005.

Reisenfeld, Suzie Rapp and Herb. October 5, 2006.

Reusing, John. April 25, 2013.

Ryan, Richard A. May, 2013.

Stewart, Judy Henke. 2013.

Stinson, Irene Neff. September, 2011.

Suhre, Frederick. 2008.

Wingard Cleon March 8, 2006.

Spring Grove Cemetery & Arboretum archives

Report of the Building Committee. Spring Grove Board Minutes, January 6, 1880.

The Cincinnati cemetery of Spring Grove: Report for 1857.